PARADISE Inc.

Texts & photographs

PARADISE Inc.

by GUILLAUME BONN

HEMERIA

PREFACE

This is a book I have been waiting to read, and the author is the person I have been longing to talk to. Guillaume, you raise very pertinent issues that are not new to the world but rather have been ignored by the world.

In the heart of East Africa, where the wilderness meets civilization, a profound struggle unfolds between humanity and the untamed. It is a saga of coexistence, conflict and adaptation, set against the backdrop of Kenya's Maasai land, where tradition is intertwined with modernity and the fate of wildlife hangs in the balance.

This book is for a project and proposal seeking solutions to the problem of human-wildlife conflict and the place of conservation in modern-day Maasai land. This book highlights the importance of community-driven conservation to conserve and manage the 70% of wildlife living outside national parks. This book seeks answers and the people to provide the right answers.

The answer is with the community.

Back to the issue of conservation and modernity. Unfolding before our eyes is a reality of what will shape conservation in the future. Unfortunately, key conservation organizations are ignoring this reality. They edit images of the Maasai community and modern elements in their stories, videos, photos, and documentaries to deceive donors into believing the land is still untouched and that conservation is the same as it was in the 1970s and 1980s.

Rapid increase in rural population means that more road and railway network, community amenities, and investments are introduced to support the growing community needs. Schools, health centres, small towns and wind turbines are spreading fast across villages. Influenced by this modernity, the Maasai are also constructing modern structures in their Manyattas, and more of these structures will increase with growing population.

The days when wildlife freely roamed the open land are long gone and will never return again. We can hope for a better future, but there is no turning back because, as it stands, the land no longer has the capacity to accommodate or revert. We, as the human species, need to accept this new reality or, at the very least, communicate that these preconceived ideas are obsolete.

A practical example in my home County is that Kajiado covers an area of 2,129,300 hectares {21,293 km²} compared to Amboseli National Park, which is the only officially gazetted area for wildlife covering 39,206 hectares {392 km²}. Currently, only one million hectares of land outside Amboseli national park are available for wildlife conservation, while the rest have been eaten-up by road and railway networks, schools, health centres, small towns and shopping centres.

Working closely with communities to create conservancies will generate direct income and create job opportunities for women and young people and help save the existing natural land before it is too late.

Thank you, Guillaume, for sharing the photo of Zebras grazing under the elevated train bridge because it is indeed a glimpse representing so many such realities already taking place in modern-day Maasai land.

Let me mention a few; I took a video of elephants drinking water in our community borehole with wind turbines in the background. This is a new investment by energy companies that you could not see a few years back, but it is now there and is planning to expand into the interior of Maasai land.

Pumping underground water for elephants, like I did during the devastating drought of 2022, was unheard of one or two decades ago, but it is now happening. The elephants got so used to water that whenever they heard the generator running, they knew the water was ready for them at the borehole, and they walked in to drink during the day.

The development of road networks in Maasai land and the emergence of modern structures by external entities, as well as those initiated by the Maasai themselves, influenced by modernity, are undeniable realities that cannot be ignored.

In the 2022 drought, I witnessed elephants walking through Kajiado town in the morning. A woman, who I presume, was coming out to throw dirty water outside of her house, was shocked to see elephants passing at her door. She threw the bowl together with the water outside and quickly went inside the house, perhaps under the bed, because she did not close the door.

We cannot stop modernity or population growth {at least not for now}. The only thing we can do is create and innovate conservation models that go with modernity and population growth by integrating pastoralism, conservation, and development. Perception is in the minds of humans, and this makes the rural poor captive to what they see happening around them. This perception has been used so well by conservation executives who arrive in big hotels in the latest 4x4 fuel guzzlers to lecture selected leaders {always selected and compromised chiefs and their cronies} on conservation.

Back in the village, villagers think that the chiefs and the conservation executives are smart and intelligent and scramble to talk or bribe the chiefs for favours because, in their eyes, they have been made to believe that without these people, they cannot do anything.

Rural villagers' morale is too low because their ideas and innovations are disregarded and sometimes appropriated, even by their governments, and also edited out of the picture of conservation to deceive donors that it is only the conservation organisations doing conservation work.

Often, we are told it is not all about money, but it is money that is editing out the photos, facilitating the travels, appropriating ideas, and even influencing the media and all other negative things meant to portray some organisations as the best suited to carry out conservation activities.

The hope in conservation lies in fully supporting community-driven conservation models. Problems like poaching are then weakened, diminishing water supplies redistributed equally, and desertification mitigated by supporting creative and innovative community conservation models that are already visible at the horizon.

On the other hand, governments are only happy with the millions of dollars collected in revenue from tourism each year, and I do not know who will tell them that they will increase tourist arrivals and the revenue by directly involving communities in conservation. Provided that the money will continue flowing, I don't think they will even care to listen. Like governments, conservation organisations are only good at stealing community conservation ideas and indigenous knowledge to make them their own. They hover all over trying to get new ideas from communities to make themselves look very creative and innovative in the eyes of their donors. Communities have the ideas and indigenous knowledge that are crucial in conservation, but they do not have the support to make their dreams come true.

The idea of creating peace with elephants is one of many good ideas from villagers that respect people's cultures and their way of life, and it is easy for them to identify themselves with.

My name is Ezekiel Ole Katato, a Maasai elder and peacemaker in Maasai land, in Kenya. I lead a council of elders who advocate for peace between human and wildlife in my village of Indupa.

For generations, the Maasai people have harmoniously shared their territory with elephants, fostering a relationship built on mutual respect and coexistence. However, the tides of modernity have brought forth unforeseen challenges, disrupting the delicate balance that once prevailed, and this is what we seek to repair.

In 2022, when elephants ventured into our village, along with fellow elders, I recognized the urgent need to educate our younger generation and create peace between the Maasai and elephants as a strategy to promote peaceful coexistence. The idea is still in its initial stages and I hope it will open the way for more modern-day conservation models in Maasai land.

Further, the peace project will raise the ideas, lessons and voices of rural communities that are currently missing in the status quo.

I hope the convergence of our views to be reflected in your book will help breathe life to the whole conservation debate around the world and also fulfil your quest of finding solutions to the human-wildlife conflict issue that I believe, can only be addressed by the communities themselves.

Ezekiel Ole Katato
Maasai Elder, Kenya

INTRODUCTION

Paradise Inc. is the result of a decades-long quest by Guillaume Bonn to witness, and to document, the final days of the great East African wilderness. What this book contains, in his photographs and his words, is the consequence of many trips over many years into the African bush as well as its towns and cities. A third generation French "African," Guillaume was born in Madagascar, and he grew up in the Comoros, in Djibouti, and in North Yemen, but it was in Kenya where he lived the longest and spent his most formative years, the place where, as he puts it, he formed his "ideas and opinions of nature and of life." It is a place he has returned to and lived for extended periods throughout his life. As a working documentary photographer over the past three decades, in Kenya and elsewhere in Africa, Guillaume has been a first-hand witness to its enduring glories and its ongoing traumas that range from its extraordinary range of human and wildlife diversity to its wars and famines and atrocious poverty. For better or worse, this is the Africa that has become his inescapable muse, a place that compels him and repels him, a bond that he describes as "le mal d'Afrique."

As a friend and colleague of Guillaume's with a shared passion for Africa, I have watched as this book has taken shape over the years; it has also been the subject of many discussions on several journeys we took together in Kenya and Tanzania. Guillaume's purpose on these trips was to show me some of the endangered wilderness areas he knew, and to introduce me to some of the people he most admired, people who were dedicating their lives to help preserve what remained: Richard Bonham, Paula Kahumbu, Ian Craig, the late Tony Fitzjohn and Richard Leakey.

Many of the changes that are taking place today in Africa are catastrophic ones. Armed conflicts, soaring human population increases, and rapidly expanding urban development have already degraded many wilderness areas and have altered the traditional coexistence between human and wildlife. Just as some of the continent's traditional human cultures are vanishing in the face of urbanization, many of its animal species are critically endangered. The onset of climate change has accelerated both the pace and the effects of these changes, leading to an urgent existential question: How much longer will the extraordinary natural environments and unique ecosystems of East Africa be able to survive?

In a meeting Guillaume and I had with him in 2021, a year before his death, the renowned paleoanthropologist and conservationist Richard Leakey shared his belief that most of Kenya's wildlife was unlikely to survive much beyond the middle of the century. The glaciers on Mt. Kenya were melting, the rivers were drying up, and the country's human population, which had quintupled in fifty years, was set to double again by the middle of the century. The next thirty to fifty years would be decisive, he said. "Overall, I'm in a very pessimistic short-to-mid-term attitude," he said. "I am not persuaded of the prospects for wildlife unless something gives, and I don't see it." Leakey's assessment was devastatingly bleak, but it had the unwelcome ring of truth. Of course, East Africa's natural environment has been under threat for a very long time. It was just over fifty years ago that Peter Beard wrote his unforgettable book, *The End of the Game*, with its various iterations published over the decades since. Documenting what he saw around him in the late Fifties and early Sixties, Beard was able to foresee the apocalyptic decline of the great East African elephant population; he accurately predicted an end to the age-old habitats and migration routes that had allowed them and the region's other remarkable wildlife species to coexist with humans since before recorded time. Beard's perceptions had a profound impact on Guillaume, who came to know him well, and worked closely with him when he was in his twenties. (Indeed, Guillaume was with Beard when he was trampled, and nearly killed, by a charging elephant, in 1996.)

Over the years since the publication of Beard's magnus opus, the standoff between man and nature in East Africa has not merely continued, it has exploded, to the extent that human society competes directly with the remaining wildlife and the natural habitats they depend upon for their survival. Wilderness areas are no longer limitless expanses, but patchworks of separate enclaves, increasingly shared with the relentlessly advancing farms, towns, cities, factories, and roads being built by human beings. How to balance it out and allow for human growth while also rescuing the animals and their habitat for almost certain extinction? A photograph taken by Guillaume of an elevated railroad bridge cutting through Nairobi National Park, a herd of zebras grazing in the elephant grass around its pillars, may be one glimpse of the looming future.

By making *Paradise Inc.* the title for his book, Guillaume is reaffirming that East Africa truly is an earthly paradise. Just as the Paradise that is the mythical realm of most of the world's major religions, he is saying, this region, in all its wondrous beauty and diversity, is a real-life repository for our collective sense of natural perfection, and a glimpse of temporal eternity. But just as determinedly, however, Guillaume wishes us to see the fragility of that paradise, the future of which now hangs in the balance. That is where the "Inc" comes in.

Guillaume inveighs, understandably, against the amoral profiteering and outright cruelty of the poachers of rhino horn and elephant ivory, but he also reserves contempt for the modern class of white-collar profiteers who build hotels on the very edges of national parks and engineer "safari experiences" for the foreign tourists who flock to places like Kenya's Maasai Mara. He reserves sharp words, as well, for those visitors who choose not to see the harsh realities that lie beyond their exclusionary zones, such as the shantytowns that ring the national parks they have paid handsomely to "explore" for a few days at a time. And if any of them wonder about the effects of their presence on the wildlife they have come to see in their luxurious Land Cruisers, or what happens to the trash that accumulates during their expensive safaris, Guillaume has some indelible reminders for them here.

> **In the end, Guillaume is saying that it is no longer possible to frame our perceptions, like photographers do, by selecting certain realities and excluding others, to suit our longstanding illusions. The time has come to face the facts, as East Africa's age-old natural landscapes and wildlife habitats inexorably disappear. *Paradise Inc.*, is therefore a requiem, and perhaps even an epitaph, but it is also a personal plea by Guillaume for the book's readers to shake off their illusions and to see things as they really are, before it really is too late.**

Paradise Inc. is not all lamentation. This book is also an ode to a land that gave birth to Guillaume and that has inspired him. There are beautiful images here. His framing of an East African river valley at dawn is unforgettable, something like everyone's idea of the Garden of Eden. There we have Guillaume's almost mystical vision of a wild Africa that is resplendent, before it became an Instagrammable image for the *Financial Times's* "How to Spend It" readers.

Guillaume Bonn is a white African of European descent, and for that very reason, he feels inevitably displaced and excluded from some of Africa's newer realities. It is an insurmountable condition.

In Guillaume's tetchy disquiet about the changes in Africa and his concerns for the future, I am reminded of another white African—the Ethiopian-born British explorer, writer and oddball naturalist Wilfred Thesiger. Born seven decades before Guillaume, Thesiger too railed against the encroachment of modernity and the destruction of Africa's old ways. Something his biographer, Alexander Maitland, wrote about Thesiger could easily apply to Guillaume: "Thesiger's impossible dream had been to preserve the near-idyllic life he had known as a boy in Abyssinia. He viewed change dismally, as a threat to the tribal people he admired, and to himself as a traditionalist and romantic who 'cherished the past, felt out of step with the present, and dreaded the future'. Such a reactionary outlook was doomed from the start and Thesiger knew it…"

Just as Thesiger's own photographs served as iconic glimpses of an Africa as it had been forever, before the ructions and paraphernalia of the twentieth century began to crush it, Guillaume's own camera lens steadies itself accusingly upon the ongoing erosion: A little pile of trash in the forest on the Maasai Mara; a magnificent lion, at repose amidst an uneven bit of bulldozed waste ground; a newly-installed gasoline pump, ready to spring into life on a roadside running through the Kenyan savannah. It is as if Guillaume is a detective, in a sense, working for the prosecution, seeking out visual evidence of the crimes being committed everywhere, all around us. As he points out these scenes, his photographs ask us to see it for ourselves, and, perhaps, to do something about it. "I am just a photographer, just an observer," says Guillaume, but what he depicts is powerful, and his message is clear.

The fact is that Africa, which was the last region in the world to be colonized, in the Scramble for Africa at the tail end of the nineteenth century, is still the continent with the wildest remaining spaces. But now, little more than a century later, we are seeing those wild spaces finally overwhelmed, as the African population surges—it is expected to double in the coming decades. But even now, Africa continues to be romanticized, fetishized, and ultimately objectified by outsiders, and by those who seek to profit from those misconceptions. In *Paradise Inc.*, Guillaume Bonn seeks to clear up the cognitive dissonance.

The clarity of perception demanded of us by Guillaume is a bittersweet one. For some reason, an anecdote comes to mind: A few years ago, on a trip to Kenya, Guillaume and I were returning to Nairobi after a few days spent in the Chyulu Hills, a wildlife reserve in the middle of Maasai country. After some hours, we reached the tarmacked highway that runs from the Indian Ocean port of Mombasa to Nairobi. Along the way, new human settlements had popped up along the roadsides. They were not unlike the messy commercial strips that festoon roads the world over, only here, they were just getting started, and the savannah that extended to the horizons beyond still had antelopes grazing visibly in the near distance. The land had not yet been carved up; it was still unfenced, but that would happen soon. Trucks carrying cargos from the coast to the capital roared noisily passed us, constantly, feeding the country's growing population.

At one point, a zebra lay dead on its side, next to the passing traffic. It was just there, a relic of the wild, amidst the gathering mess that people create with their roads and vehicles and buildings. It was a sad sight, of course, but also, somehow, a thrilling one. After all, it was not just any dead animal but a *zebra*, a most extraordinary creature, and a reminder that in Africa, the wild, though endangered, still existed.

Jon Lee Anderson
Dorset, England

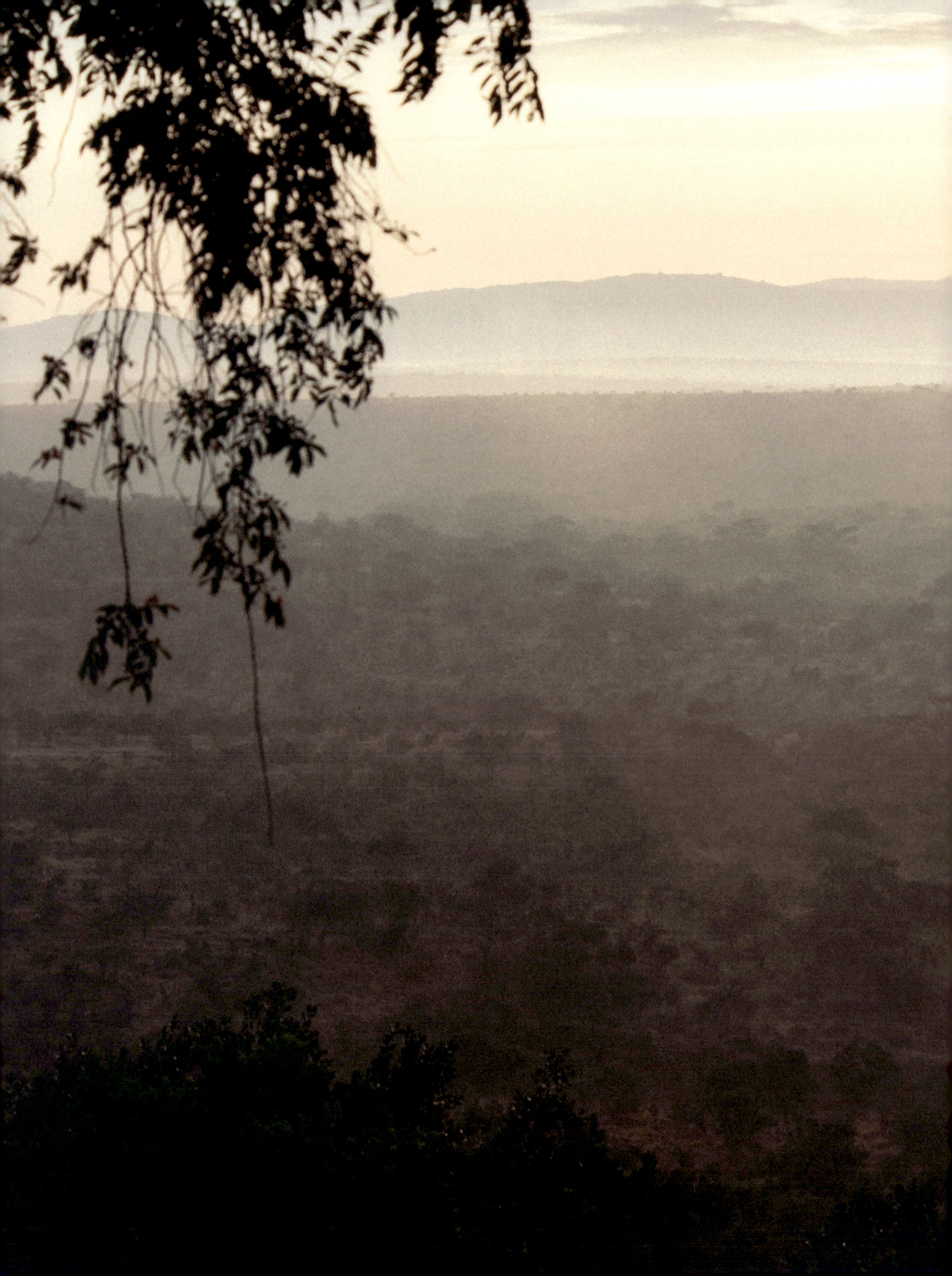

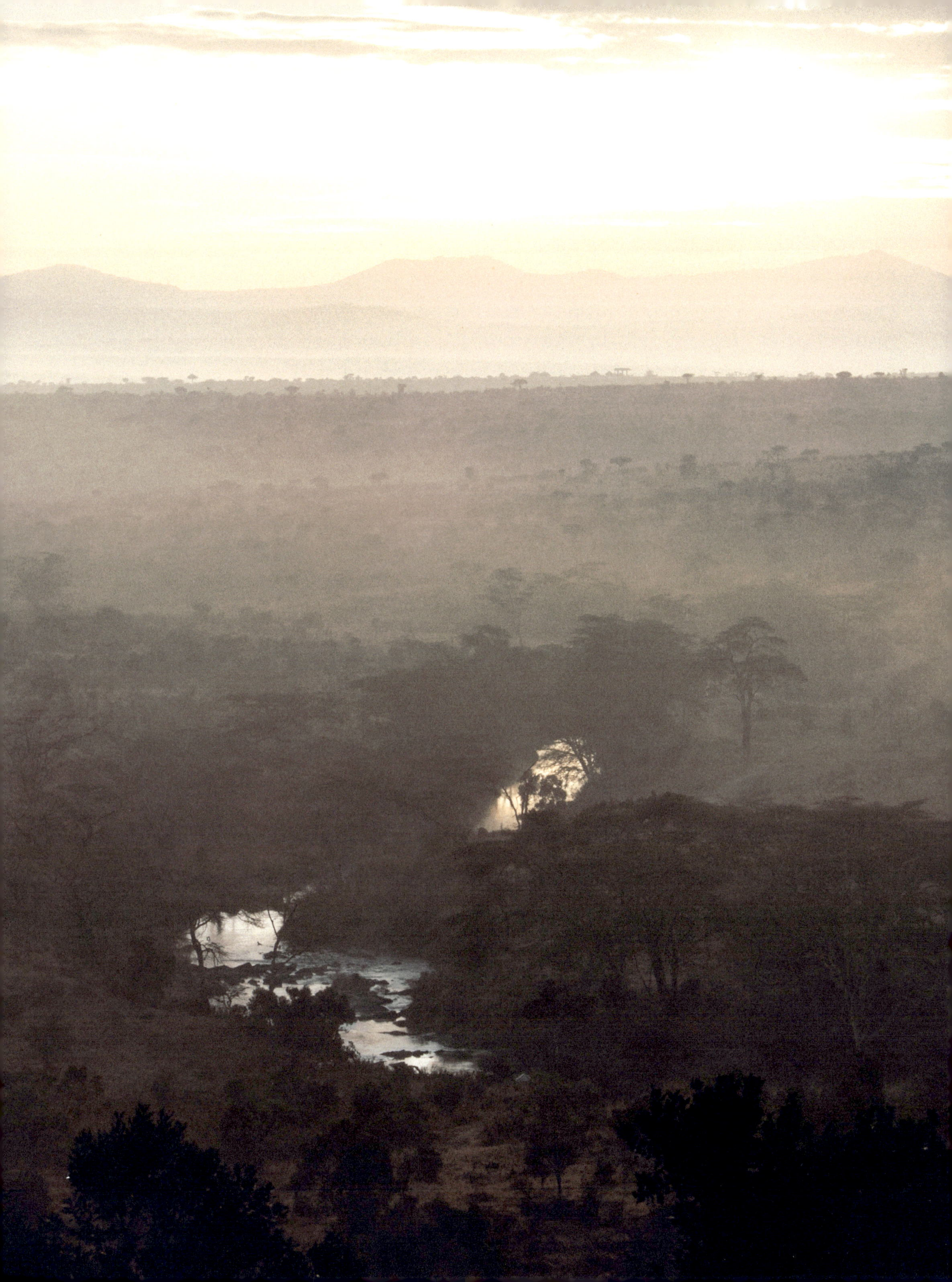

I have been trying for a long time to come to terms with the changes that are transforming Africa. We are made to believe that progress is a good thing, that mobile phones and the latest new car will make us all happier and our lives will be better. Along with these things, skyscrapers, highways, parking lots, and all the other accoutrements of consumerism (for maximum profit) have changed Africa and the rest of the world, sometimes disastrously.

I have seen remote communities where the wholesale imposition of Western culture was eroding traditional, more sustainable ways of life. It's easy to overlook that the landscapes we now see as commonplace were once vibrant ecosystems—forests, rivers, pristine beaches, or the sacred grounds where rhinos once gave birth.

Not so long ago, humans needed protection from wildlife and now all the remaining wild habitats and its wilderness are in imminent danger of being lost forever. I despair at the thought of the billions spent over the years in all forms of feel-good conservation campaigns given to NGOs that have failed to save anything. I grapple with finding a path forward out of any status quo perpetuating corrupt systems and how to convey that the complexities of conservation cannot be easily resolved with money or good intentions.

How does one document the subtle nuances of destruction created by the modern world? How do I capture and photograph the final vestiges of an older world transitioning into a new one? How do we comprehend that we are irreversibly losing generations of accumulated human wisdom, where both humans and wildlife once coexisted harmoniously?

The chapter *No Man's Land* is an attempt to show that Africa stands as the last frontier where you can see so clearly the gradual impact overpopulation is having on the planet, while explaining at the same time the continent's complexities in the pursuit of creating better understanding and knowledge with the foolish dream and hope to save it and to save us all.

NO MAN'S LAND

How do you make the unseen seen

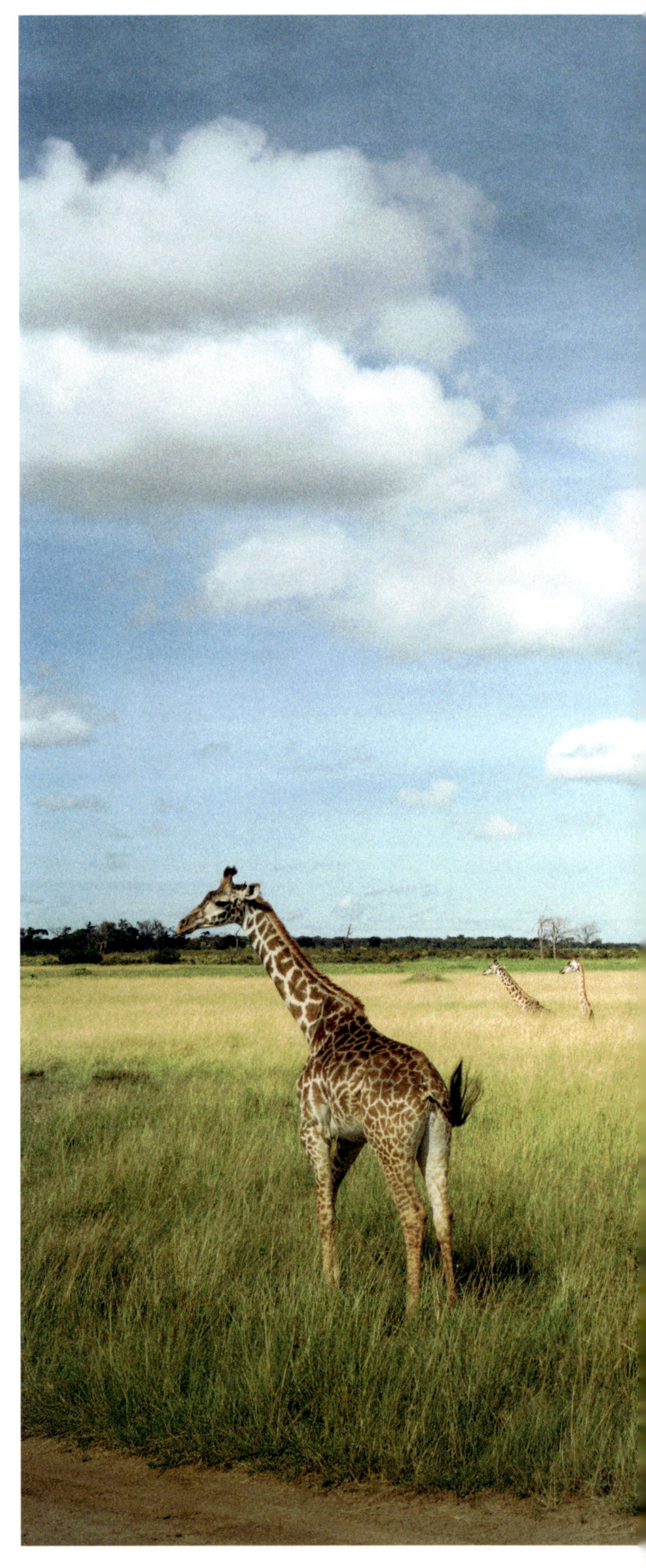

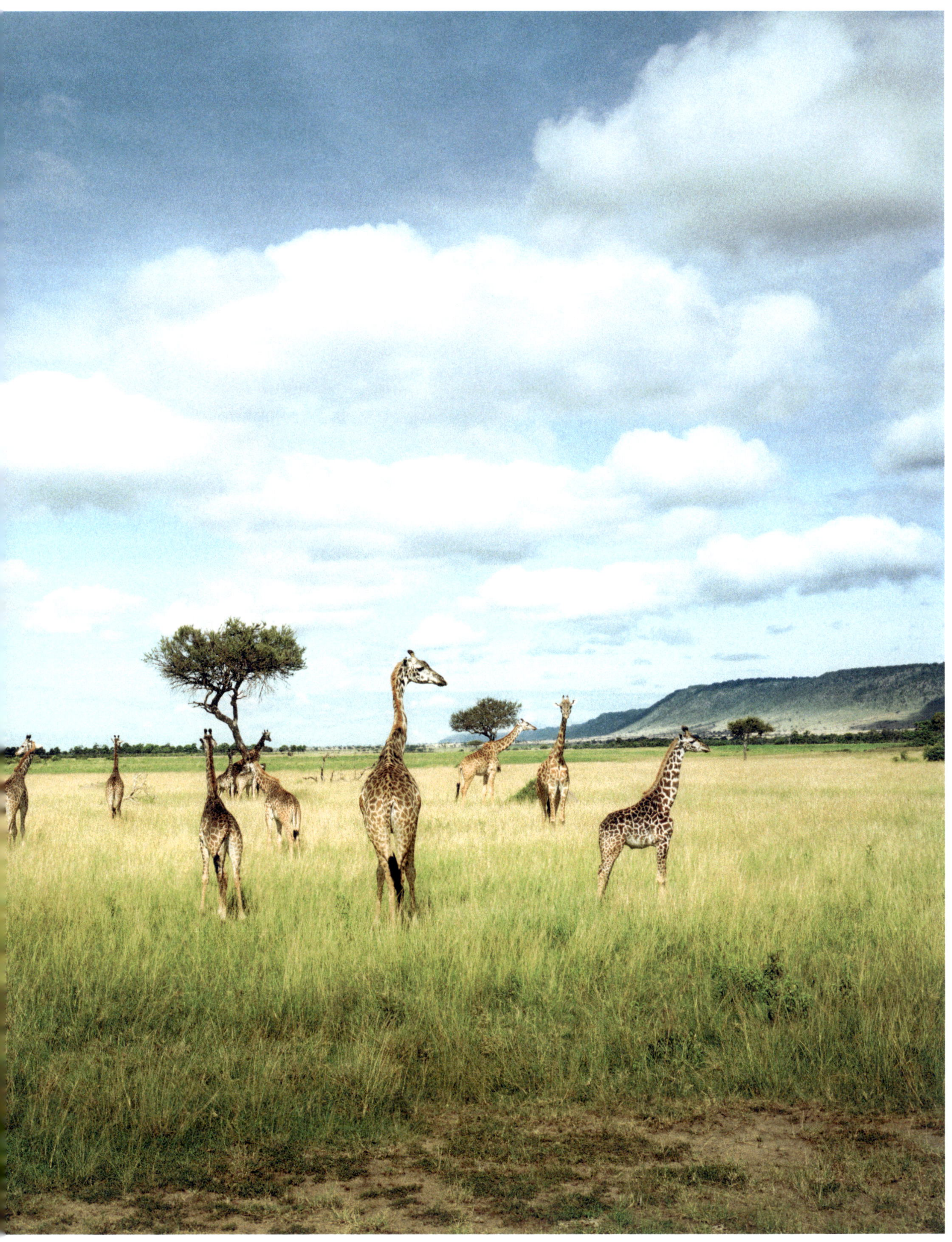

Many cities still consist of a mix of
rundown buildings constructed decades
ago, left unmaintained or unimproved.
Simultaneously, newly erected high-rises
are funded through foreign aid loans,
giving rise to corruption, kickbacks, and
a mounting foreign debt. This trend enables
nations such as China to expand their
influence and control over the continent.

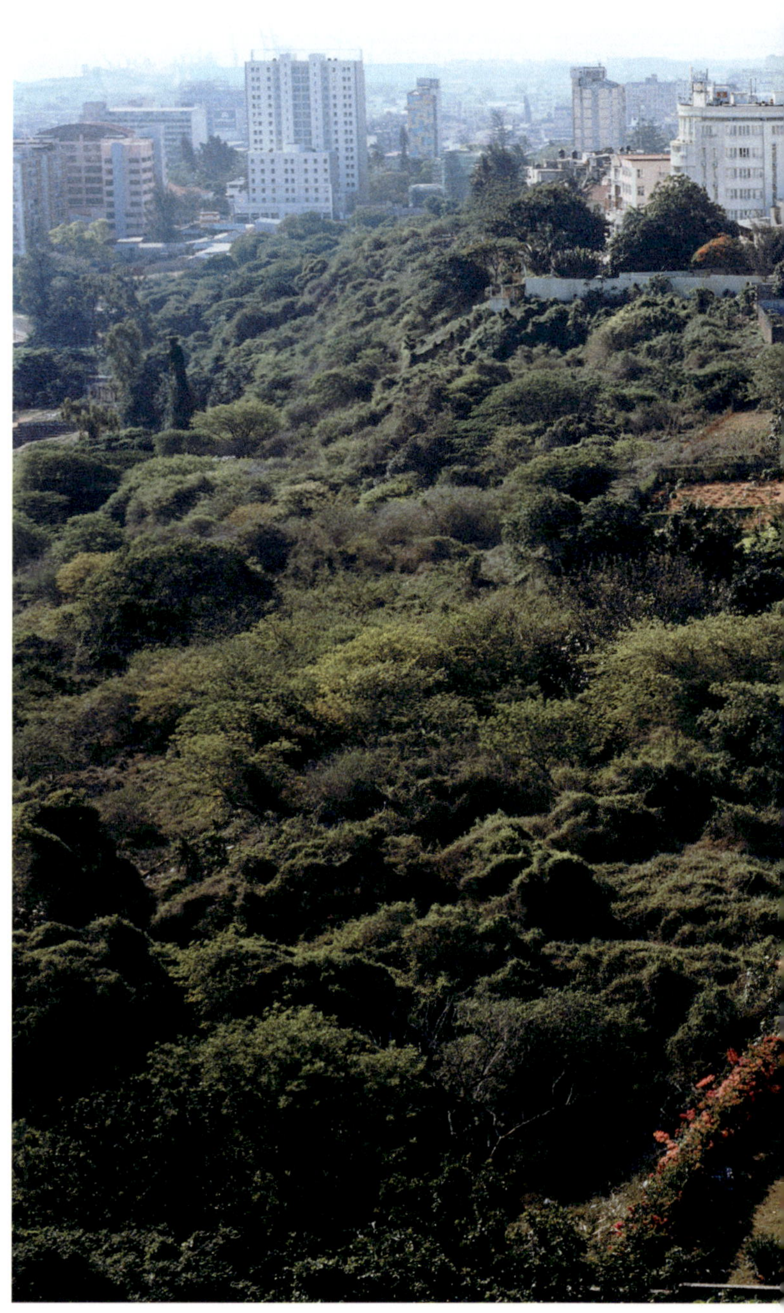

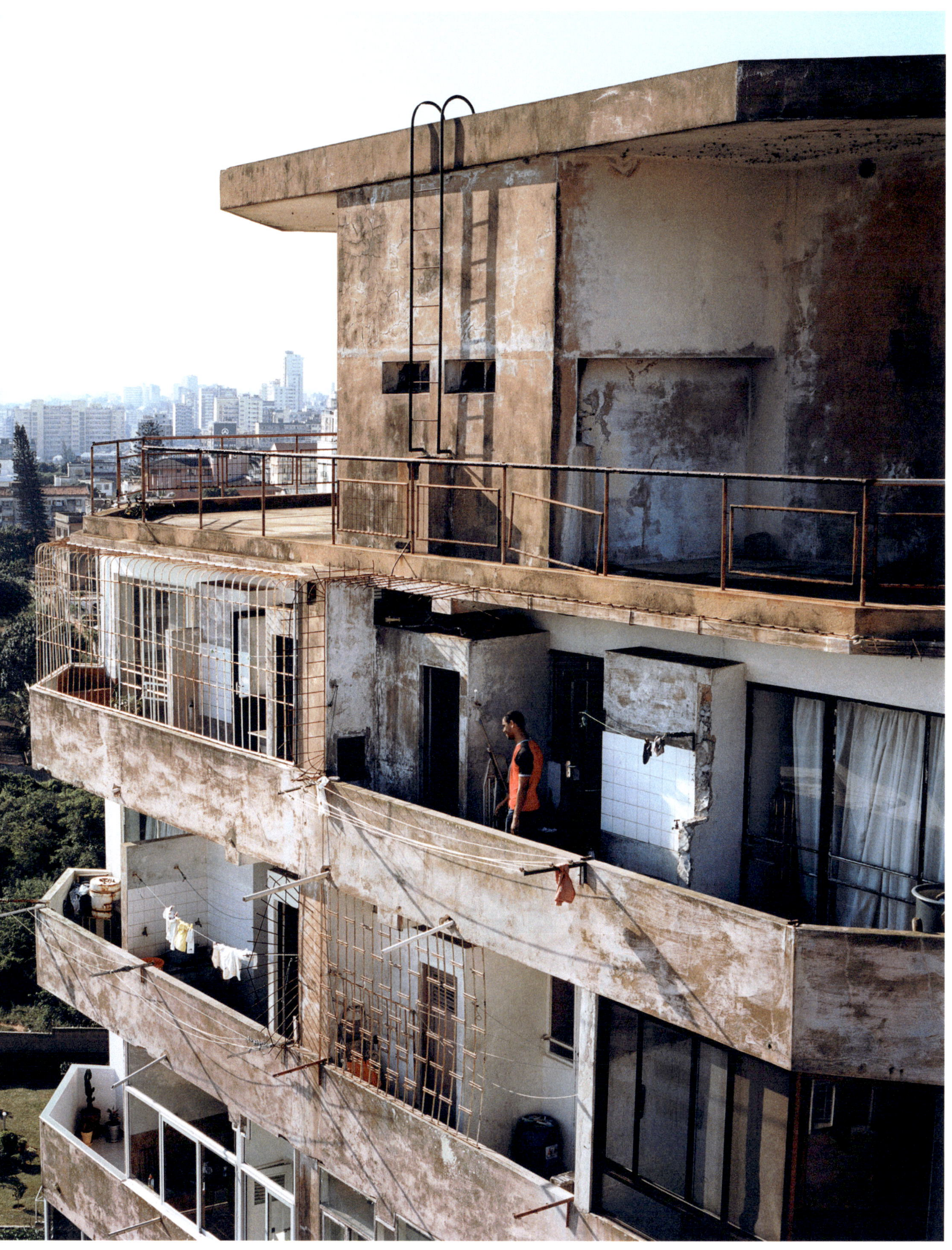

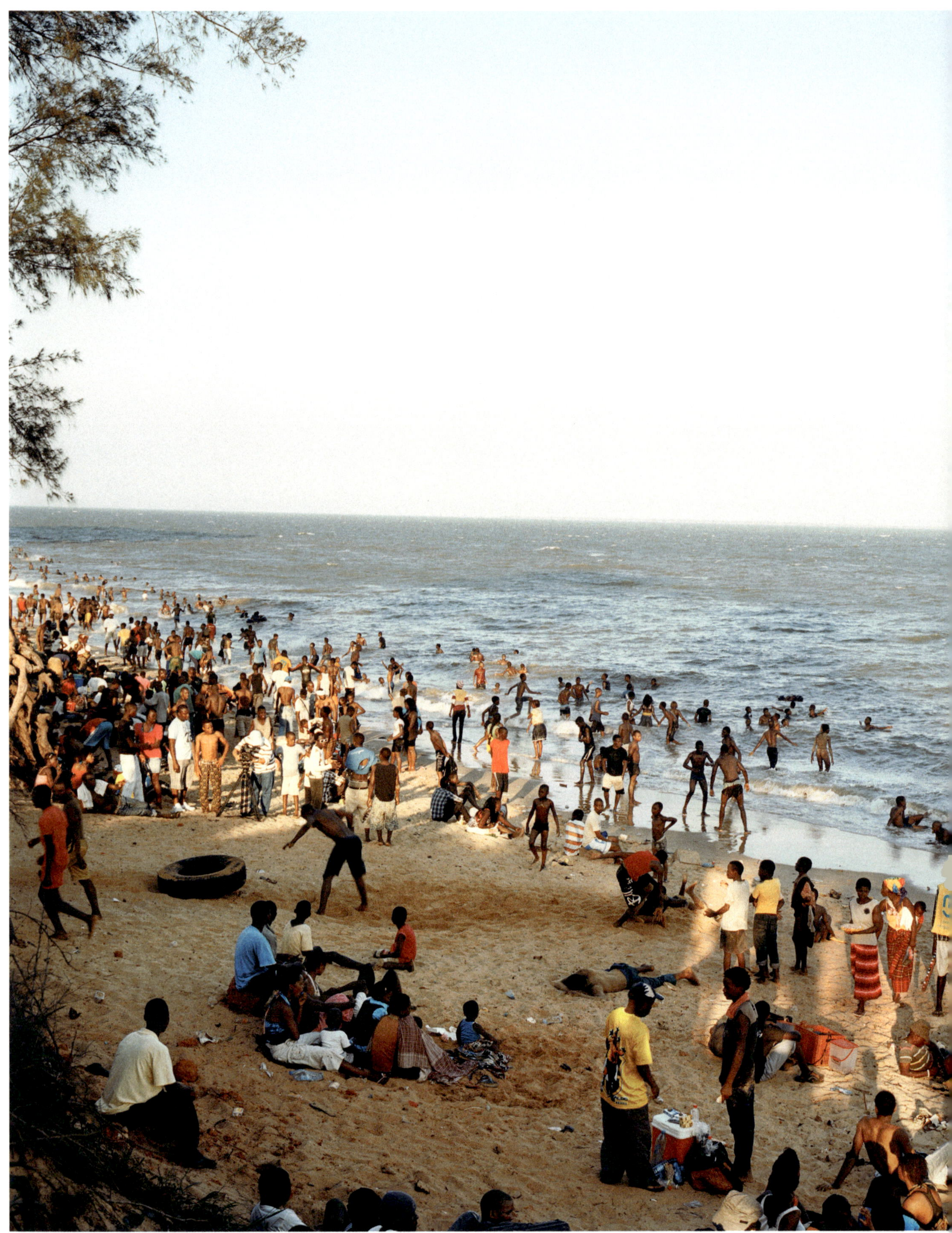

On a Sunday afternoon, families and friends gather to unwind at a public beach located just beyond the city limits.

Projections indicate that by 2050 the continent will host a minimum of 25% of the global population, a significant increase from the less than 10% recorded in 1950. This surge will inevitably escalate the demand for resources, exerting pressure on the dwindling wilderness habitats and their resident wildlife.

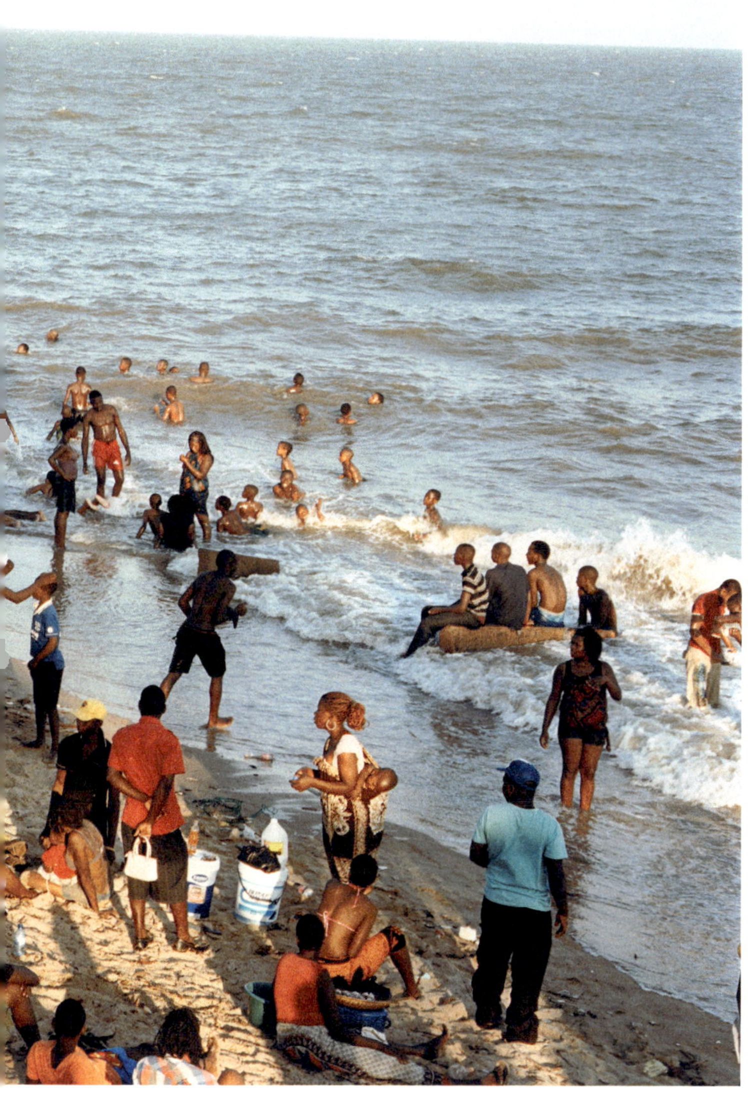

The Maasai Mara National Reserve is a unique wildlife conservation haven famous for its spectacular natural diversity of wildlife and is the premier Kenya Safari location in East Africa, offering visitors numerous reasons to visit this animal paradise.

The ecosystem of the reserve is on the brink of imminent collapse due to substantial investments from hoteliers and camp operators. Moreover, the reserve, which is the habitat for 25% of Kenya's wildlife, is confronted with the issue of high visitor numbers that pose a significant threat to the remaining balance of the ecosystem.

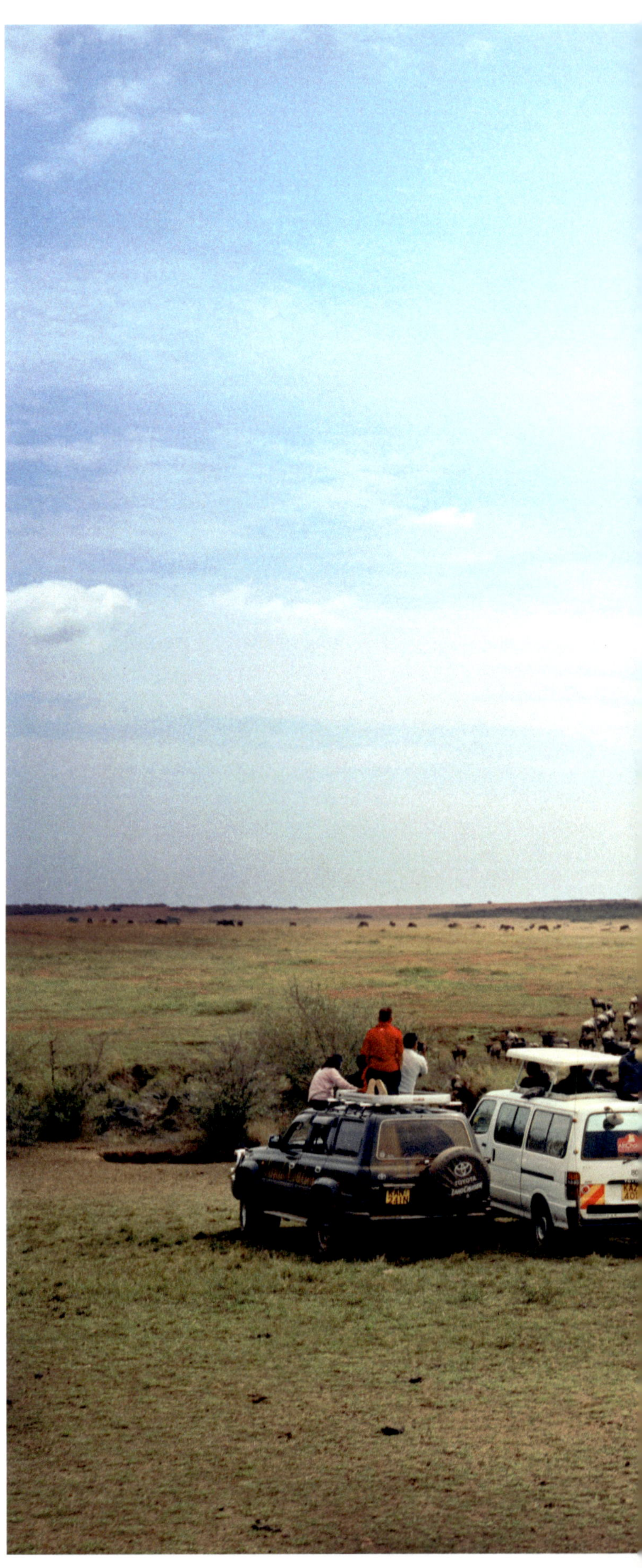

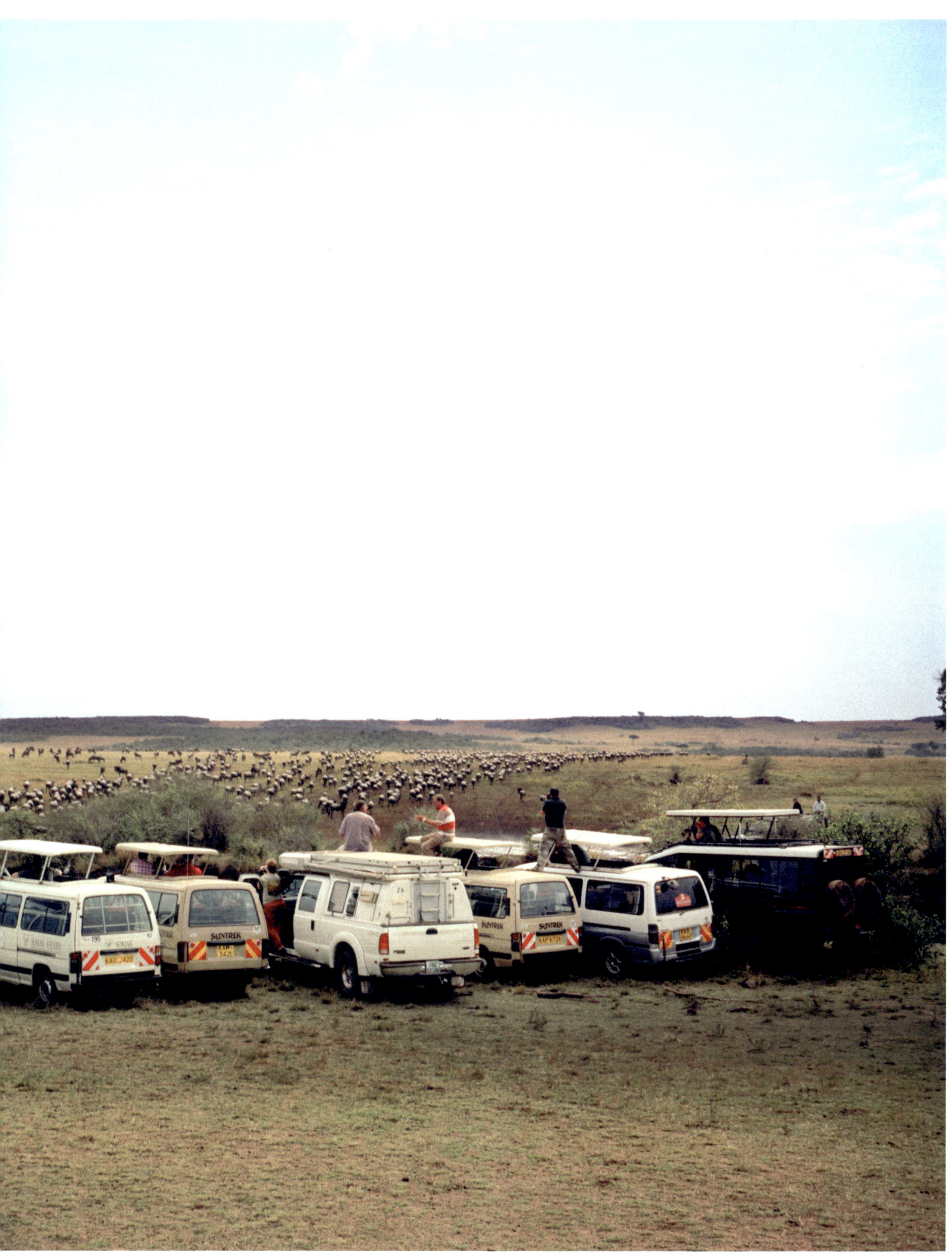

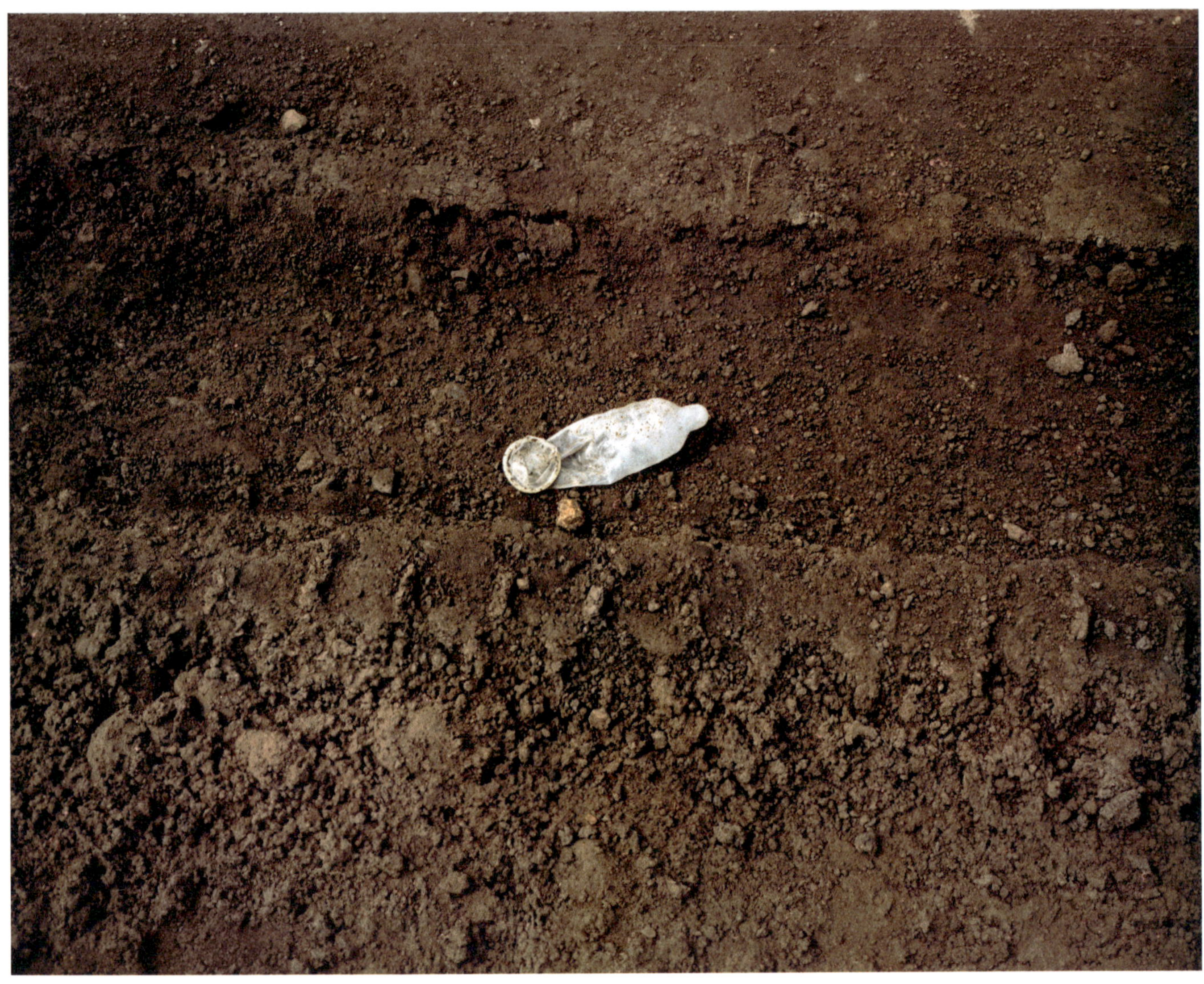

On my journey to witness segments of the magnificent migration, my attention was drawn to an unexpected sight — a discarded condom lying on the roadside, proof that we are no longer in an only exclusive wilderness area but one that is under immense human pressure. The Great Migration entails the awe-inspiring movement of over a million wildebeest from Tanzania's Serengeti to the adjacent Maasai Mara Reserve in Kenya.

This phenomenon stands as one of the most spectacular displays of wildlife behavior globally. It unfolds annually, with the creatures' primal instincts propelling them toward lusher landscapes in accordance with the climatic rainfall patterns across the Serengeti-Maasai Mara ecosystem.

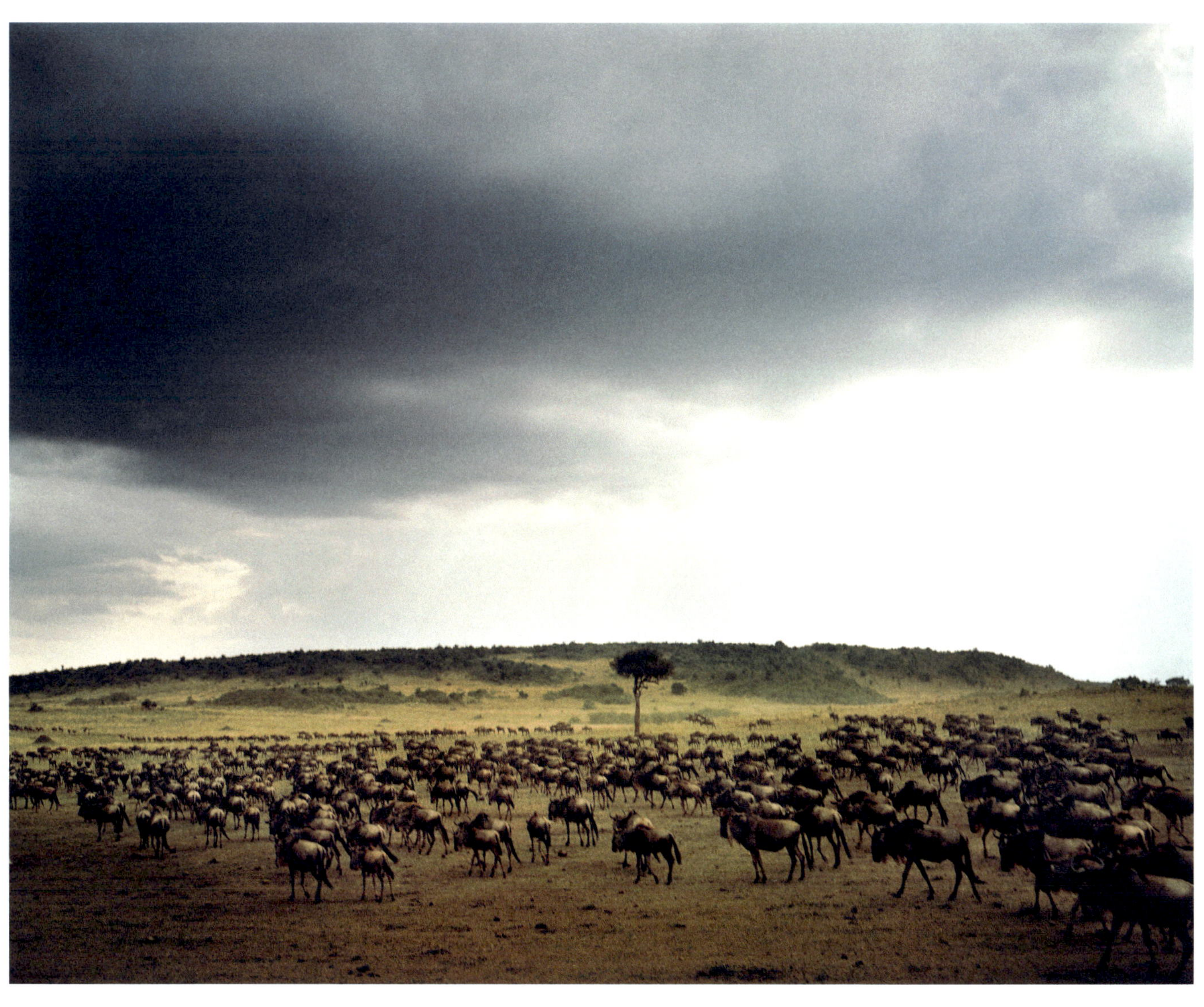

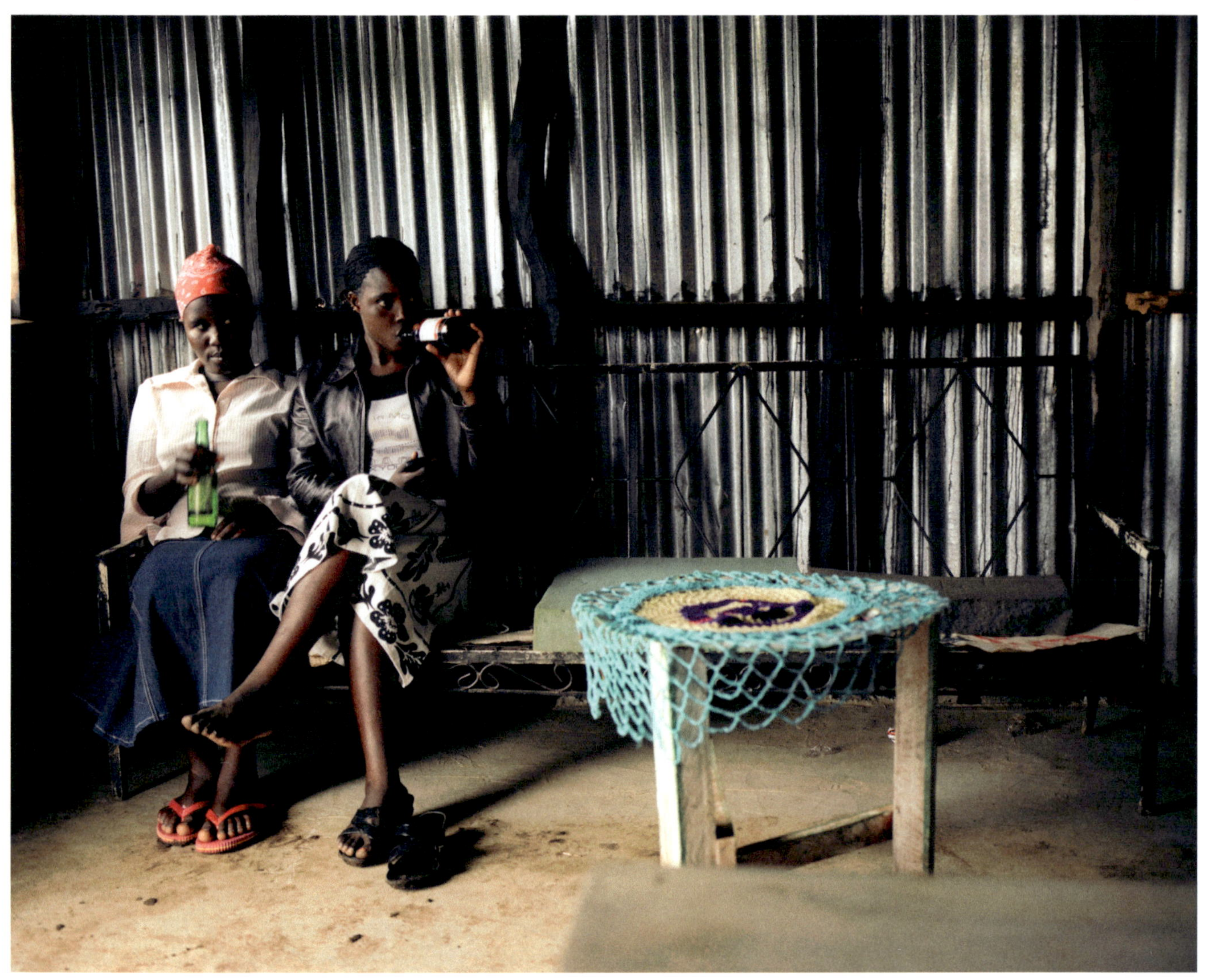

In an unmonitored settlement situated within a conservation area
bordering the Maasai Mara game reserve, prostitutes eagerly await
clients arriving from nearby lodges where they work. On the next
page, within the game reserve, a chef employed by a neighboring
lodge is preparing breakfast for clients who are soon to return
from their early morning hot air balloon ride.

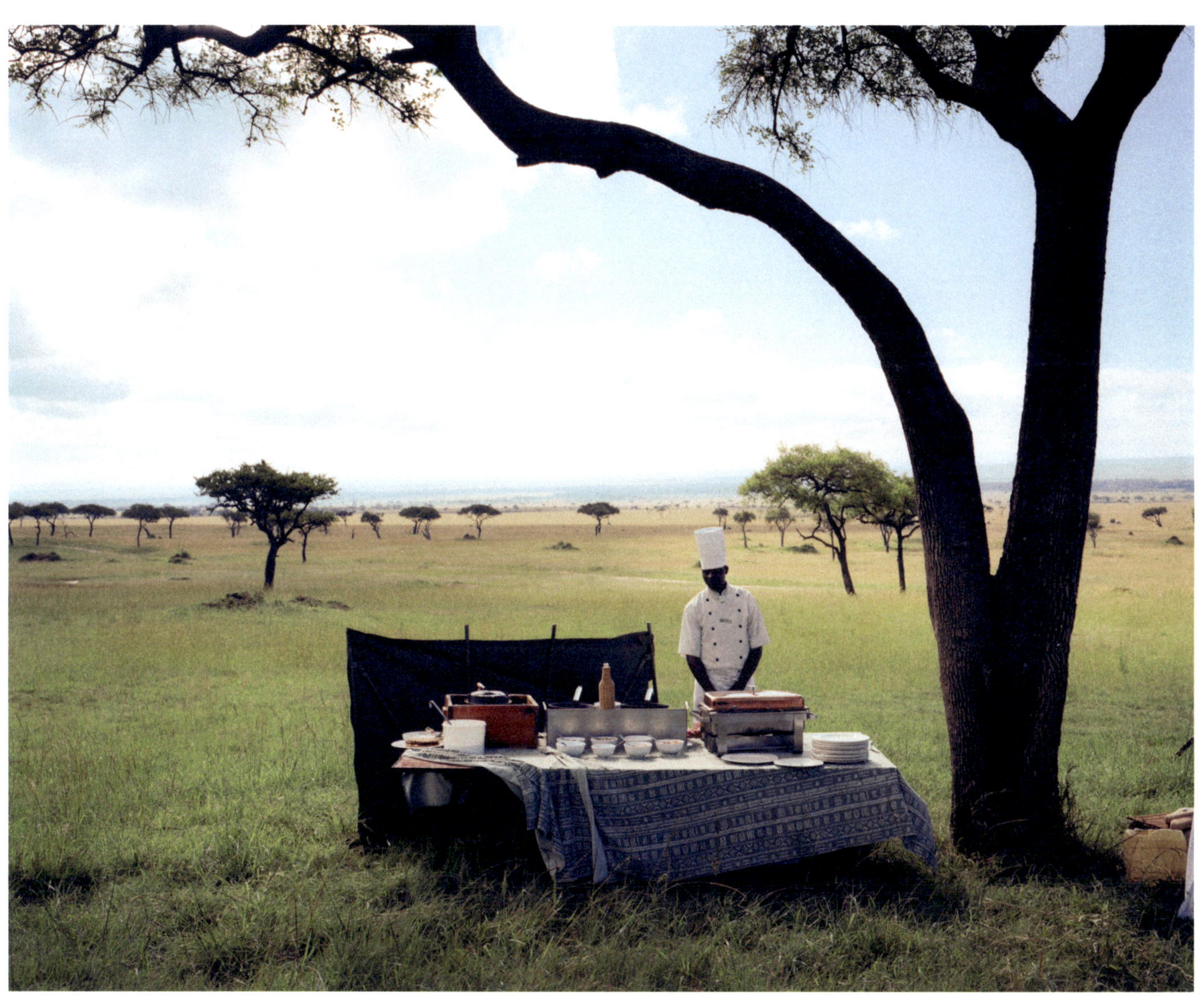

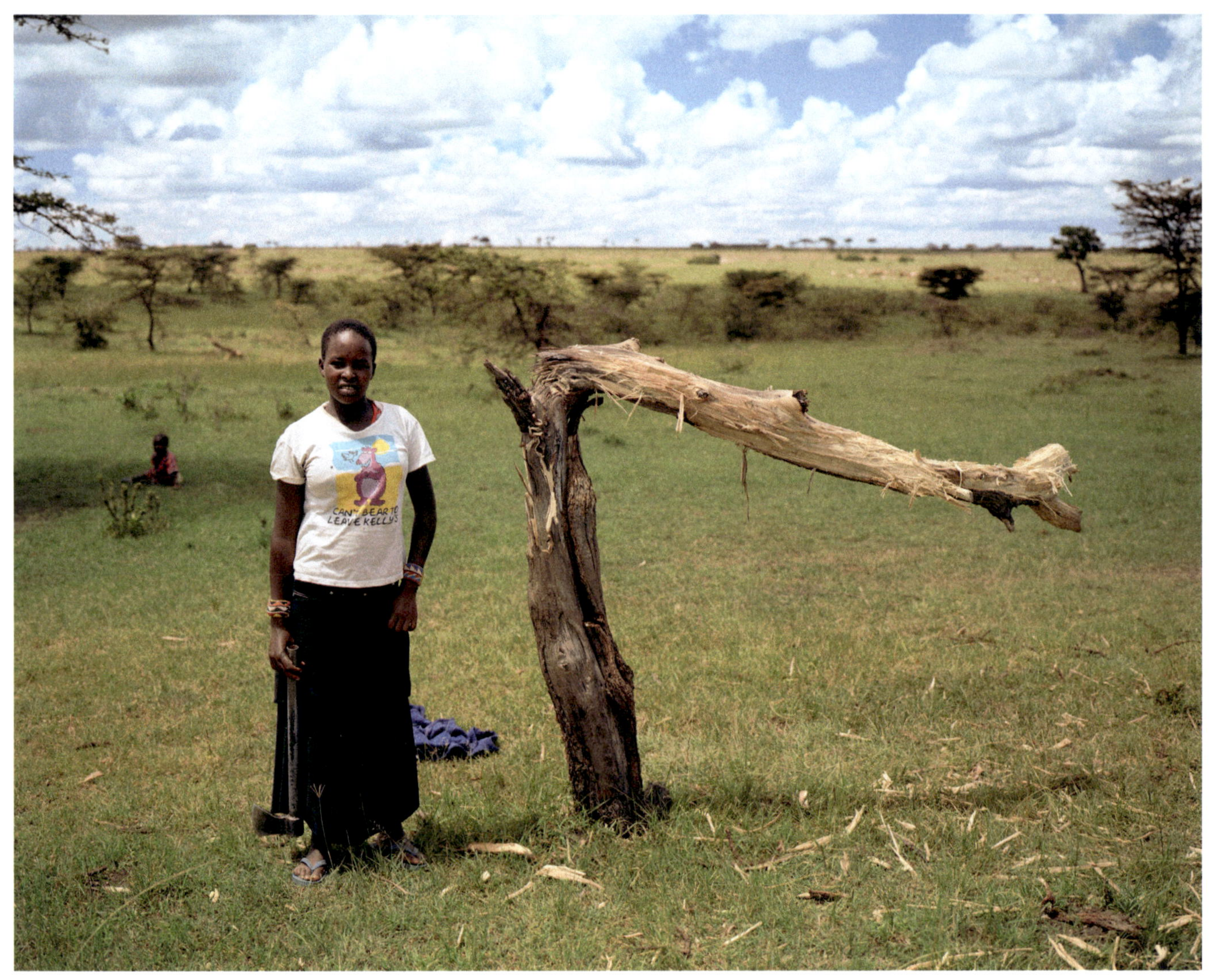

A woman is chopping down a tree on the outskirts of the Maasai Mara
game reserve, intending to use it for charcoal to prepare meals
for her family or to create a fire on chilly nights. According
to a study conducted by the World Wildlife Fund for Nature from
1989 to 2003, wildlife losses were staggering, reaching up to 95%
for giraffes, 80% for warthogs, 76% for hartebeests, and 67% for
impalas. The study attributes this decline in animal populations
to the growing human settlement in and around the reserve.

The human pressure is not only over taking the wilderness space
where the wildlife is, but it is also eradicating all the trees
and vegetations that giraffes, impalas and all non predators
animals feed on.

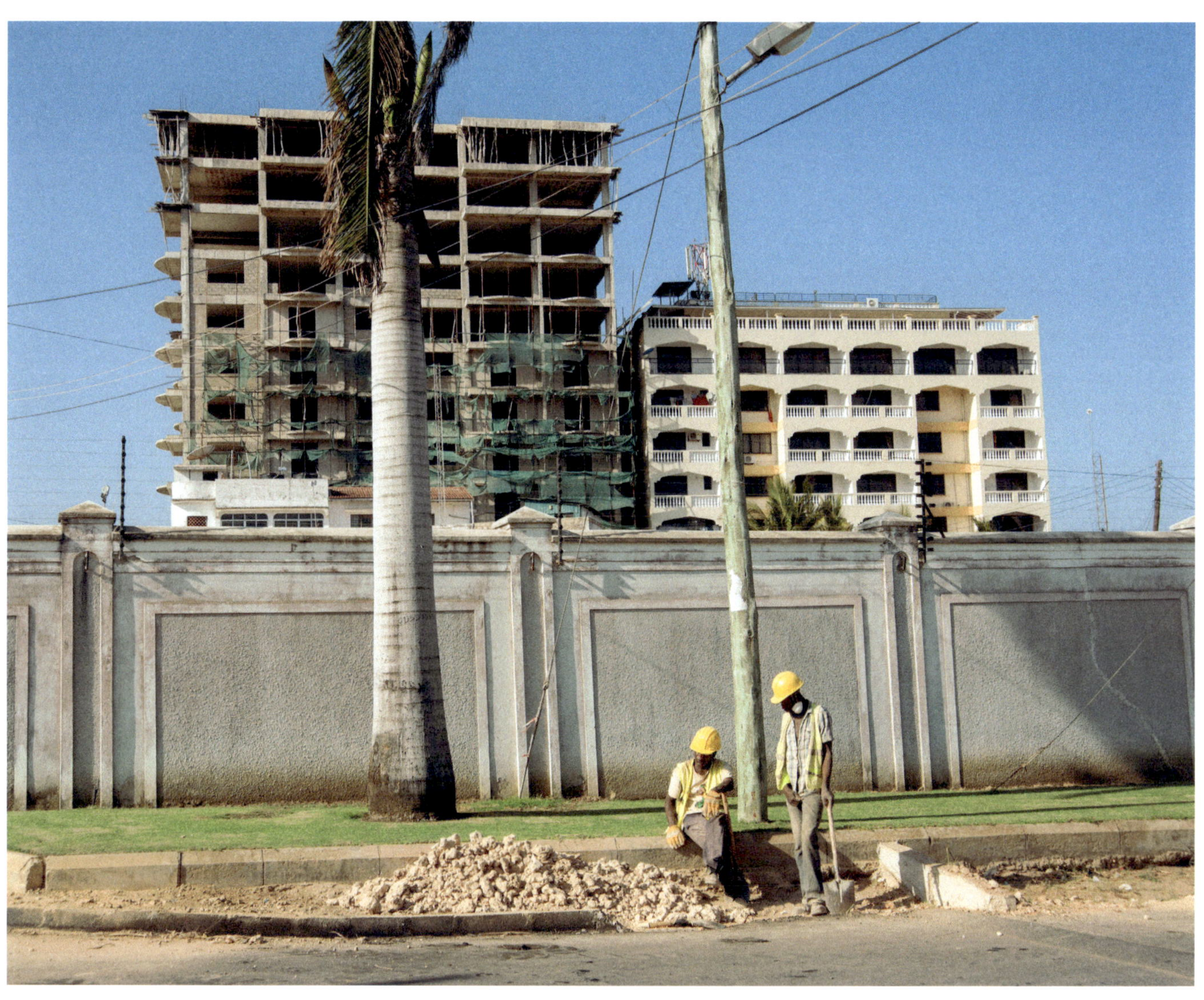

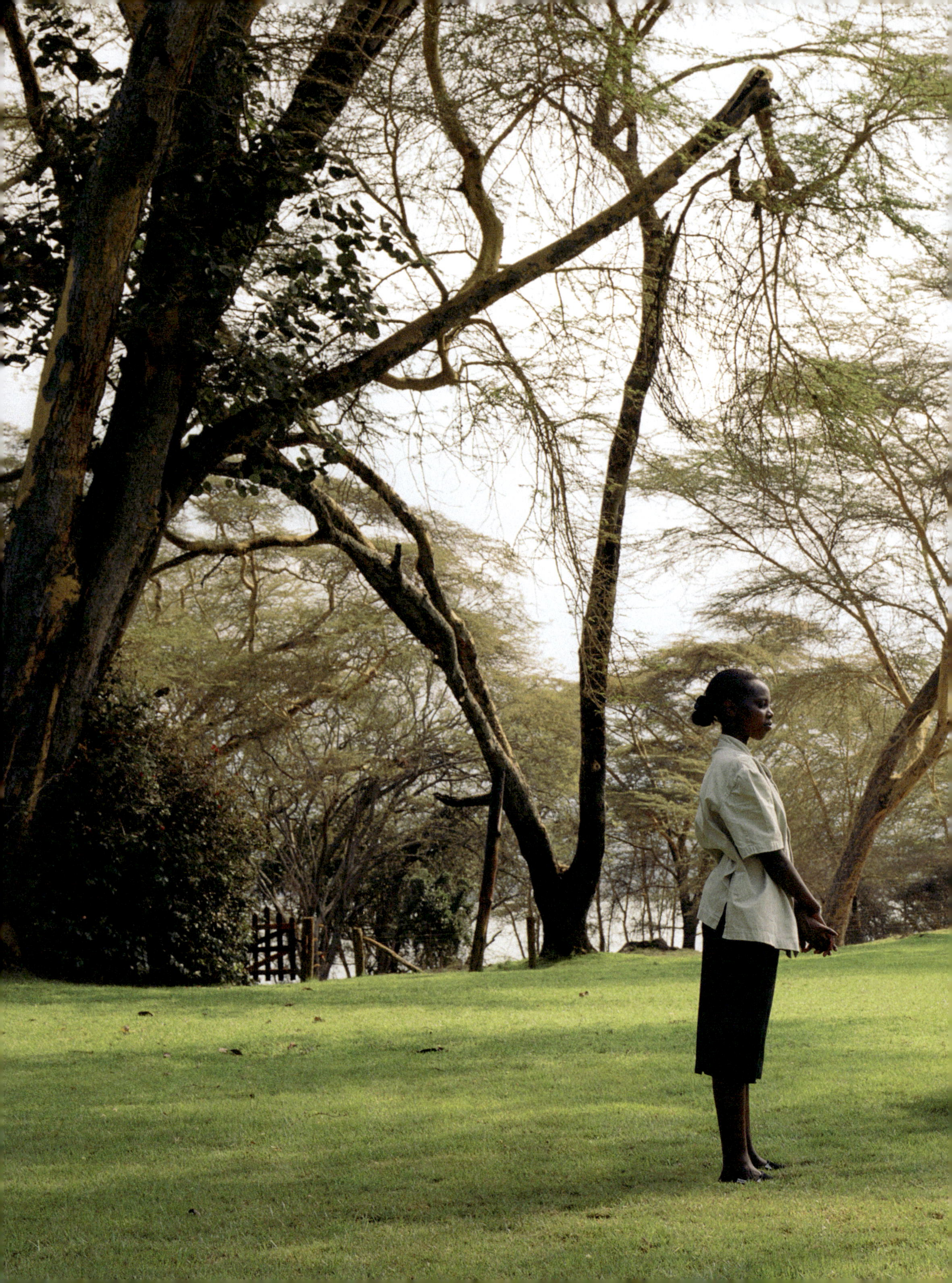

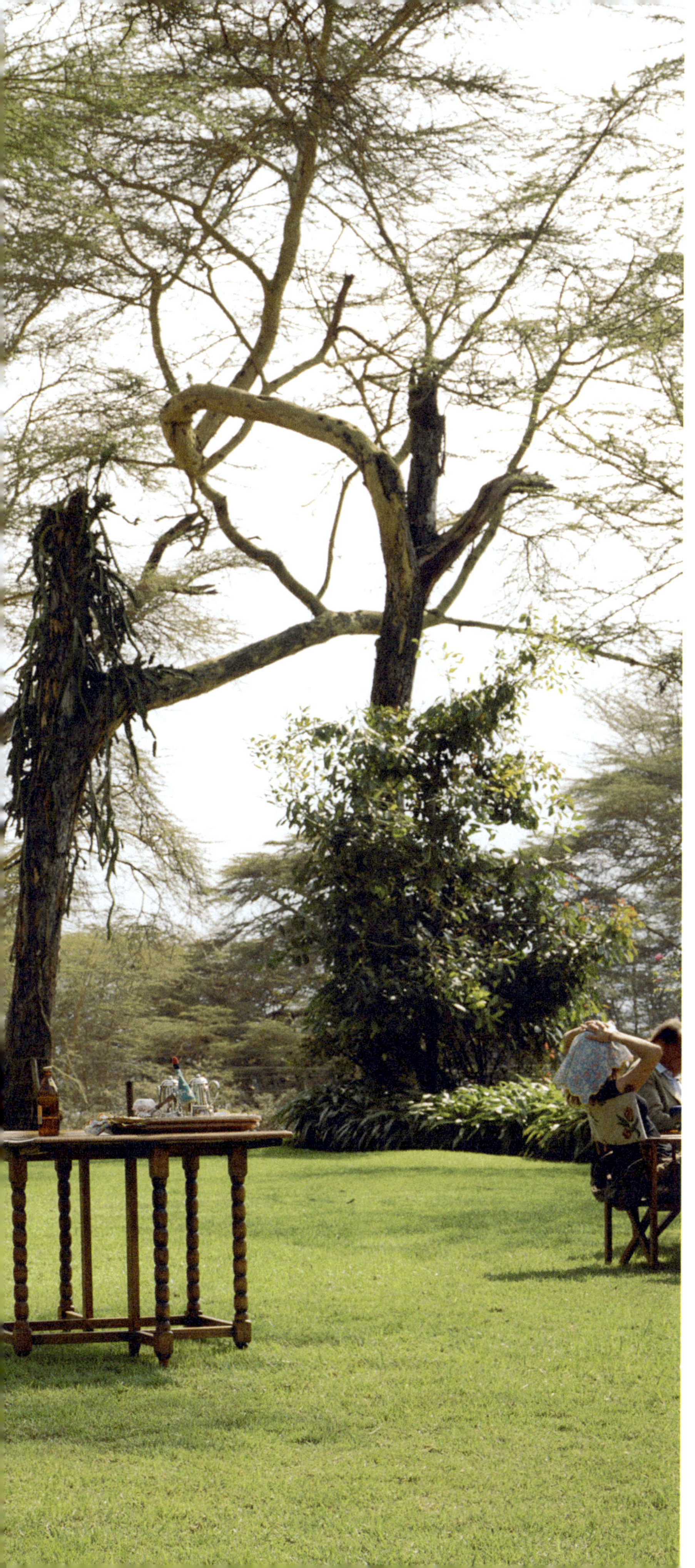

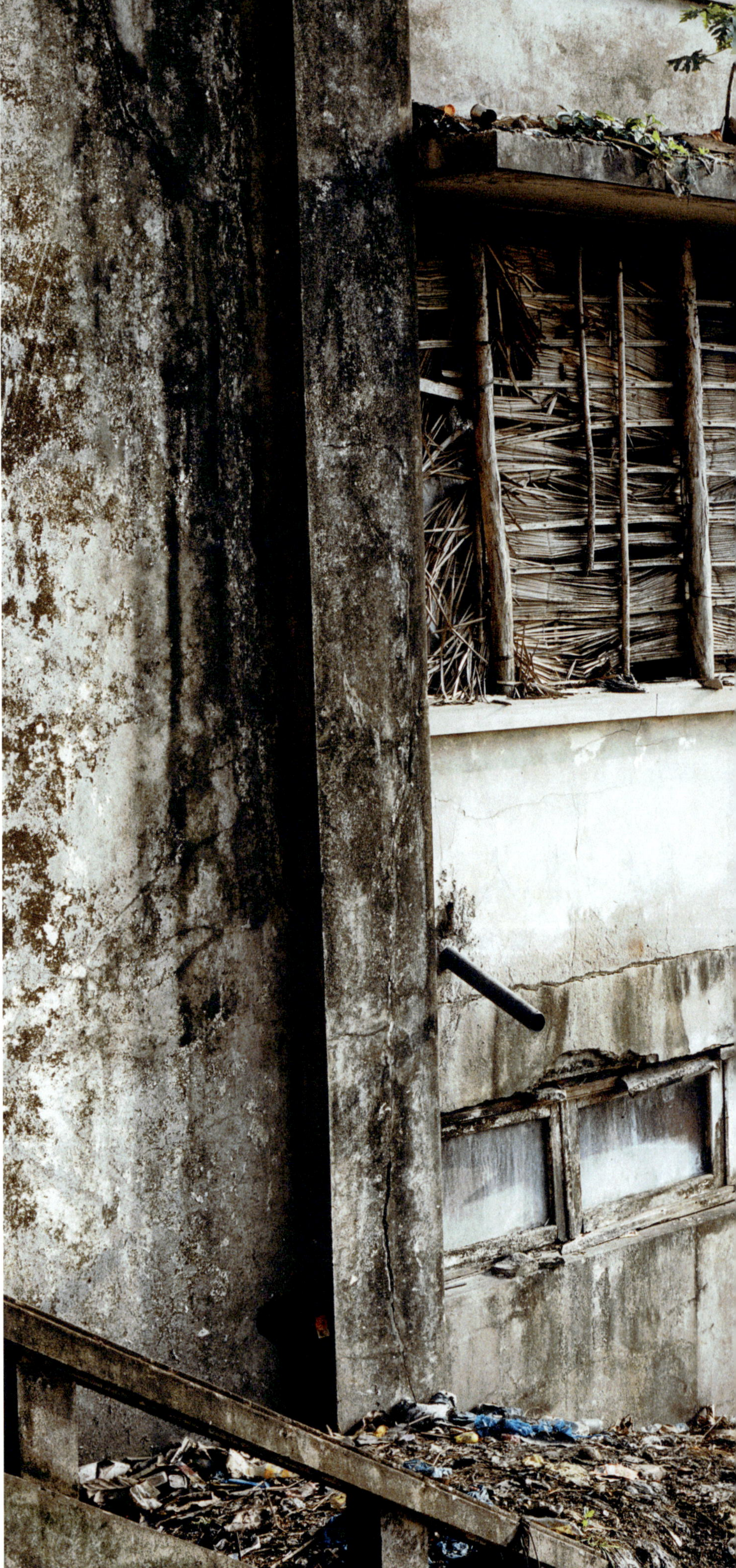

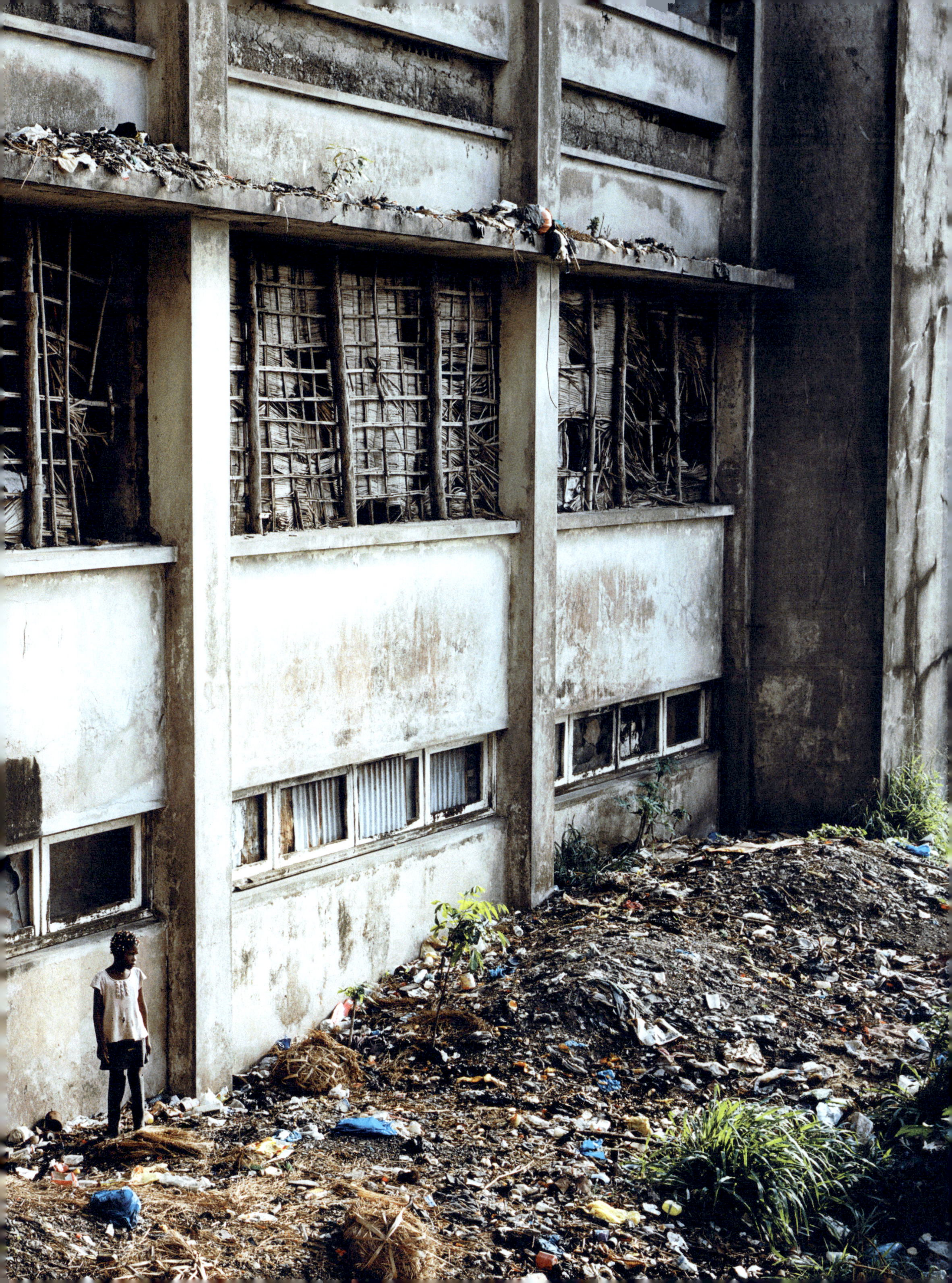

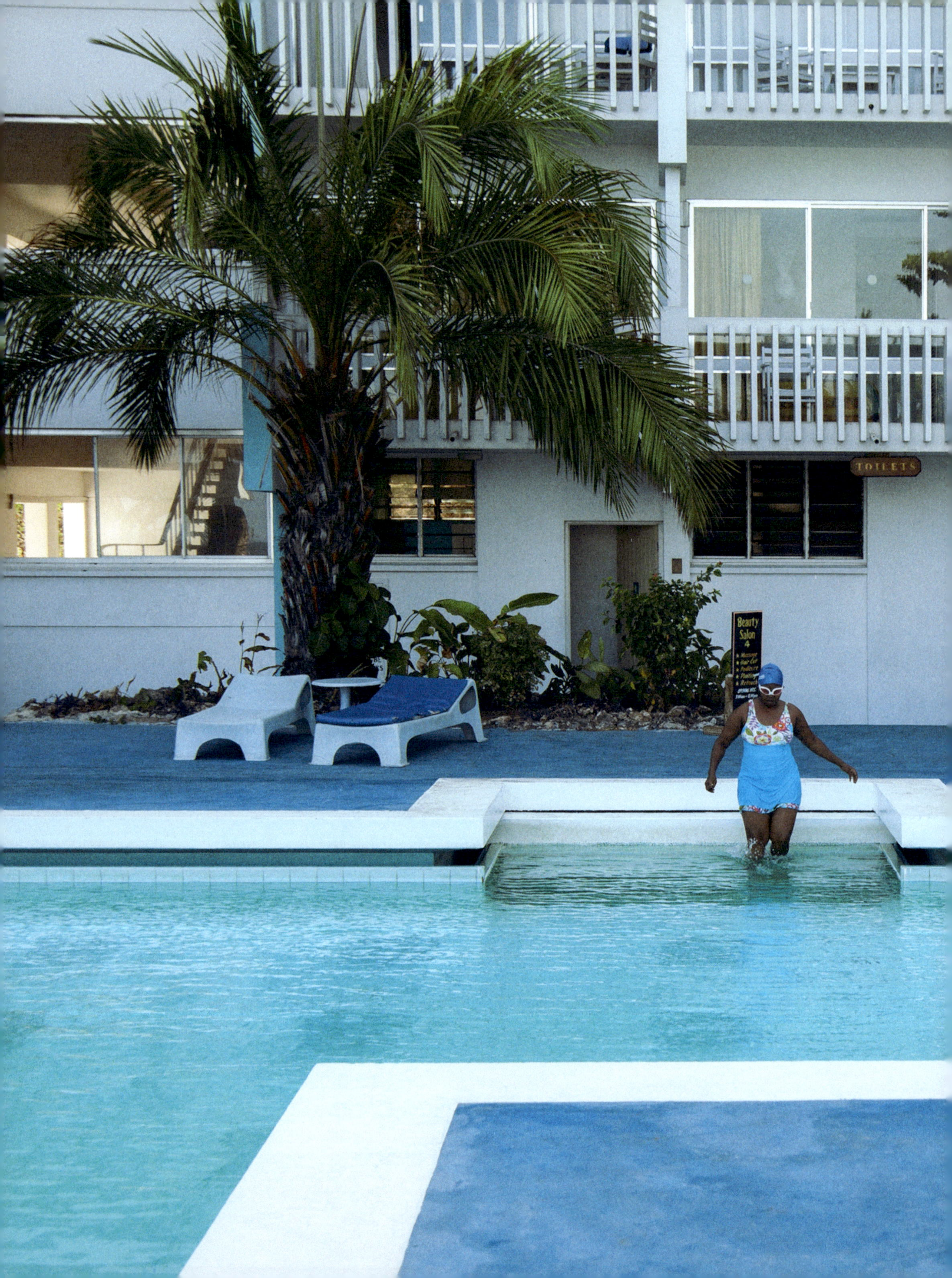

TOILETS
Beauty
Salon
4

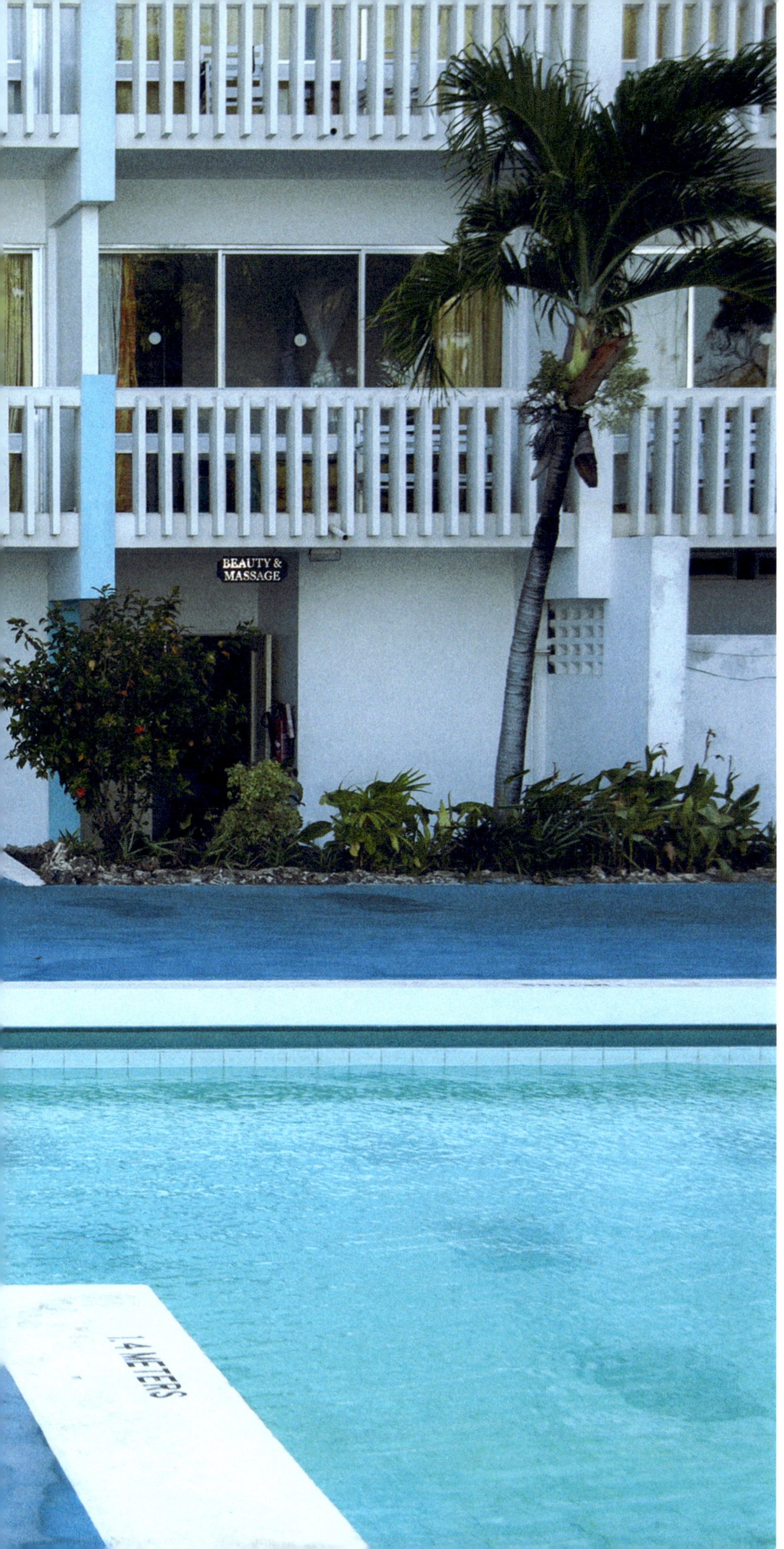

BEAUTY &
MASSAGE
1.4 METERS

Unmonitored settlement situated just outside one of the main entrance gates of the Maasai Mara National reserve.

The majority of wildlife species, 83.7%, counted in the last WWF 2021 report, in the Maasai Mara Ecosystem live outside of the reserve with only 16.2% in the protected areas in the Maasai Mara National Reserve.

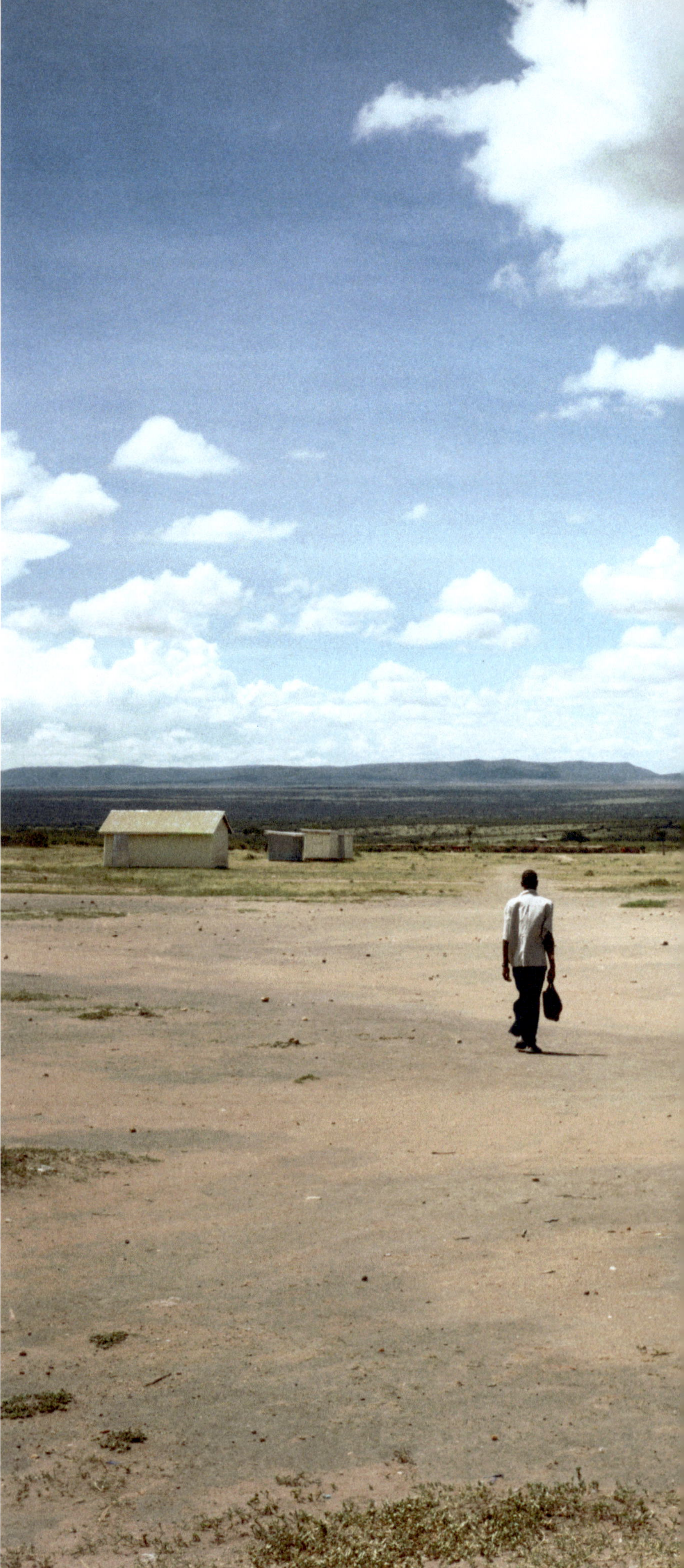

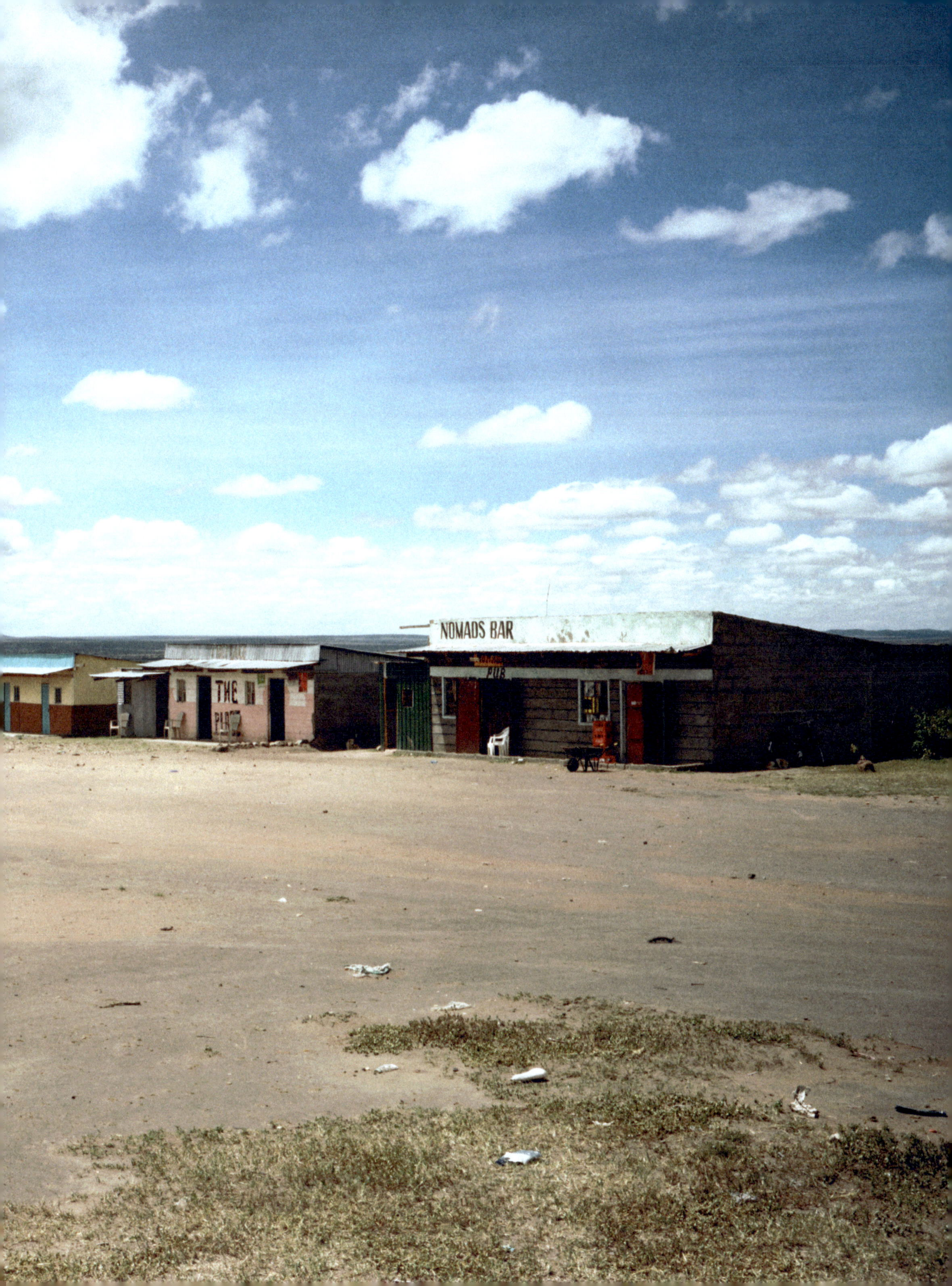

NOMADS BAR
PUB
THE
PUB

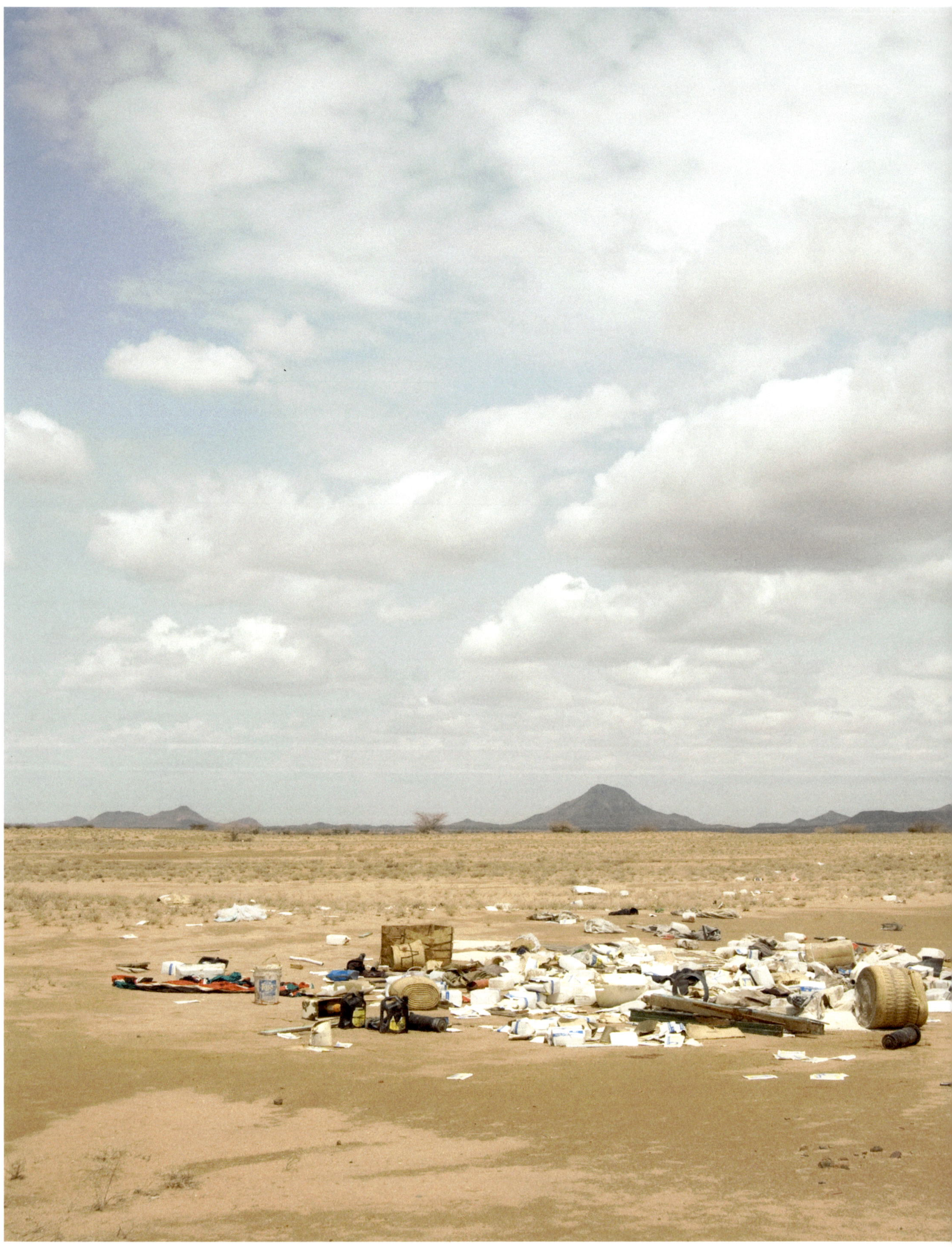

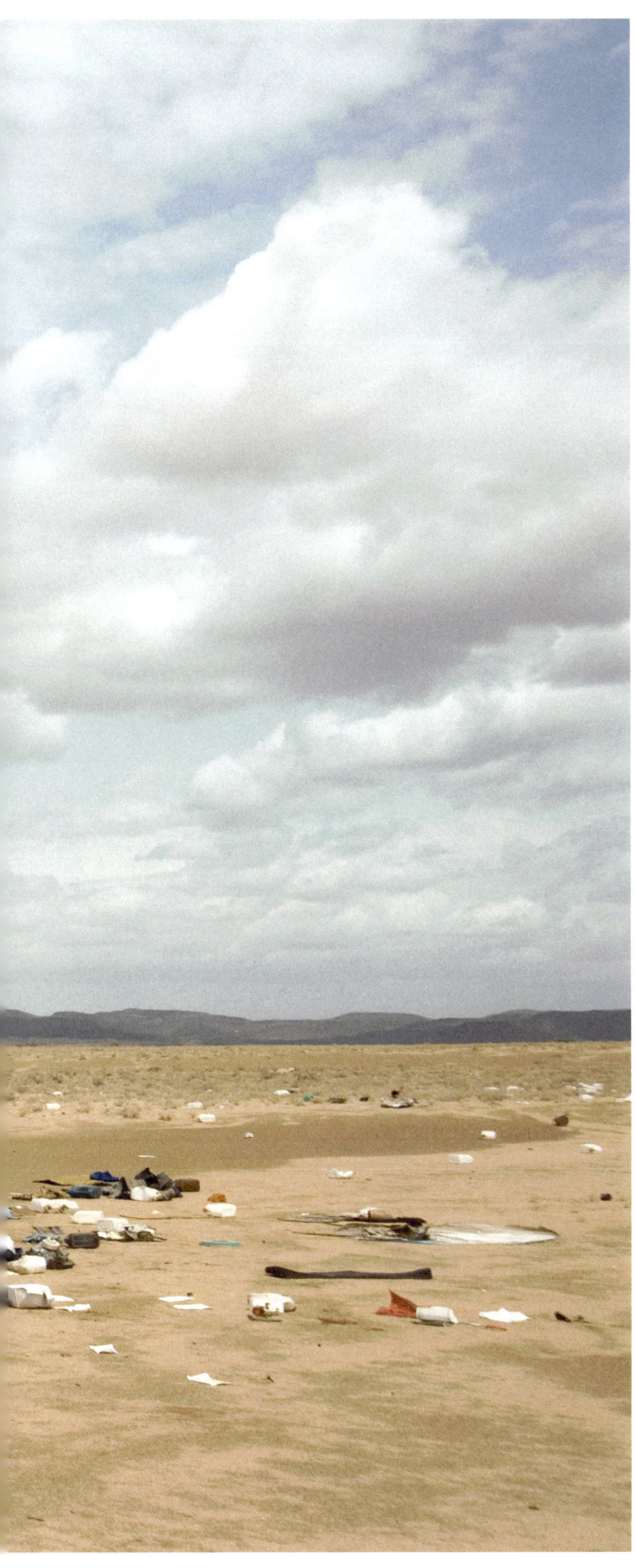

Developing nations have long asserted their rightful claim for compensation due to the devastating impact of climate change. Essentially, they are urging affluent countries to cease their reckless emissions of greenhouse gases, which contribute to the intensification of extreme weather events, prolonged droughts, and more destructive hurricanes, resulting in widespread devastation that incurs billions of dollars in costs.

I sincerely hope that a recent agreement reached by the United Nations to establish a fund aimed at aiding impoverished nations in dealing with climate-related disasters exacerbated by the pollution emanating from affluent nations will not absolve the latter from their responsibility to cease the degradation of their own habitats, ecosystems, and wildlife, and to curtail their pollution output. It must not allow them to behave as if these problems have never occurred or never existed.

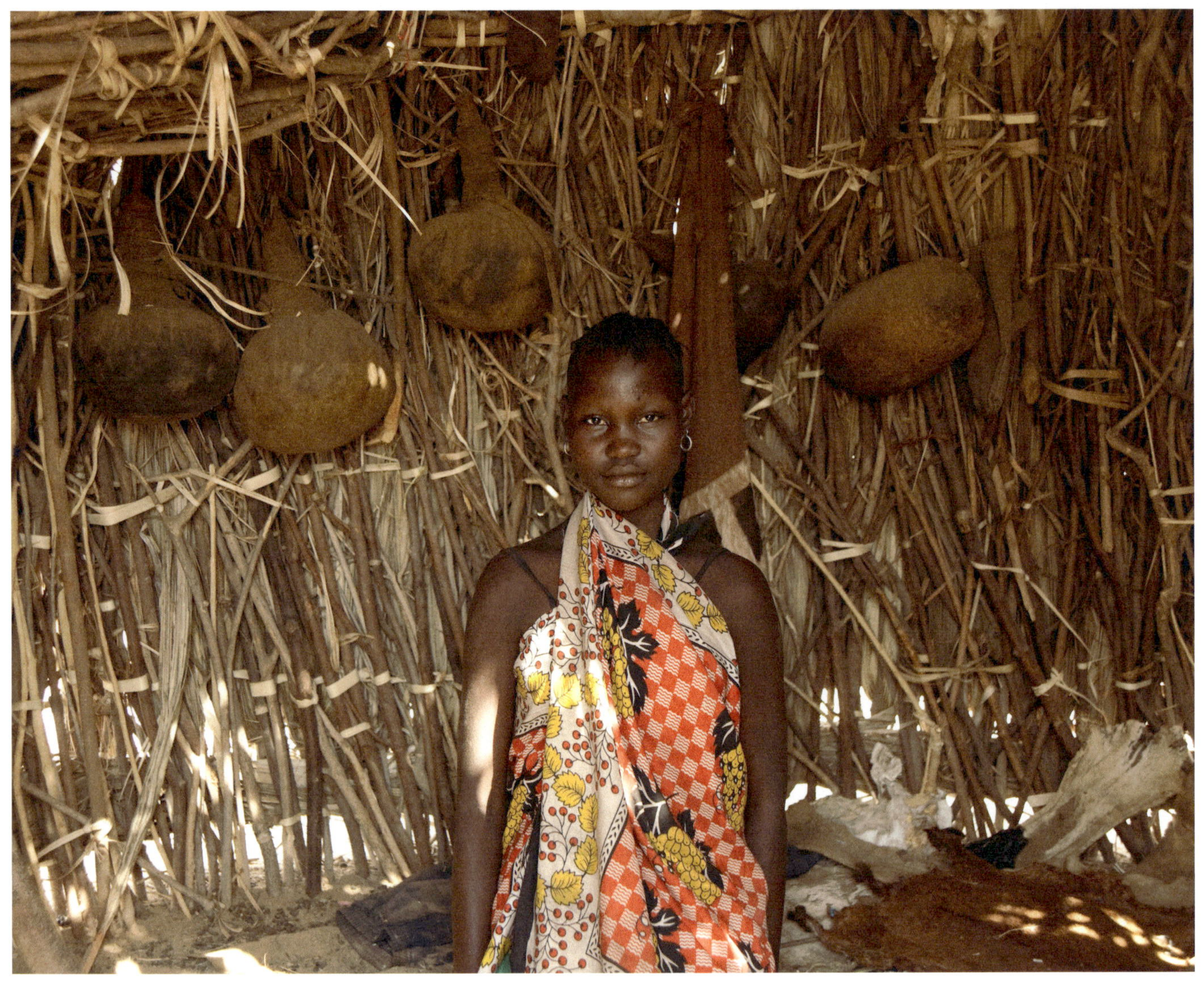

Turkana County stands as an arid, economically deprived, and
secluded region, long overlooked by successive administrations.
It is a place where pastoral communities continue to adhere
to traditional lifestyles, as depicted in this photograph.
However, recent oil discoveries in the area have ushered in
a wave of development, exemplified by the newly constructed petrol
station on the following page—a prominent symbol of progress.

Yet, security concerns in Turkana persist, rooted in the complex
dynamics of tribal politics. The distribution of firearms over the
years has exacerbated tensions between tribes, serving as a tool
for political manipulation. If these issues are not addressed,
the region could potentially evolve into a hotspot for conflicts
over oil resources.

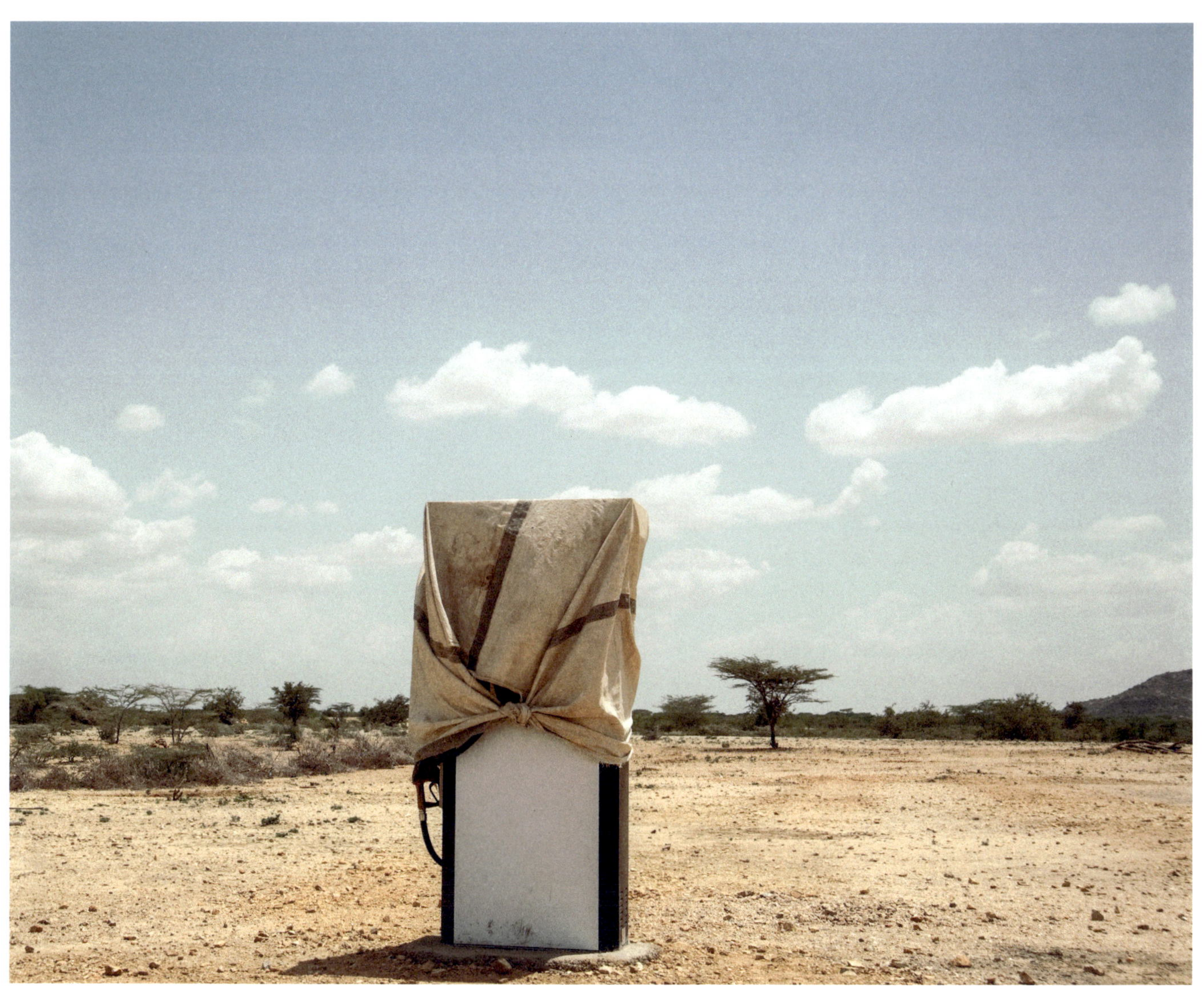

Turkana County lies at the crossroads of Kenya's blurred borders with Ethiopia, Uganda, and South Sudan. This arid region has historically been overlooked by successive Kenyan administrations. In recent years, Turkana County has gained significant attention from both the Kenyan government and investors. This interest was piqued after reports surfaced about a British-owned oil exploration company discovering approximately 250 million barrels of crude oil in the area.

The prospect of oil revenue is viewed as a potential solution to poverty in a region where nine out of ten people live below the poverty line. However, beneath the optimistic rhetoric, the current political and security landscape in Turkana County bears a striking resemblance to the conditions that ignited the insurgency in Nigeria's Niger Delta.

Is there any corner of the world where petroleum extraction has occurred without transforming the surrounding area into an environmental catastrophe?

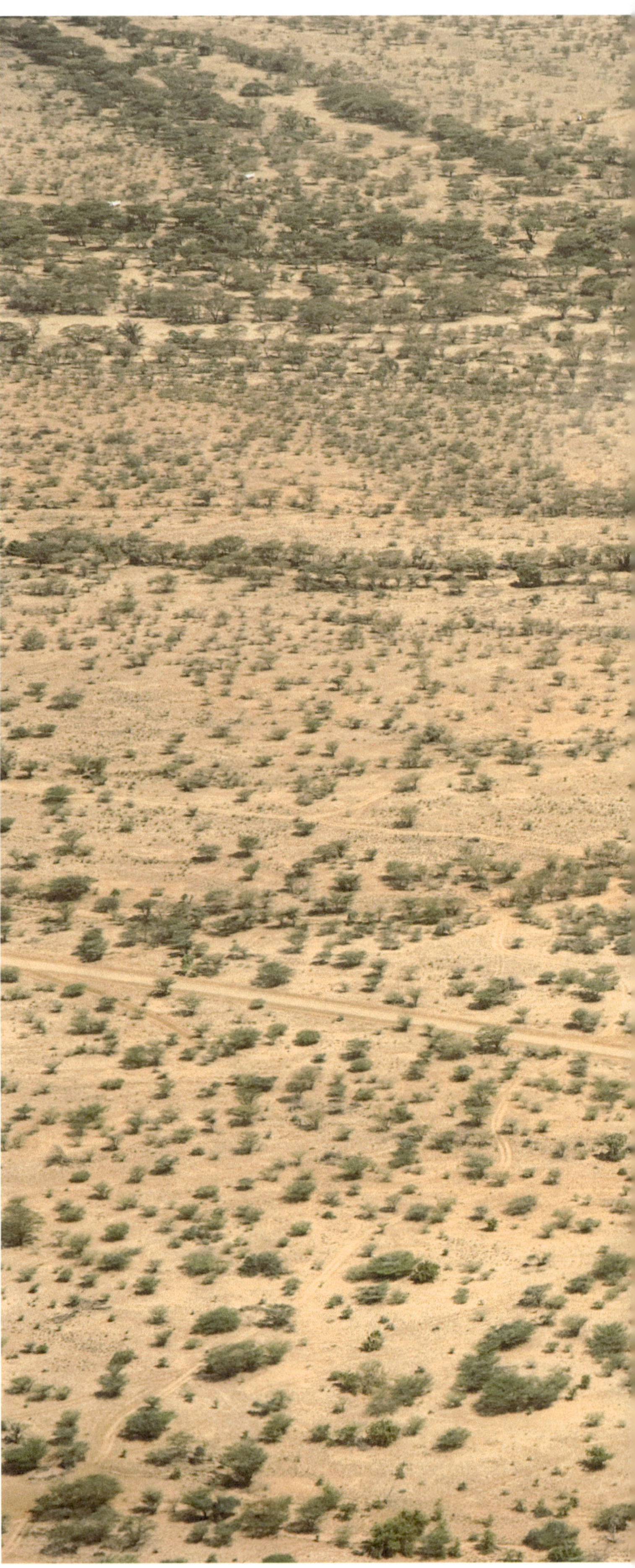

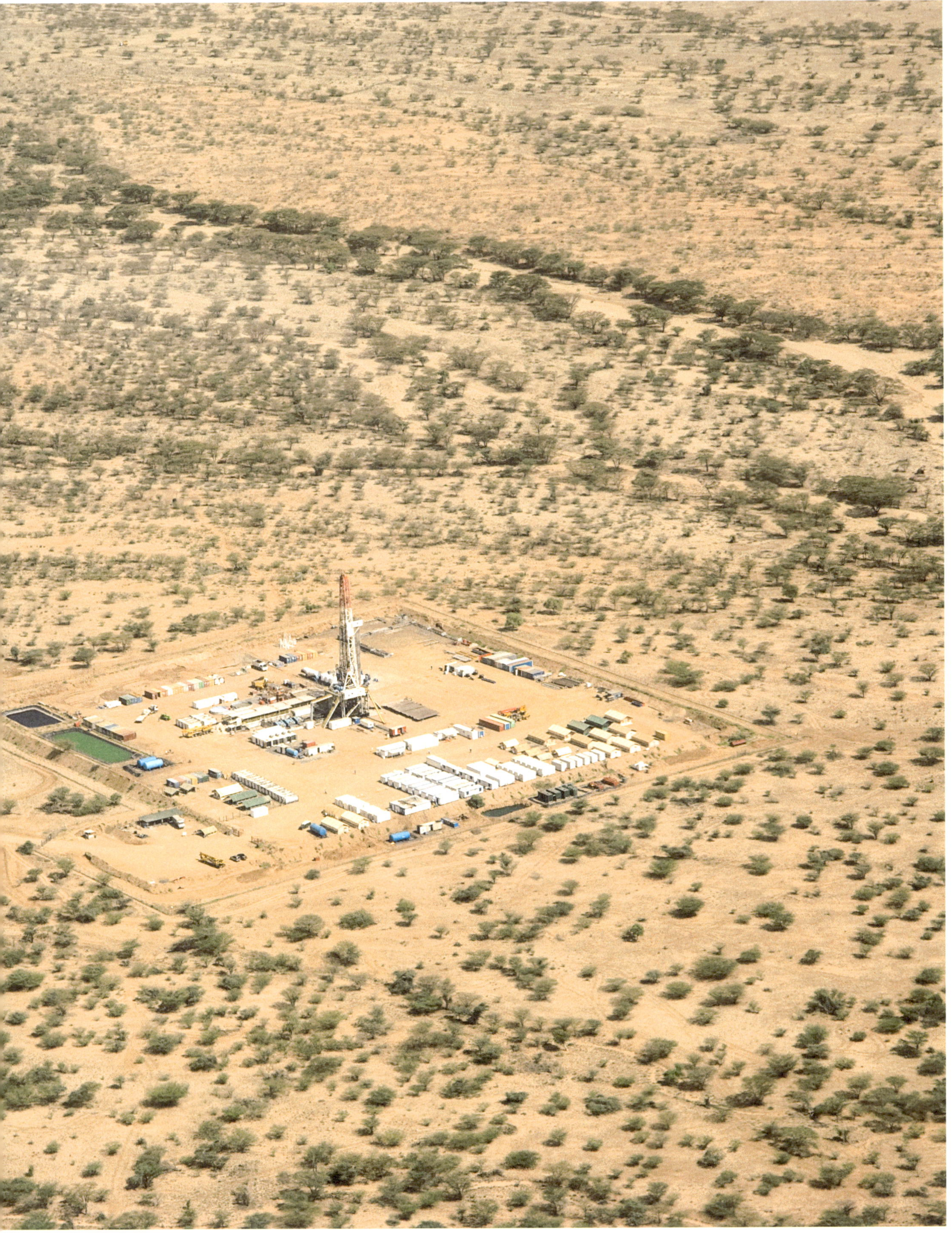

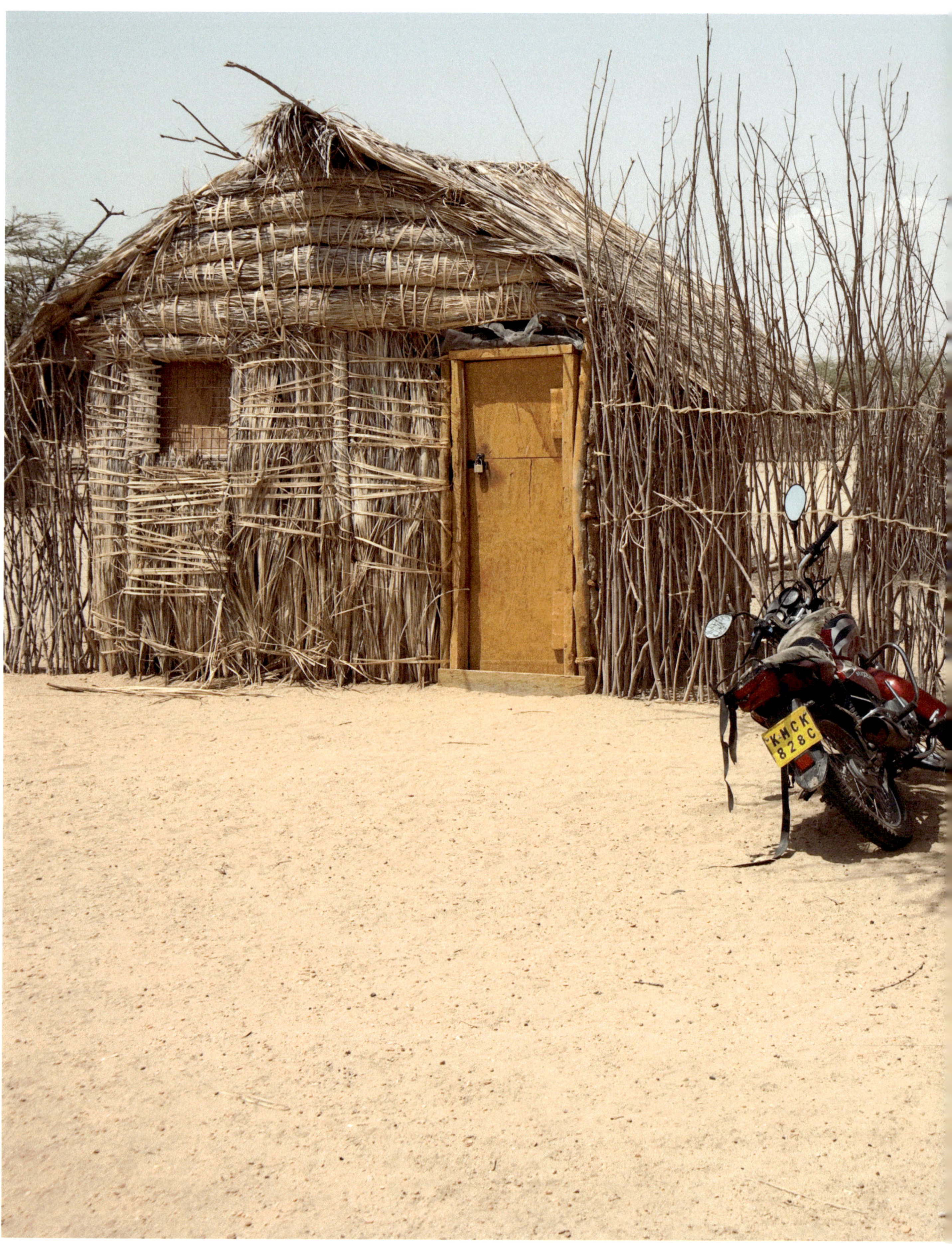

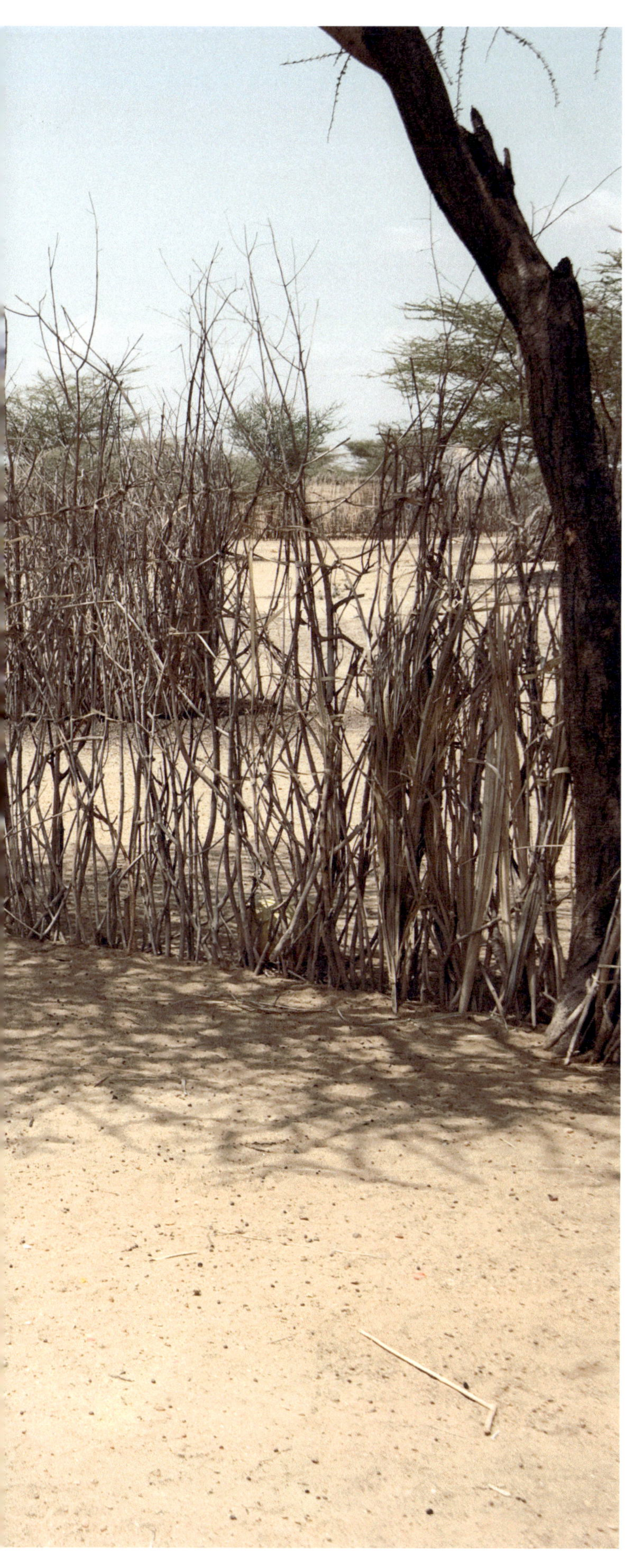

Not too long ago, this hut bore no resemblance to a house; it lacked windows and a door secured with a padlock to deter intruders.

Traditional lifestyles revolved around communal well-being, where resources were shared and decisions were made collectively for the benefit of all. Trust formed the foundation, and in challenging times, survival hinged on unity. However, things changed with the introduction of capitalist Western ideals, driven by the pursuit of profit on the continent.

In my opinion, this photograph stands as one of the finest I've ever captured, vividly illustrating the gradual and inexorable march of what we commonly refer to as progress.

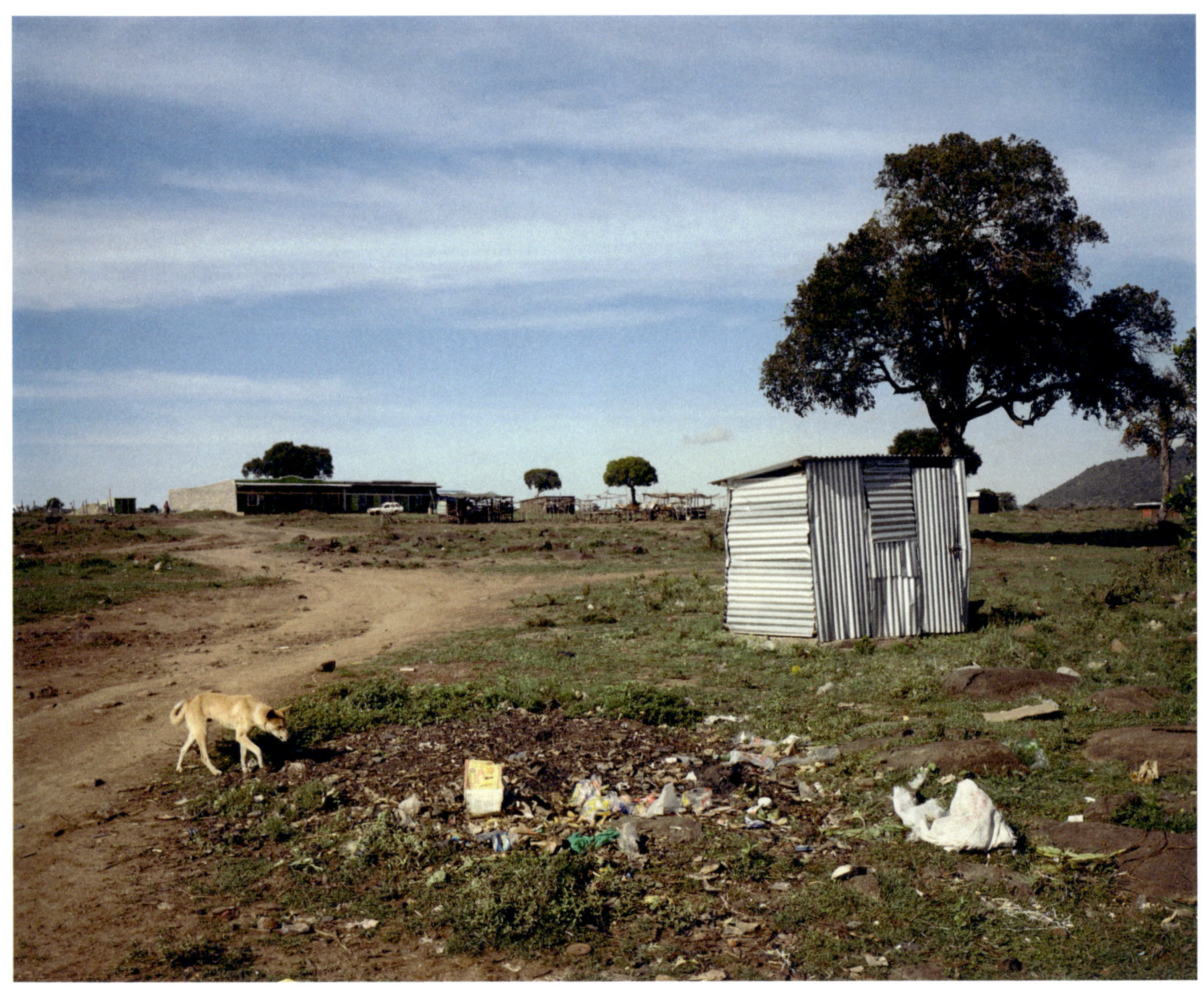

A dog wanders through Mara Rianta, a settlement of corrugated iron sheets nestled in a conservation area adjacent to the Maasai Mara game reserve. Typically, these unmonitored residences are allowed to proliferate because they play a vital role in supporting an economy driven by the personnel of luxury lodges within the reserve. These individuals visit to unwind during breaks, shop at local food stores, engage in activities such as playing pool (as shown on the following page), or grab a drink.

Some might even seek less savory pursuits, like hiring a prostitute, given that their wives and families are not local residents. Over time, these unauthorized dwellings evolve into shanty towns, posing a threat to the habitat and its wildlife through pollution and poaching.

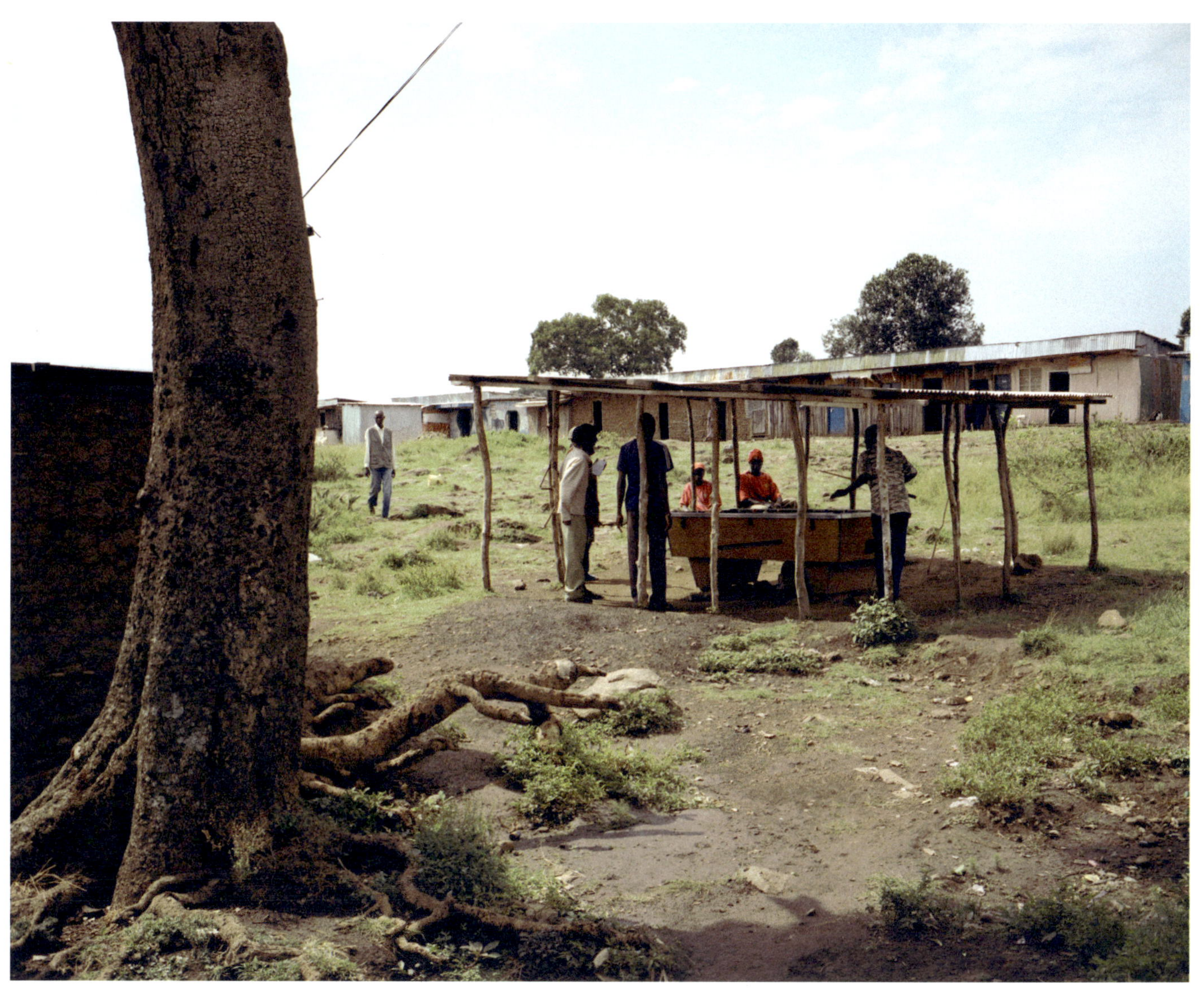

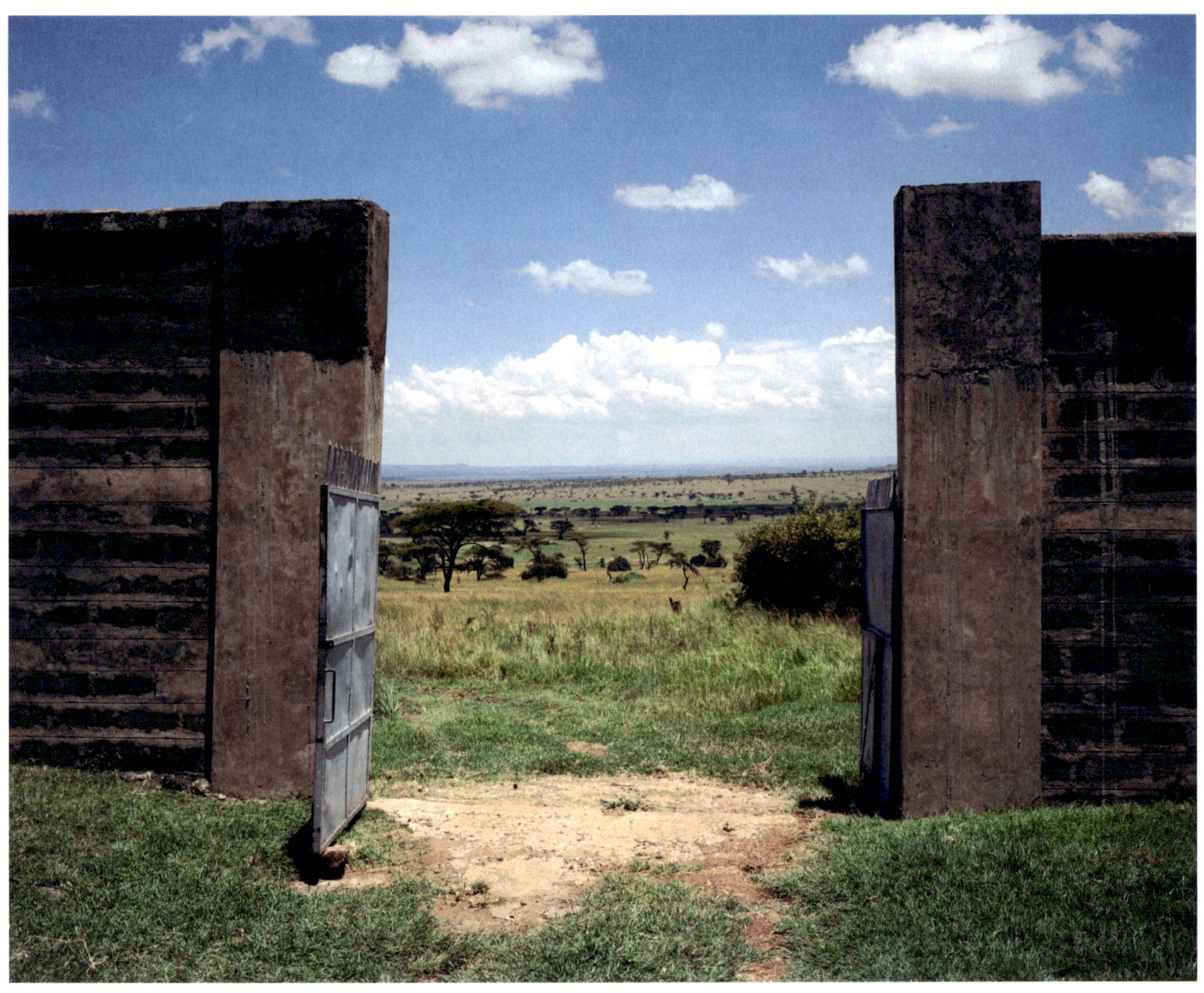

This gate stands as an official border post of the Maasai Mara Game Reserve in Kenya, situated alongside the Serengeti National Park in Tanzania. I can't help but ponder how such a blatantly disrespectful structure toward the environment was permitted to be erected in this renowned game reserve. It truly reflects poorly on the commitment to maintaining a long-term vision for preserving this significant area.

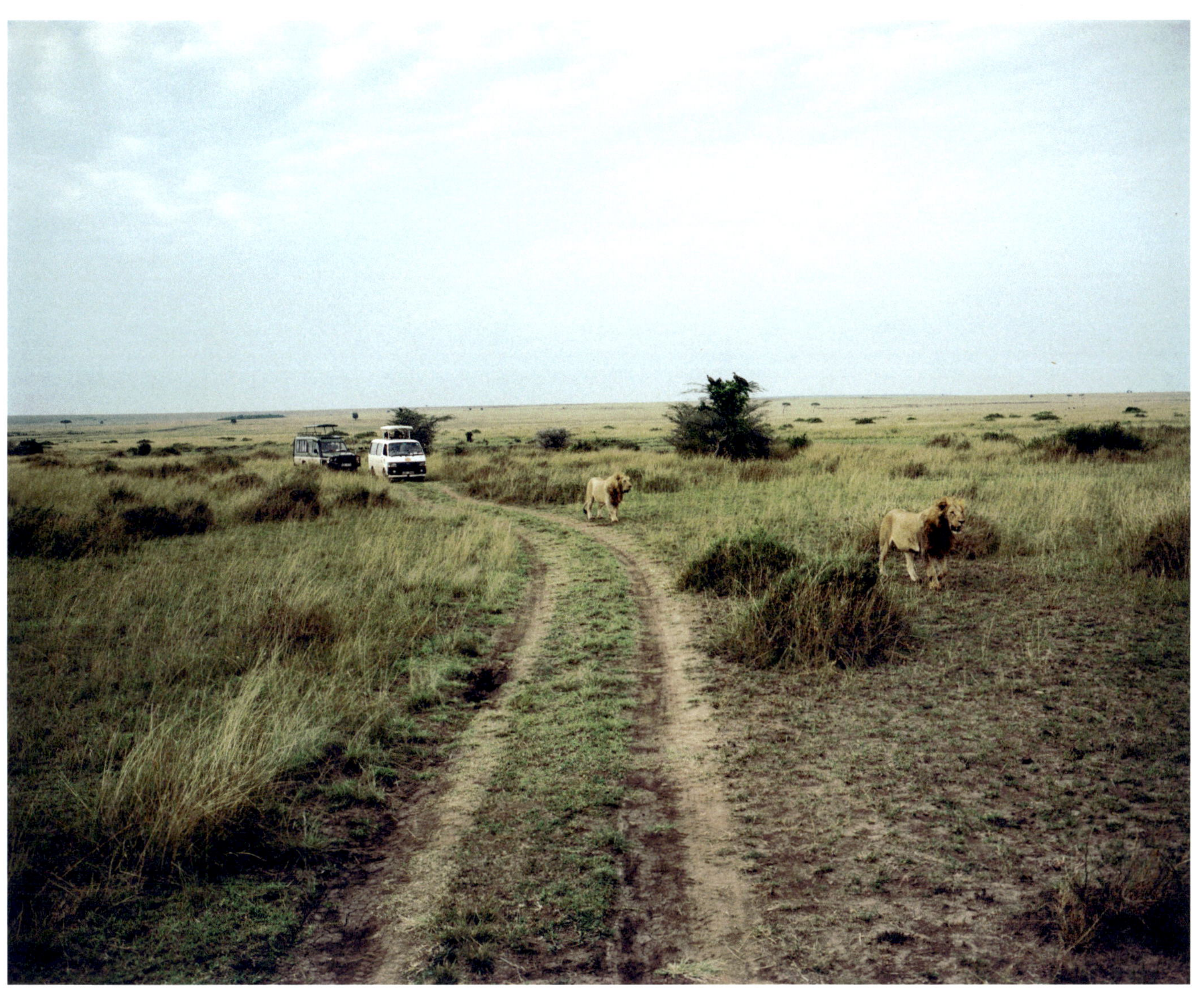

Finding places in East Africa where your safari experience doesn't resemble a visit to an open zoo is increasingly challenging. However, the allure lies in the fact that these animals still roam freely in their natural, picturesque habitats. The encroachment of human populations and the prevalence of poverty around National Parks exert significant pressure on the diminishing wilderness.

Additionally, the booming demands of tourism, coupled with local corruption, have facilitated the construction of an excessive number of hotels, surpassing the already strained capacity and intensifying the stress on wildlife.

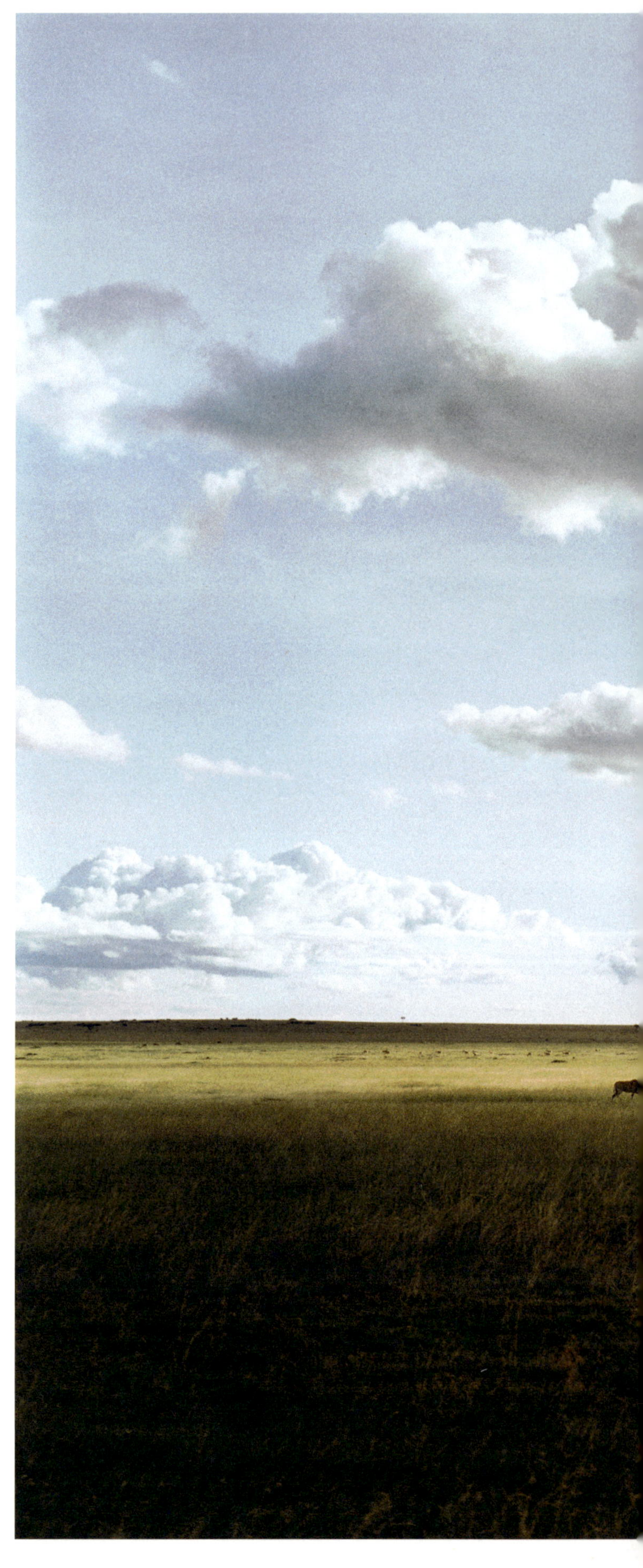

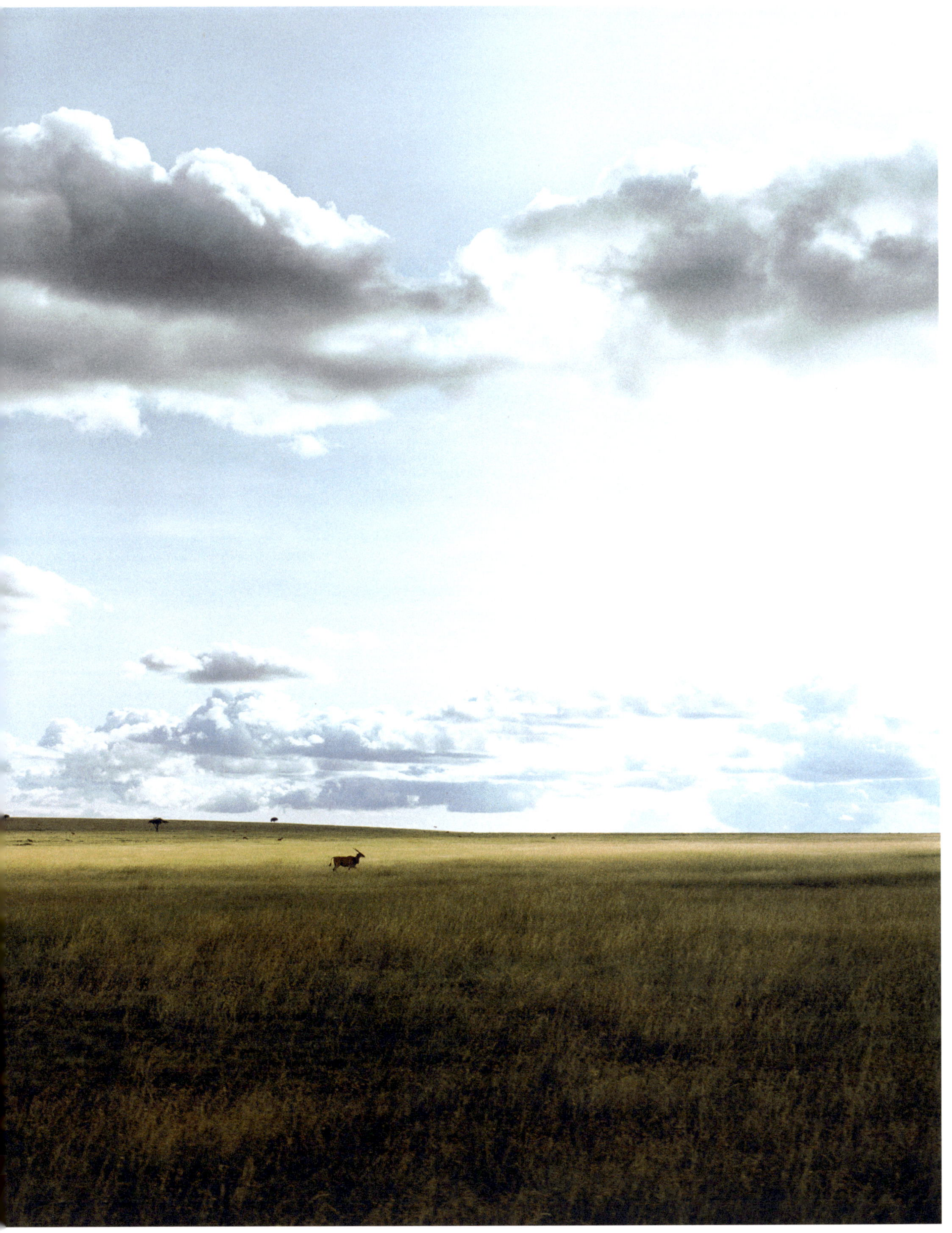

The swimming pool is undergoing
cleaning and preparation for the
guests of this lodge, situated just
beyond the official boundaries
of the Maasai Mara game reserve.

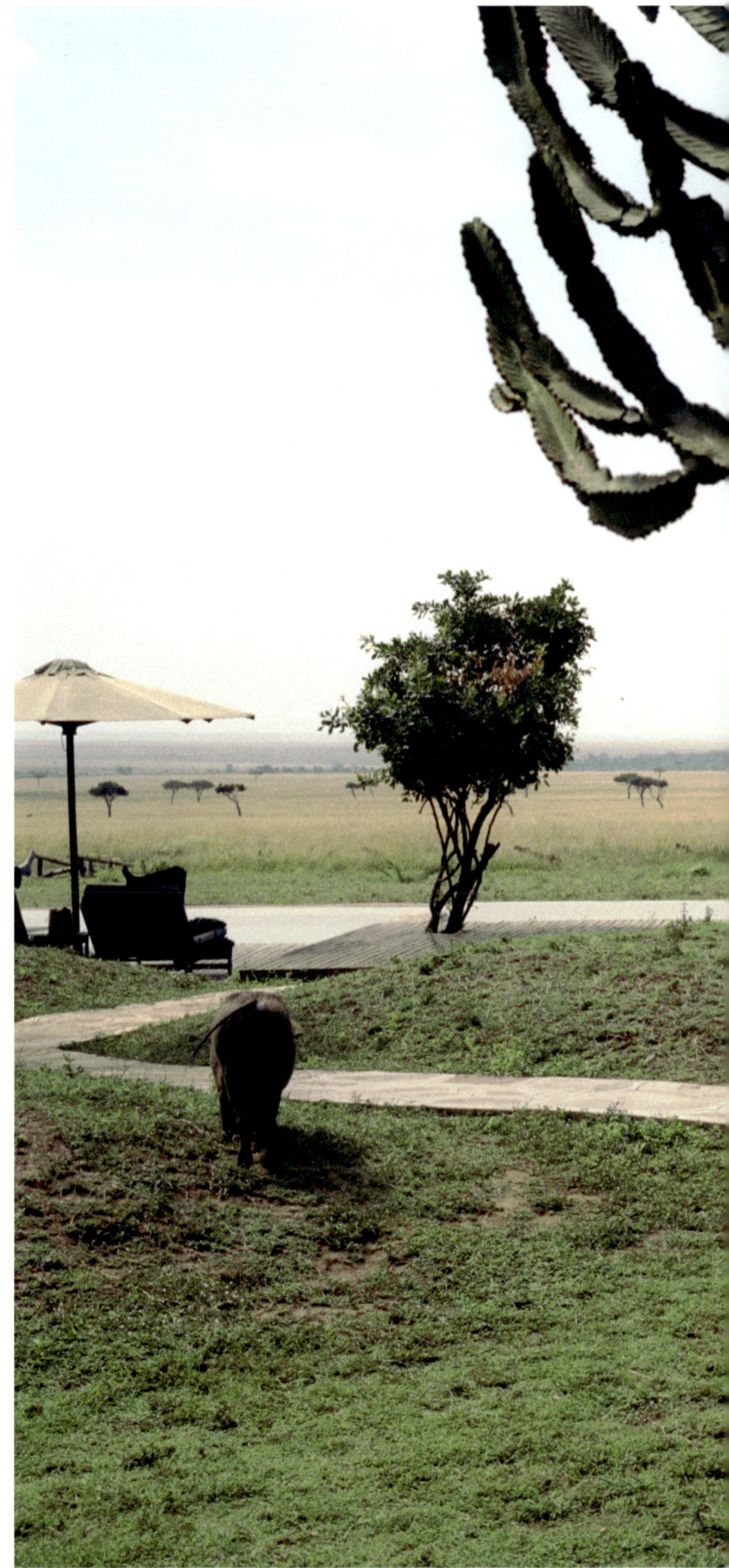

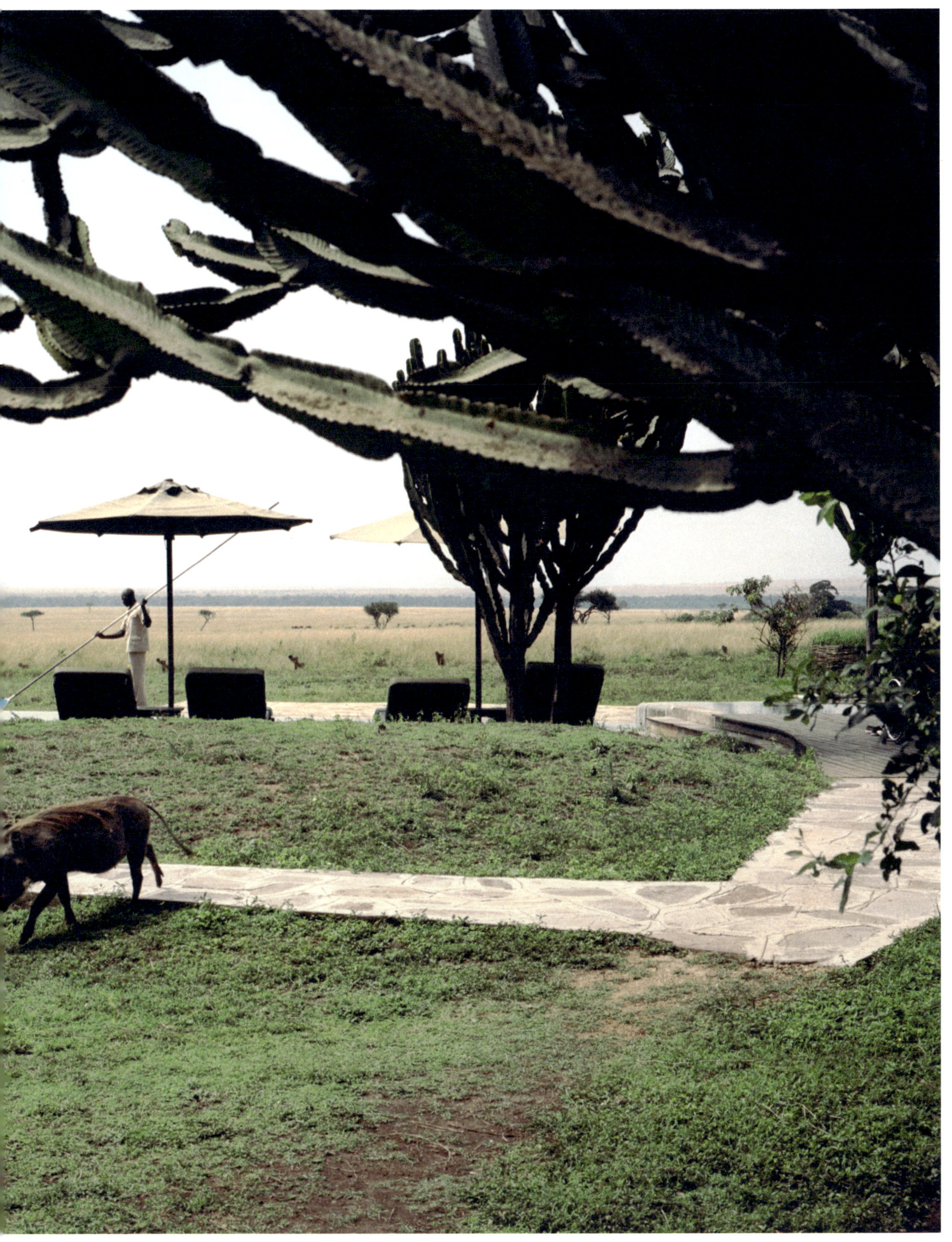

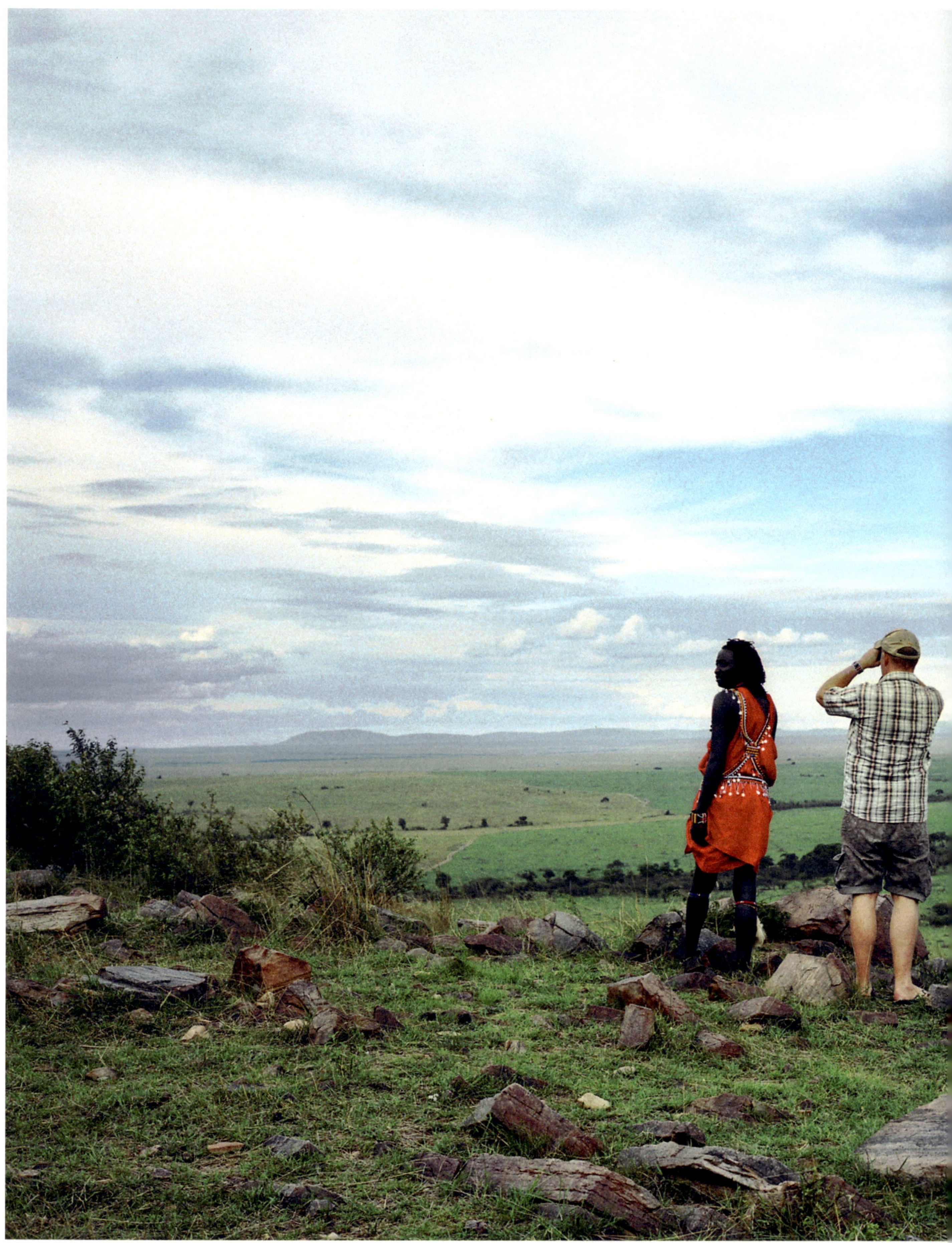

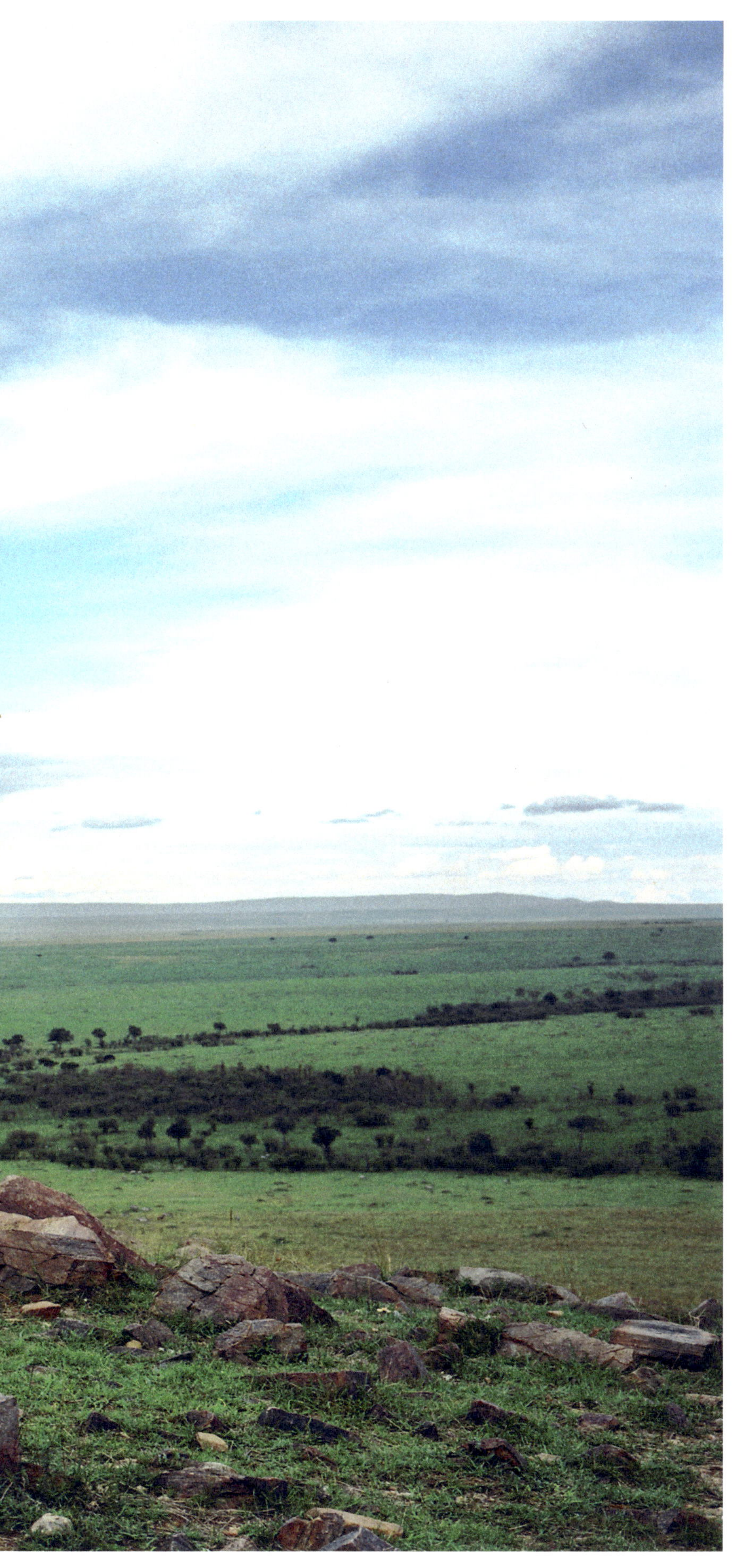

A tourist and his guide, adorned in a Maasai traditional attire.

When I captured this photograph, it was uncertain to me whether the guide was indeed Maasai or if he had been instructed by his employer to dress in such a manner for commercial reasons, creating the illusion that the client was being led by one of the world-renowned tribal warriors.

A warthog is foraging amidst the refuse of
a prestigious five-star lodge located on the
periphery of the Maasai Mara game reserve.

The reserve's ecosystem is facing strain
due to substantial, frequently illicit
investments from hotel proprietors and
camp operators. Unfortunately, due to
widespread corruption, these ventures
persist unchecked.

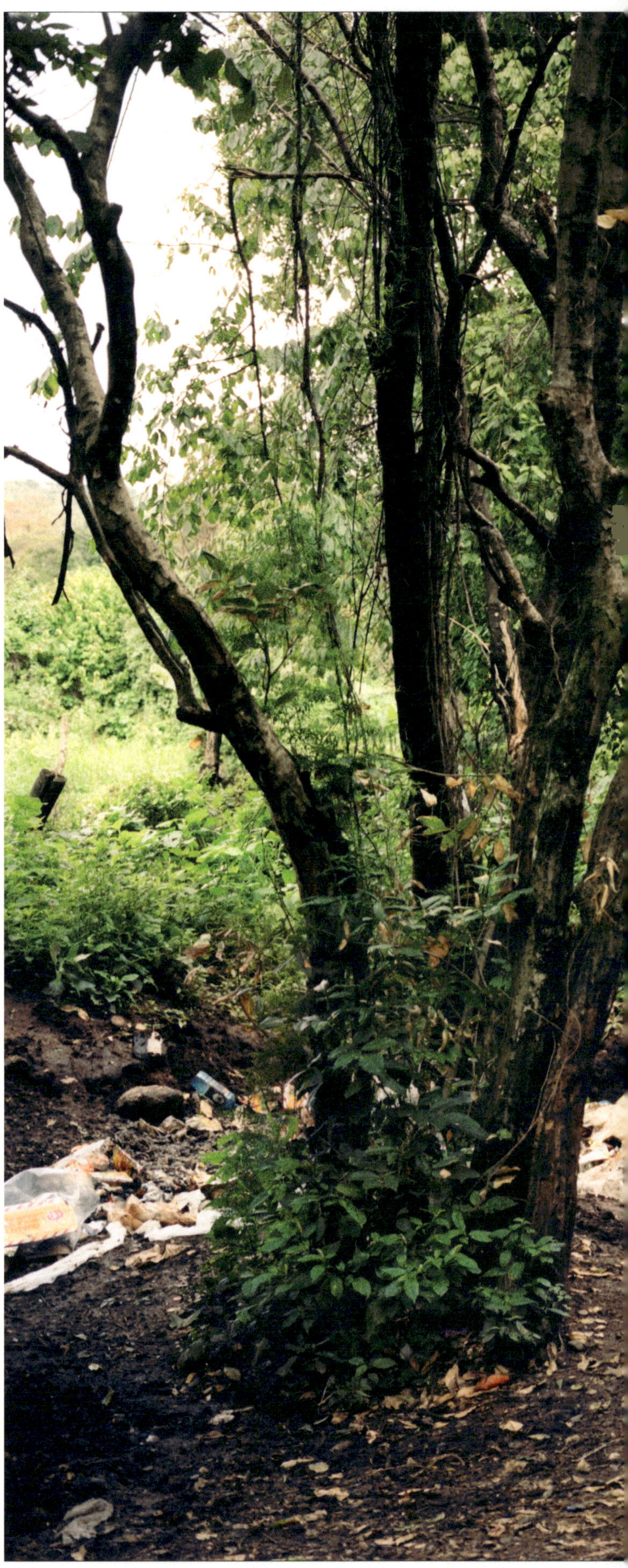

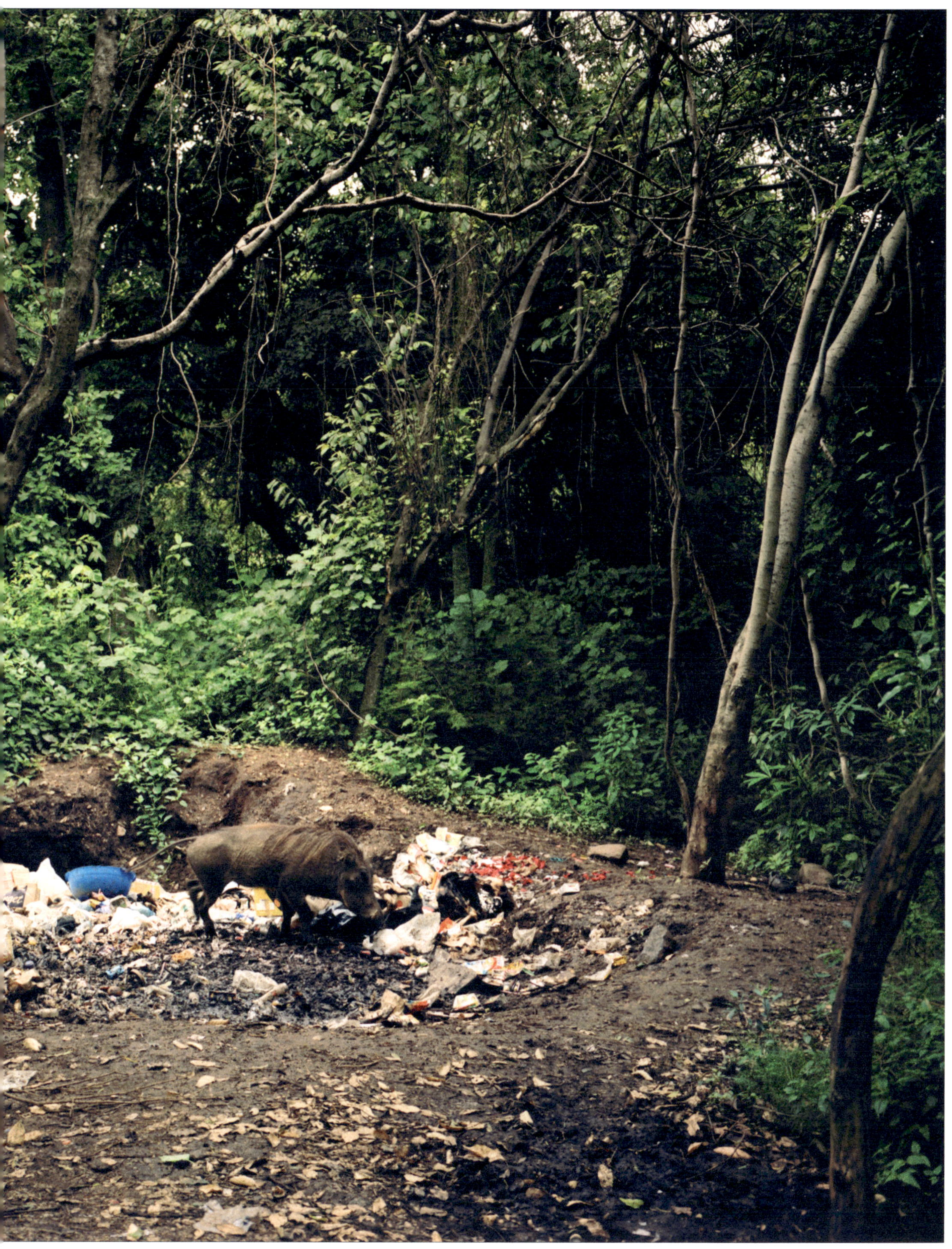

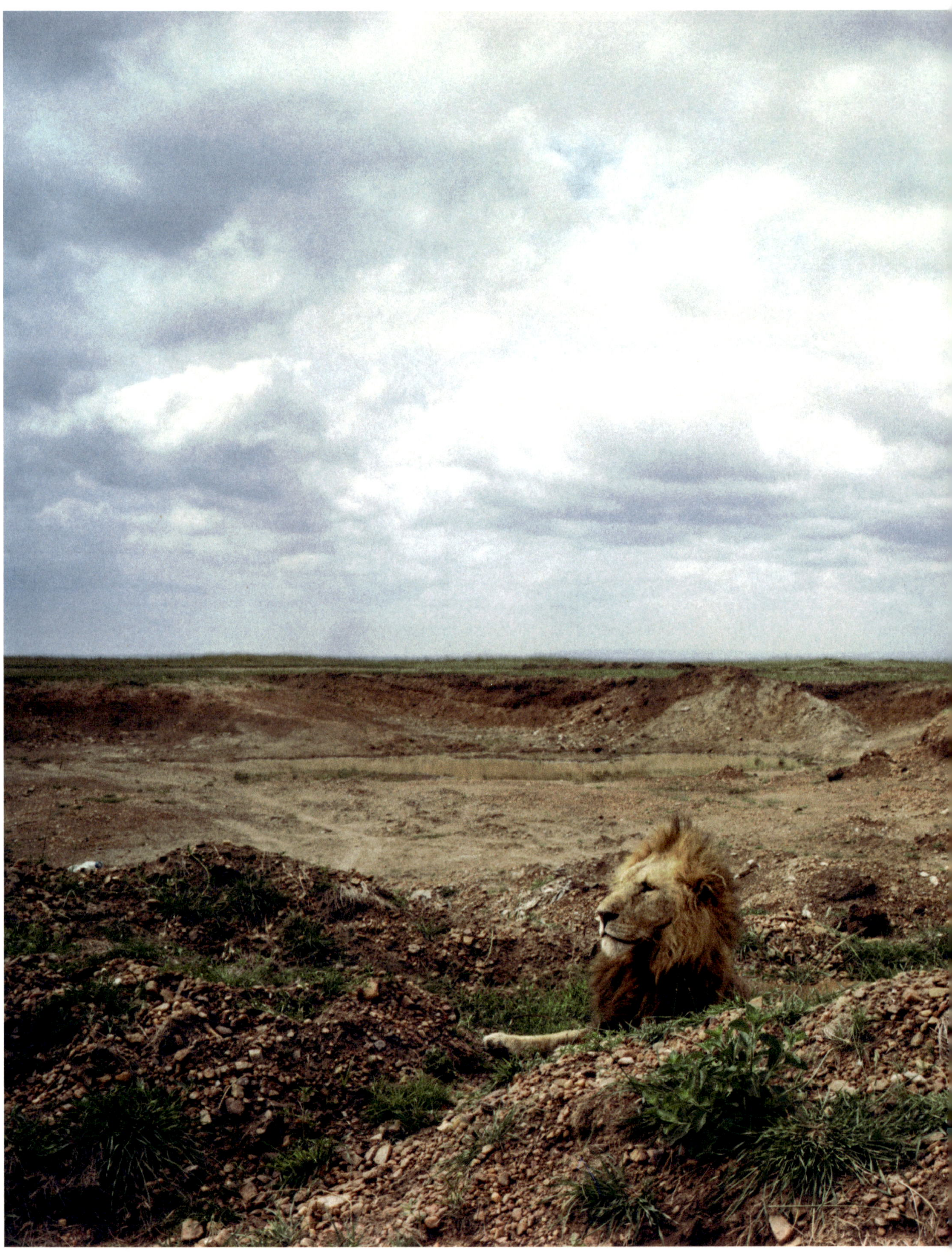

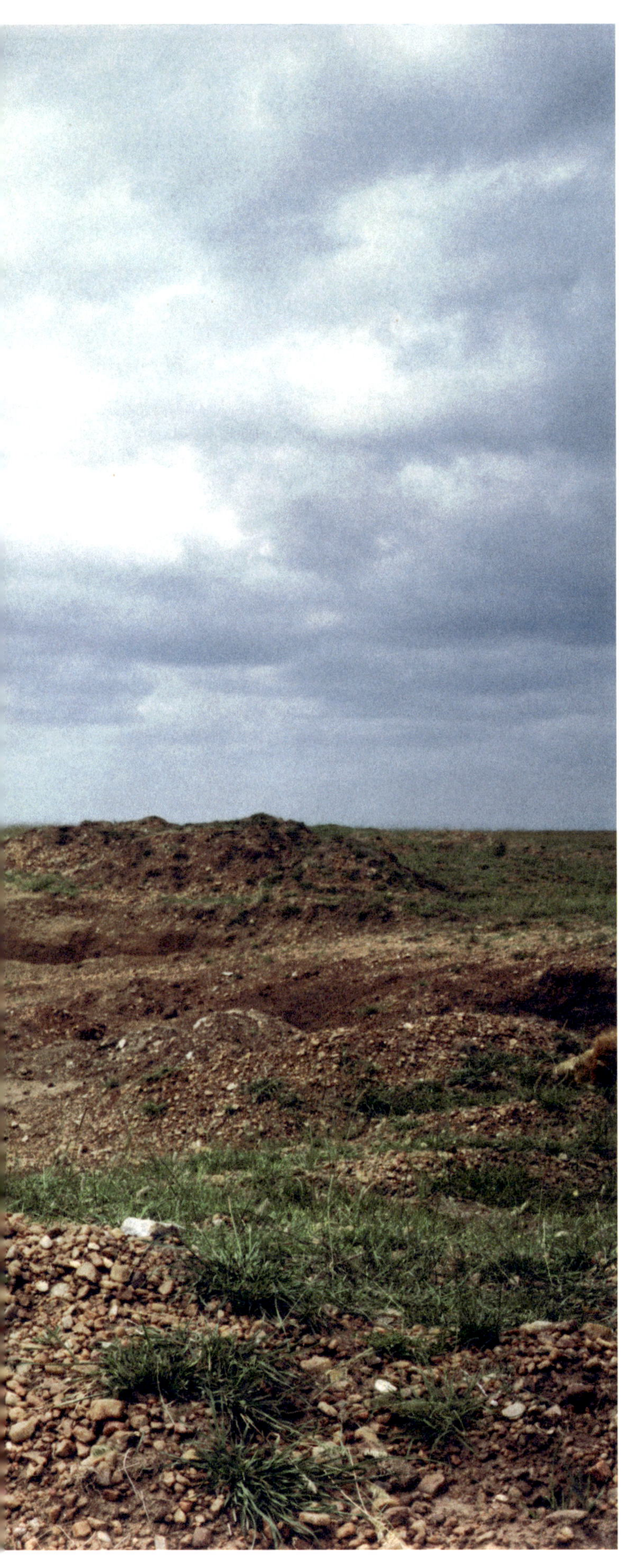

A man-made quarry lies just beyond the confines of the Maasai Mara game reserve, serving as a resource for the construction of new human settlements. The region outside the reserve's borders acts as a habitat where wildlife seeks fresh grazing grounds or engages in hunting activities.

The reserve's limited size proves insufficient to support the entire wildlife population, resulting in frequent human-wildlife conflicts. For instance, elephants venture into the area to raid small vegetable farms, prompting landowners to retaliate by resorting to lethal means such as spears or poisoned arrows.

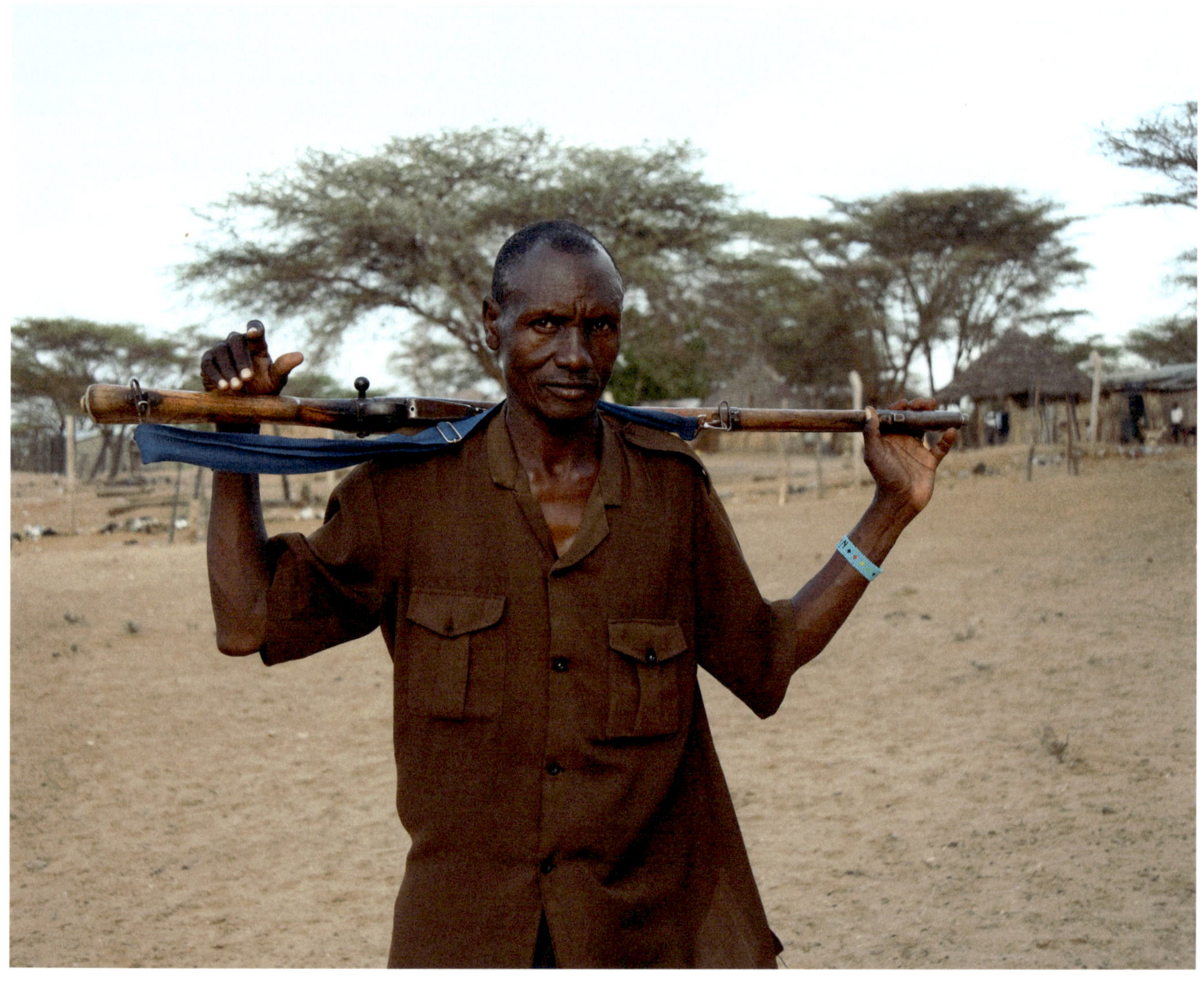

Numerous individuals throughout Turkana County have received
firearms from the Kenyan government to defend themselves against
potential assaults by the neighboring Pokot tribe, particularly
during incidents of cattle-rustling raids. Those who receive
these firearms are automatically enlisted in the Kenyan Police
Reserve (KPR), established in 1948 to aid the regular Kenya Police
in upholding law and order.

In the rural areas of Kenya, the KPR frequently constitutes the sole
law enforcement presence. Additionally, politicians representing
each tribe are legally distributing guns for political advantages,
thereby perpetuating tensions in the region.

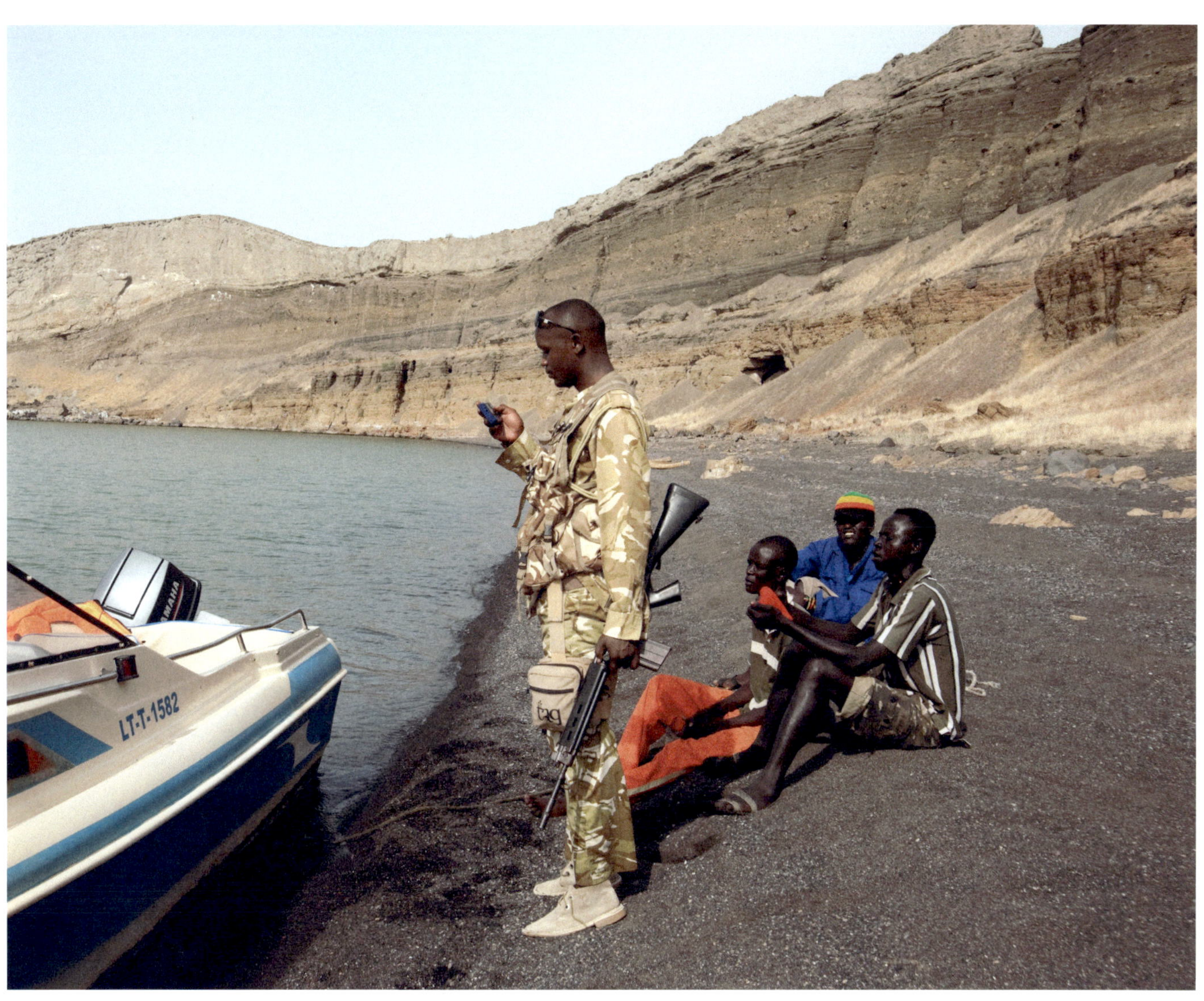

A Kenyan Wildlife Service officer intercepted poachers who were illegally fishing on Central Island, a protected national park area within Lake Turkana. The officer promptly called for a boat to collect them.

Kenya embraced Pentecostalism in the '70s through missionaries from Nigeria, America, and Canada. Departing from traditional practices, like testimonies, speaking in tongues, and dance, they aimed to amplify the Holy Spirit's presence.

These methods offered hope to neglected communities, resonating strongly despite criticisms of leaders exploiting their authority for personal gain. In places like Lodwar in Turkana county (in this photograph), where poverty and illiteracy affect over 80% of the population, Pentecostalism has a robust following.

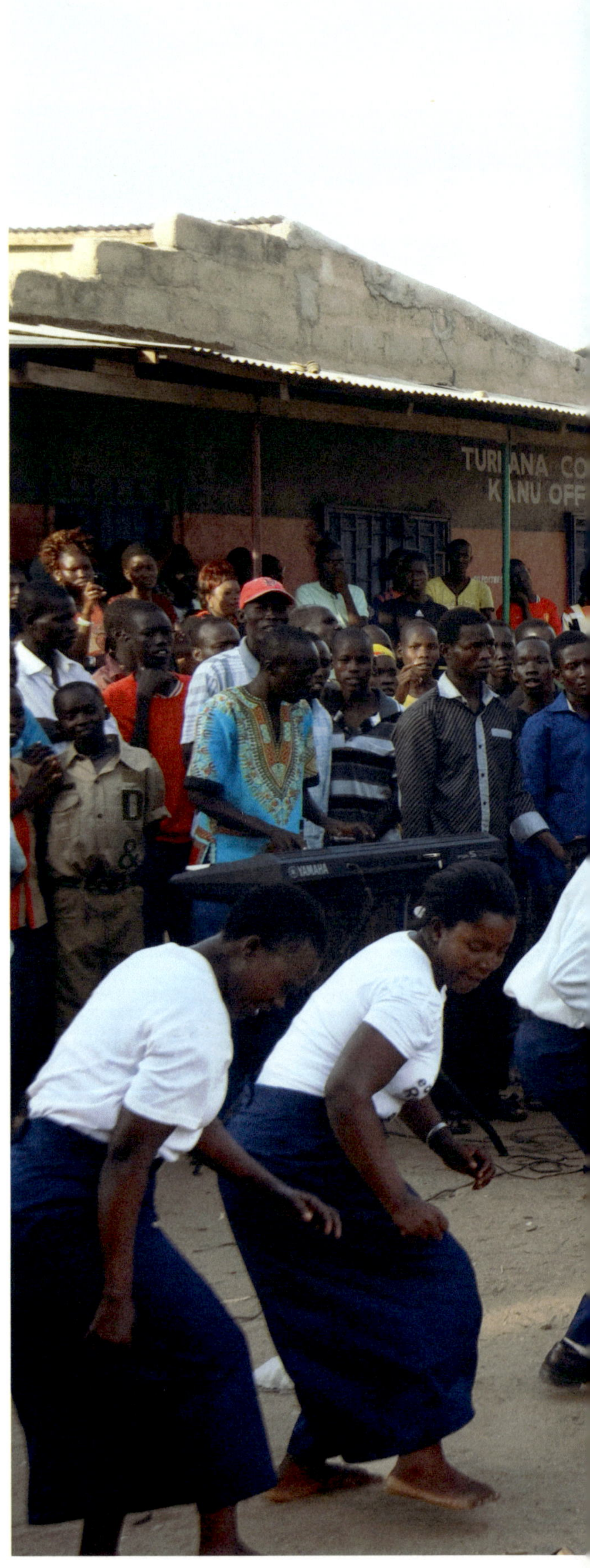

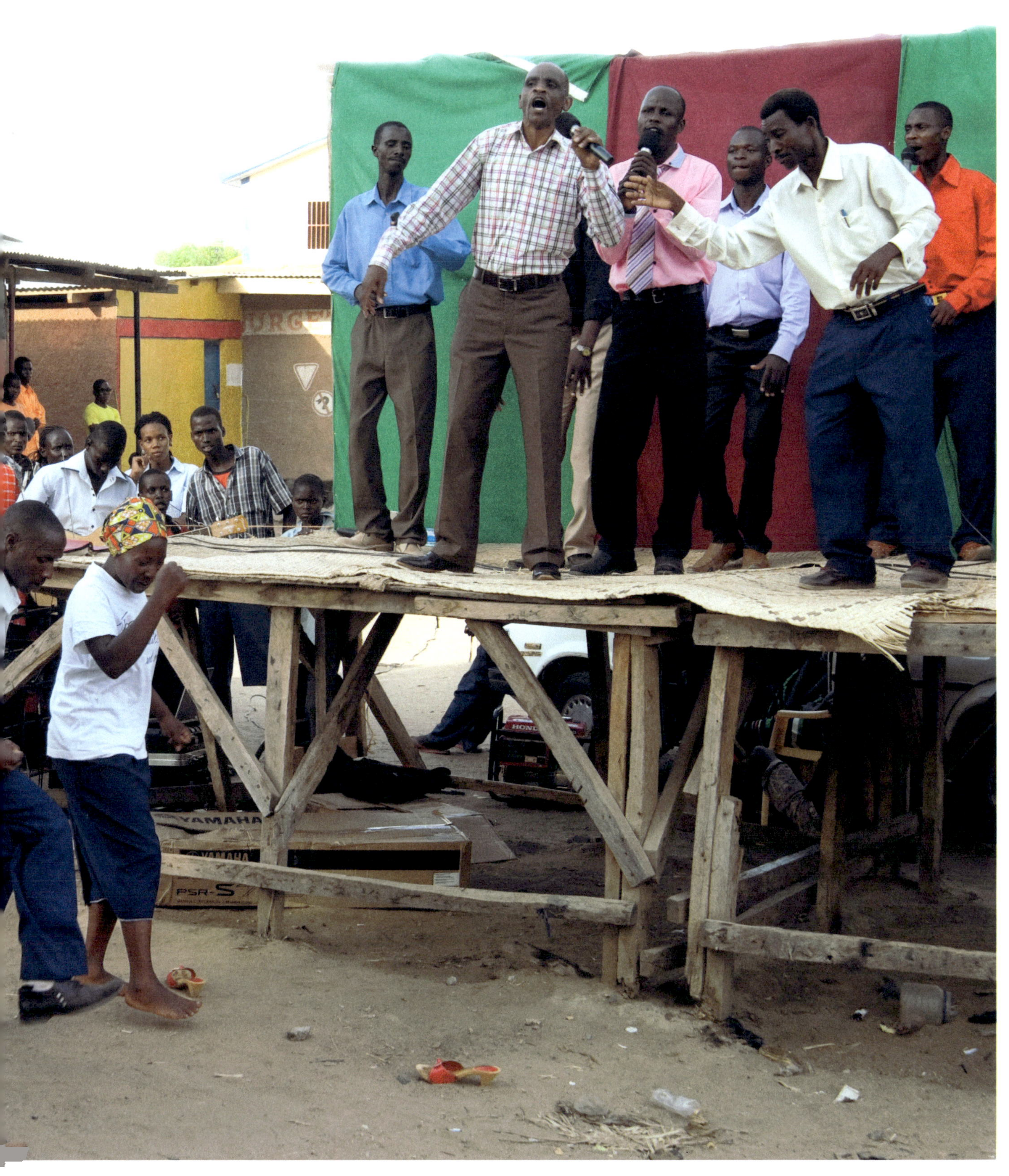

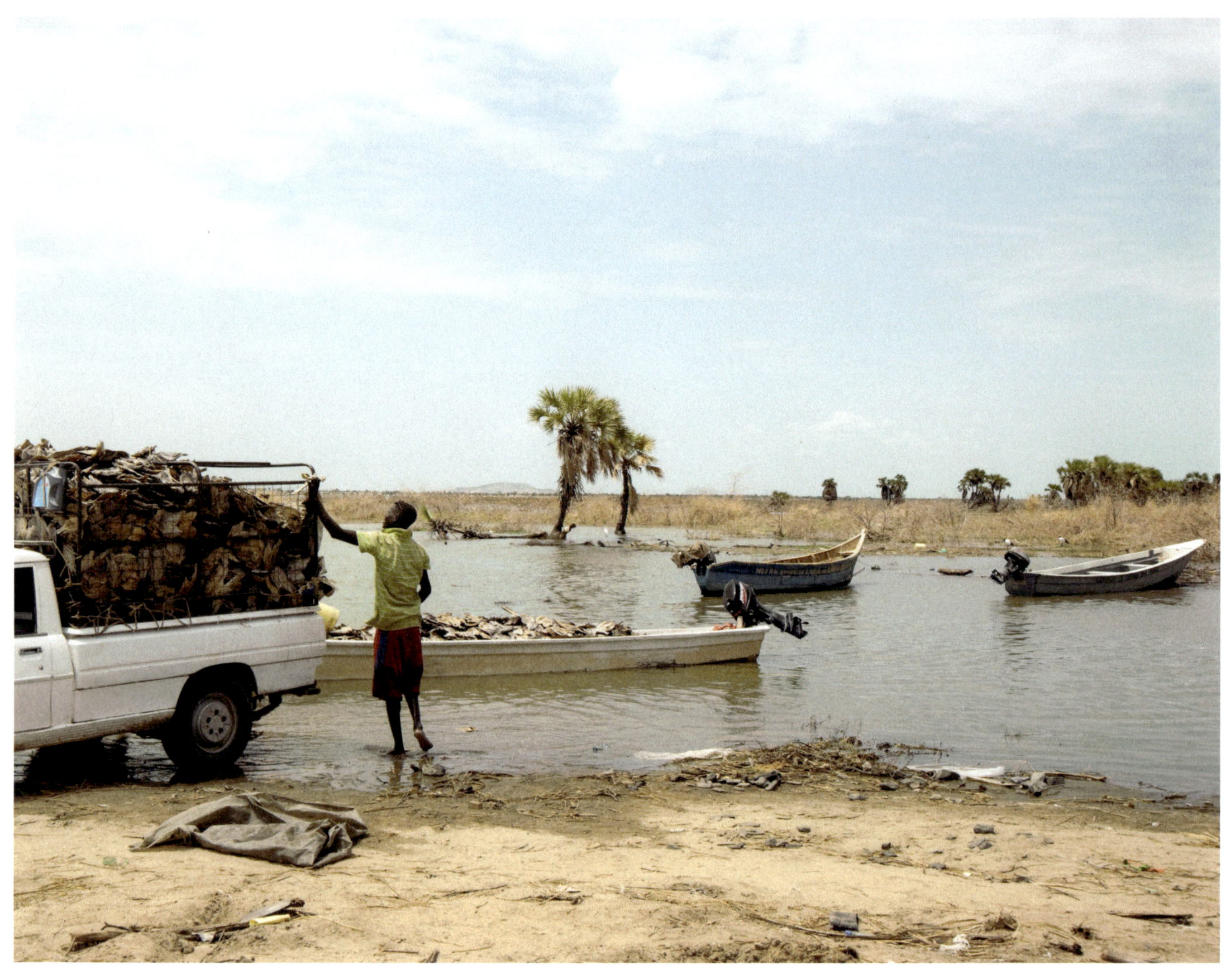

At Kalokol fish-landing bay in Kenya's Turkana region, a man loads
dry fish onto his truck. Fishmongers compete for smaller fish
like tilapias to sell locally, while middlemen swiftly load the
best catch into their vehicles. Many brokers travel from Kitale,
300km away, enduring days-long journeys due to poor roads.

Despite the challenges, the lucrative sale of fish in Nairobi
restaurants for significant profit, drives excessive fishing
in this mismanaged region. The poor roads limit market access,
exacerbating limited livelihoods and widespread poverty.

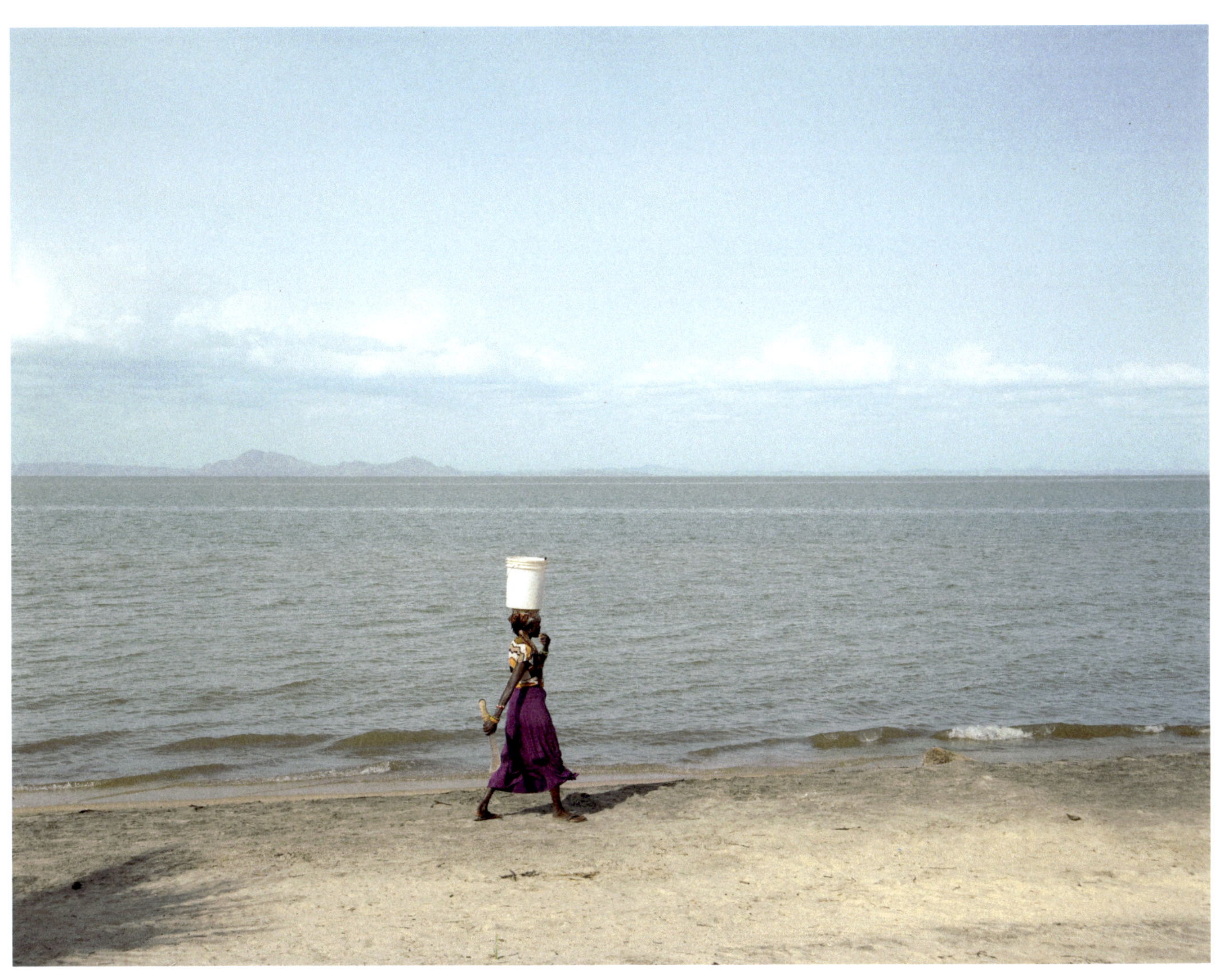

A hippopotamus residing in a man-made water dam, situated well beyond the legal confines of a game reserve, finds itself encircled by various human activities.

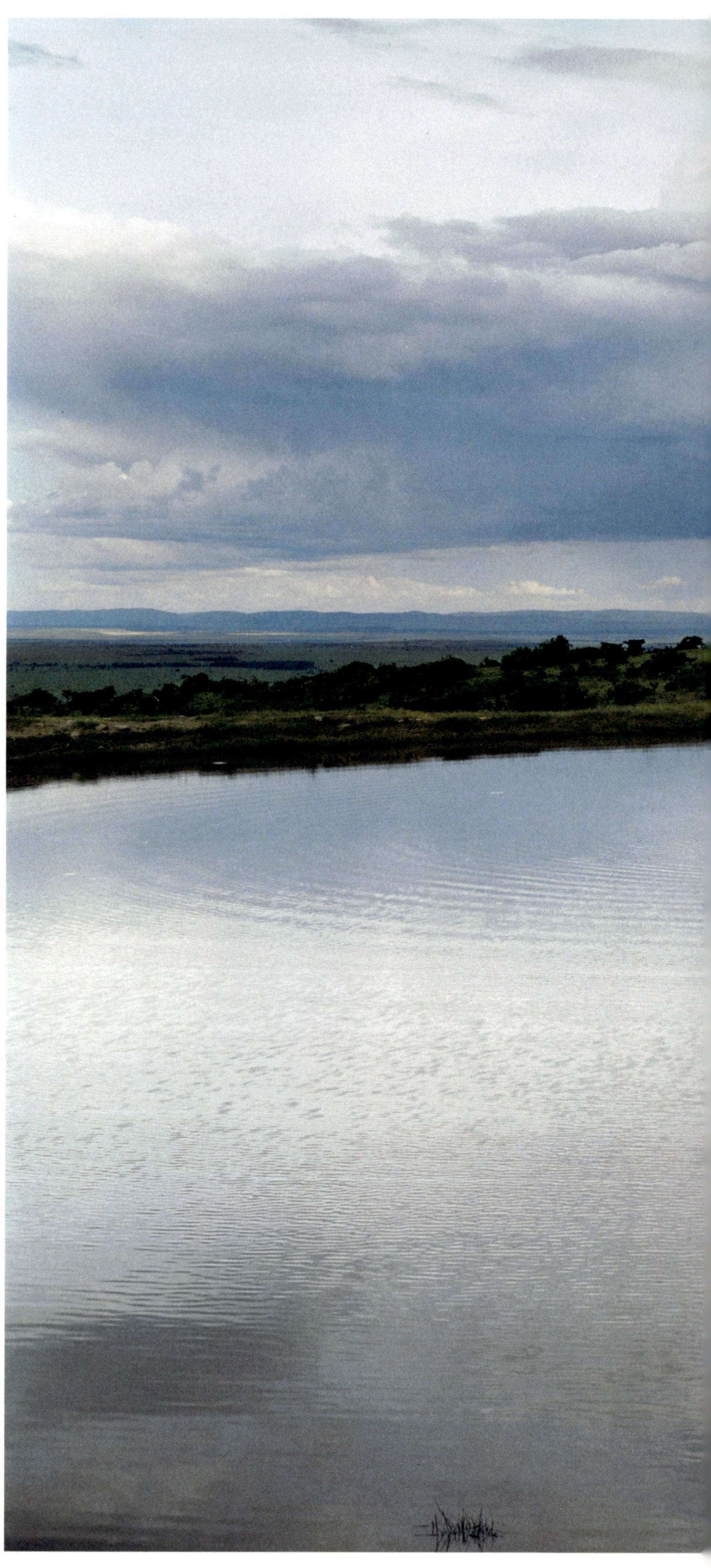

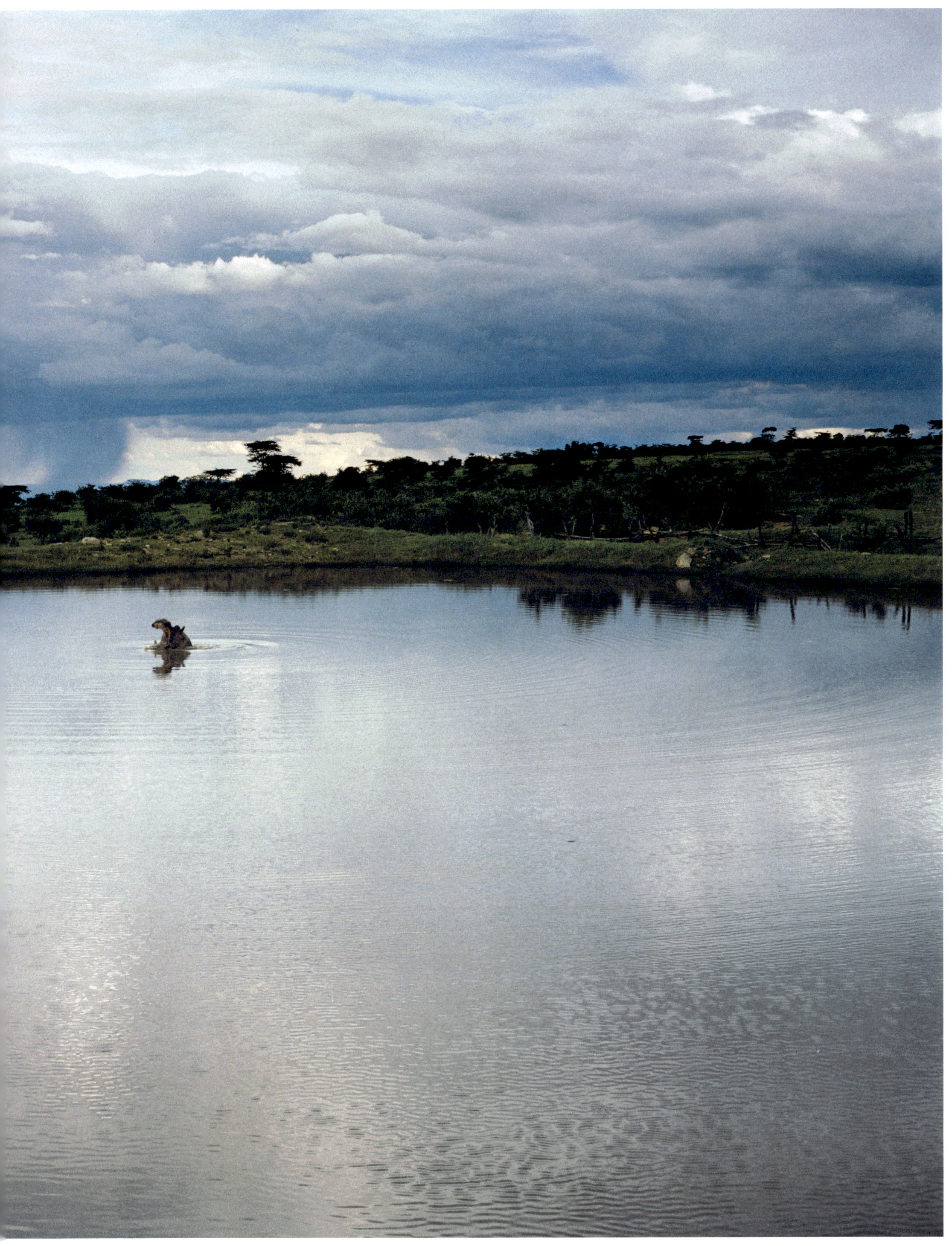

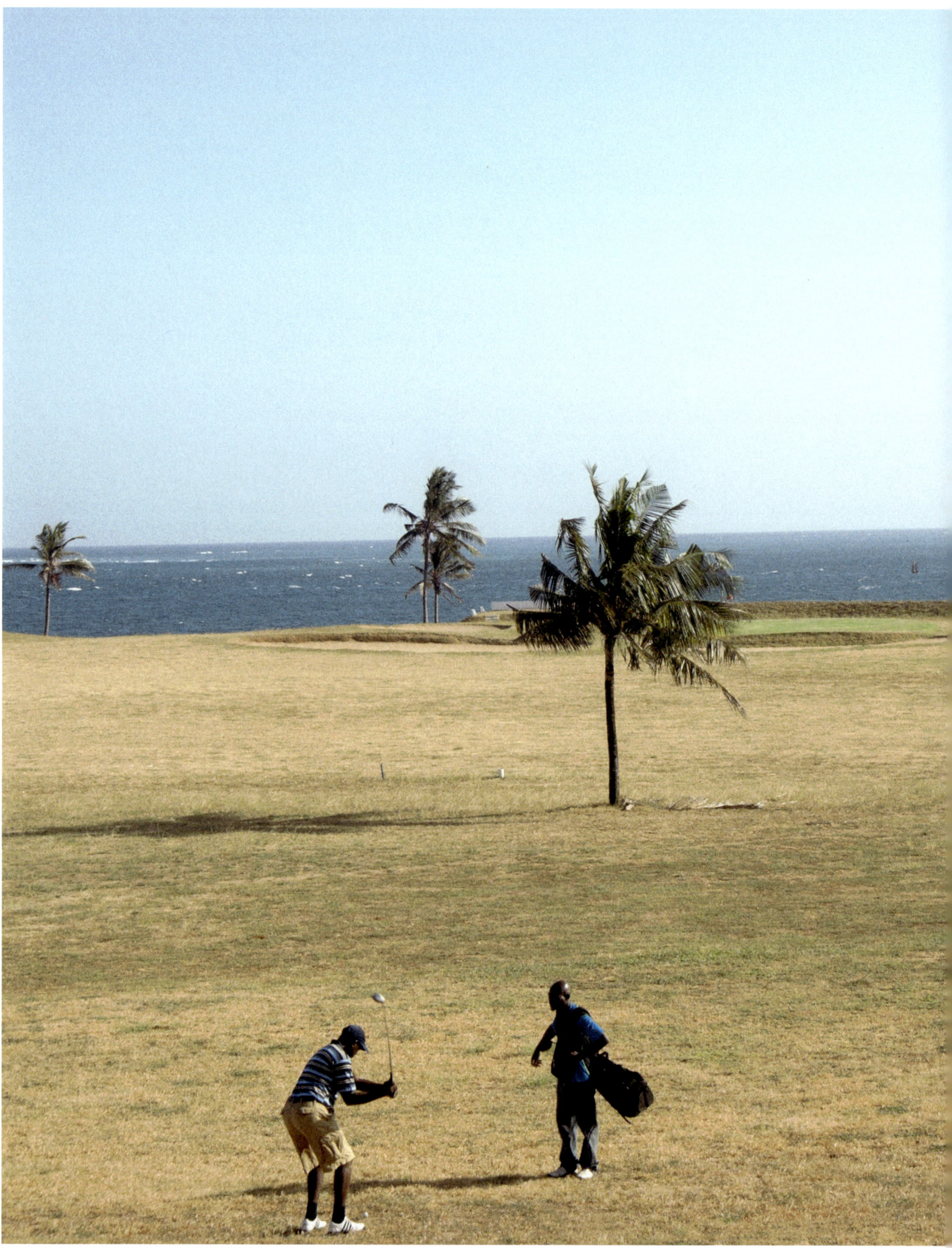

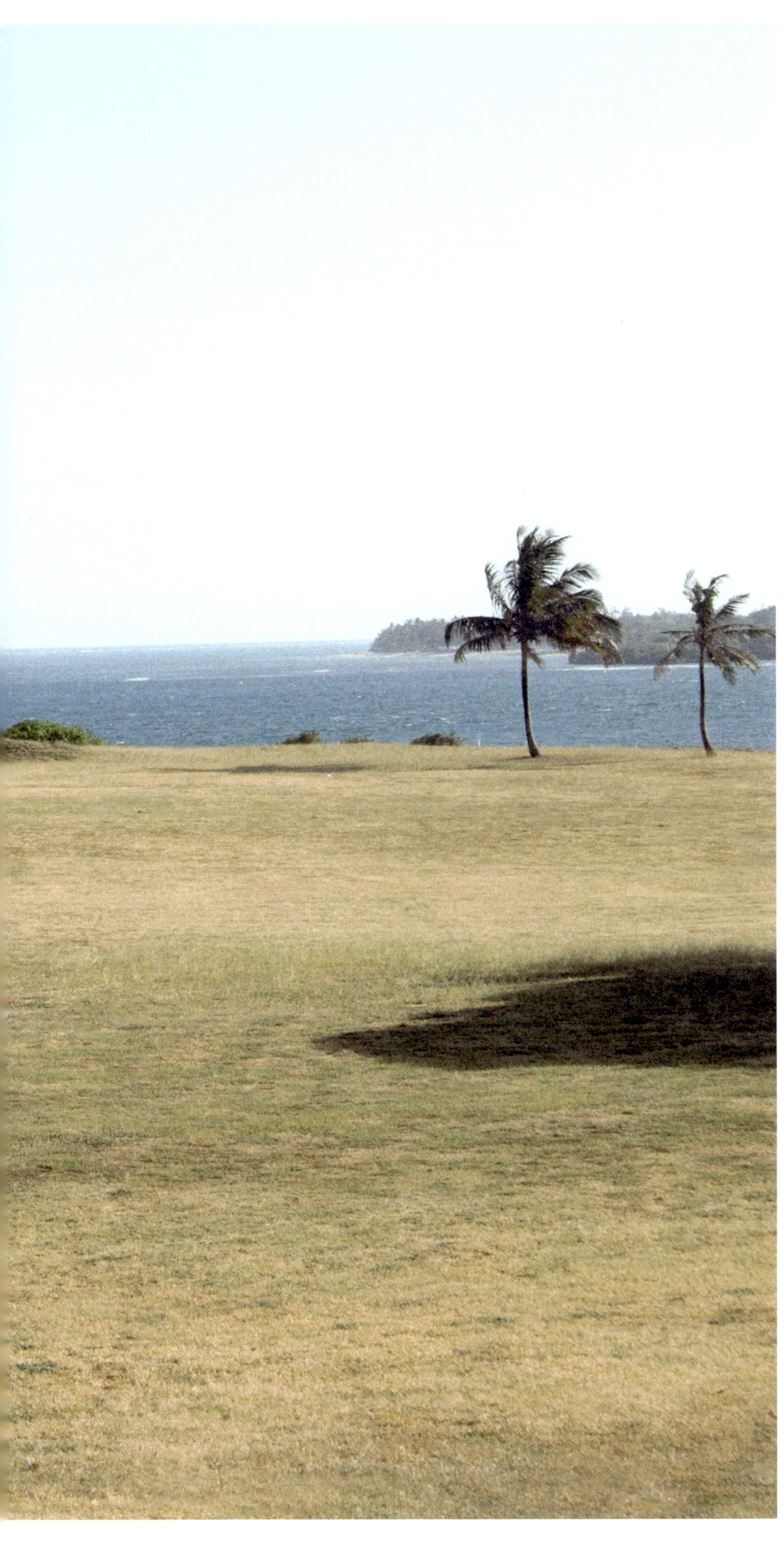

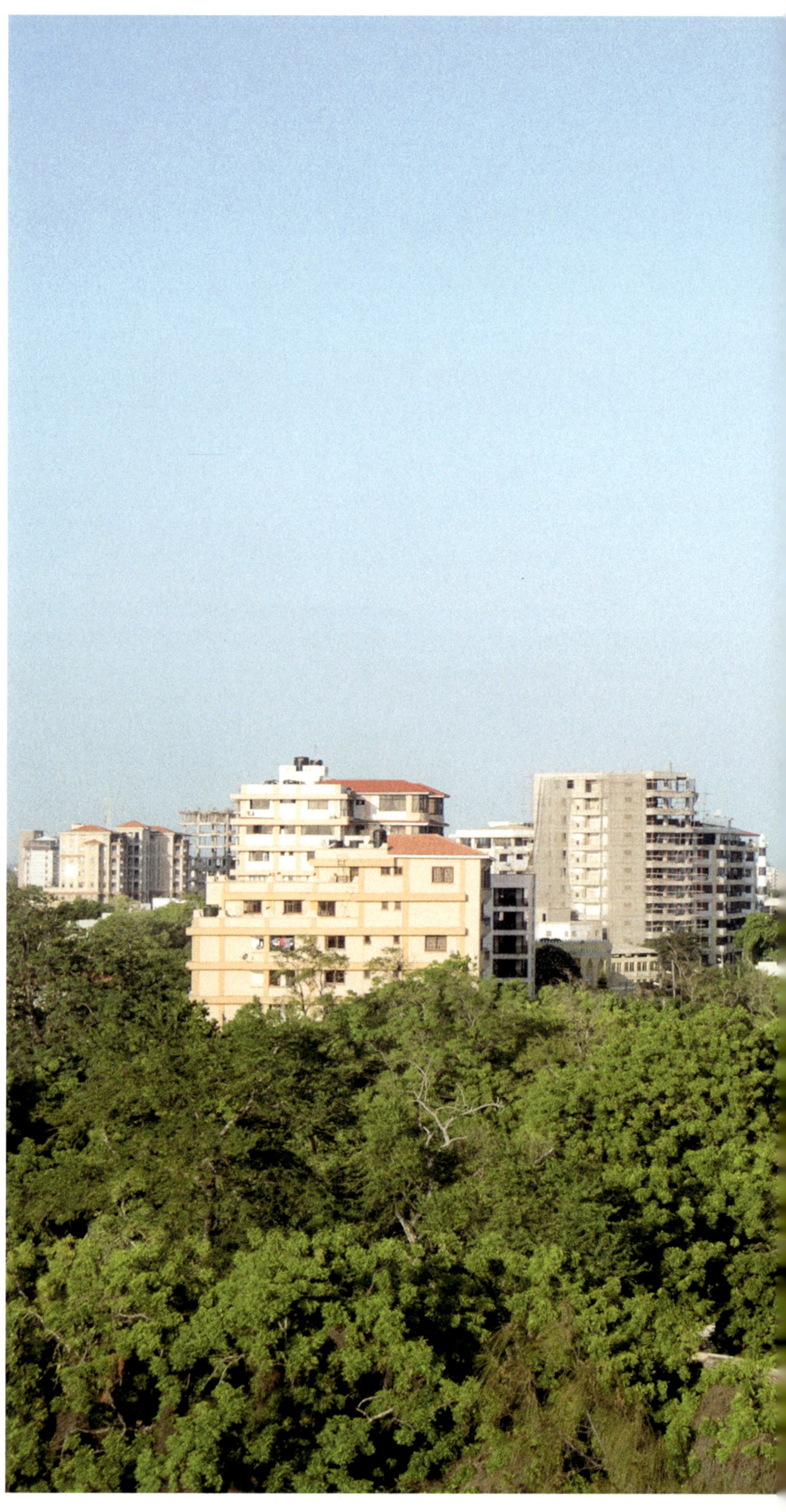

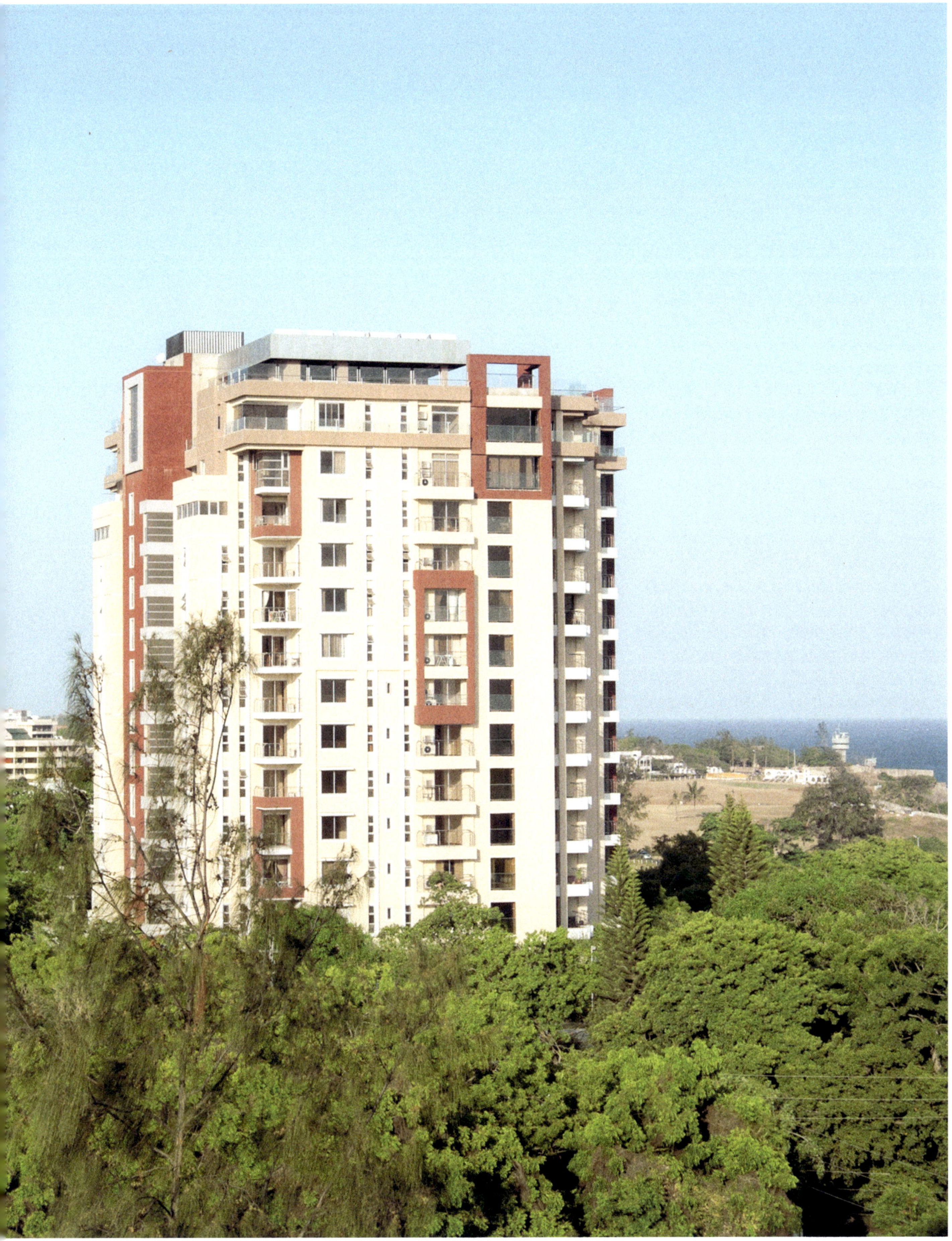

The reality is that these animals are destined to be imprisoned in large open-air zoos. Fences are going up all over East Africa, as much as to keep people out as to keep animals in. The clash between humans and animals for living space will have disastrous consequences, unless we stop pretending that our problems are any different than theirs.

The ghettos we have created for animals are reflections of the concrete jungles we are busy constructing for ourselves. Jungles of waste and pollution, Africa's problems are not unique, all over the planet human pressure is forcing us all to live in an increasingly over crowded and over stressed environment.

We have to wake up and recognize that we cannot do it alone, that human beings are just one link in a complex chain of life, that their future and ours is up to us.

Peter Beard, 1982

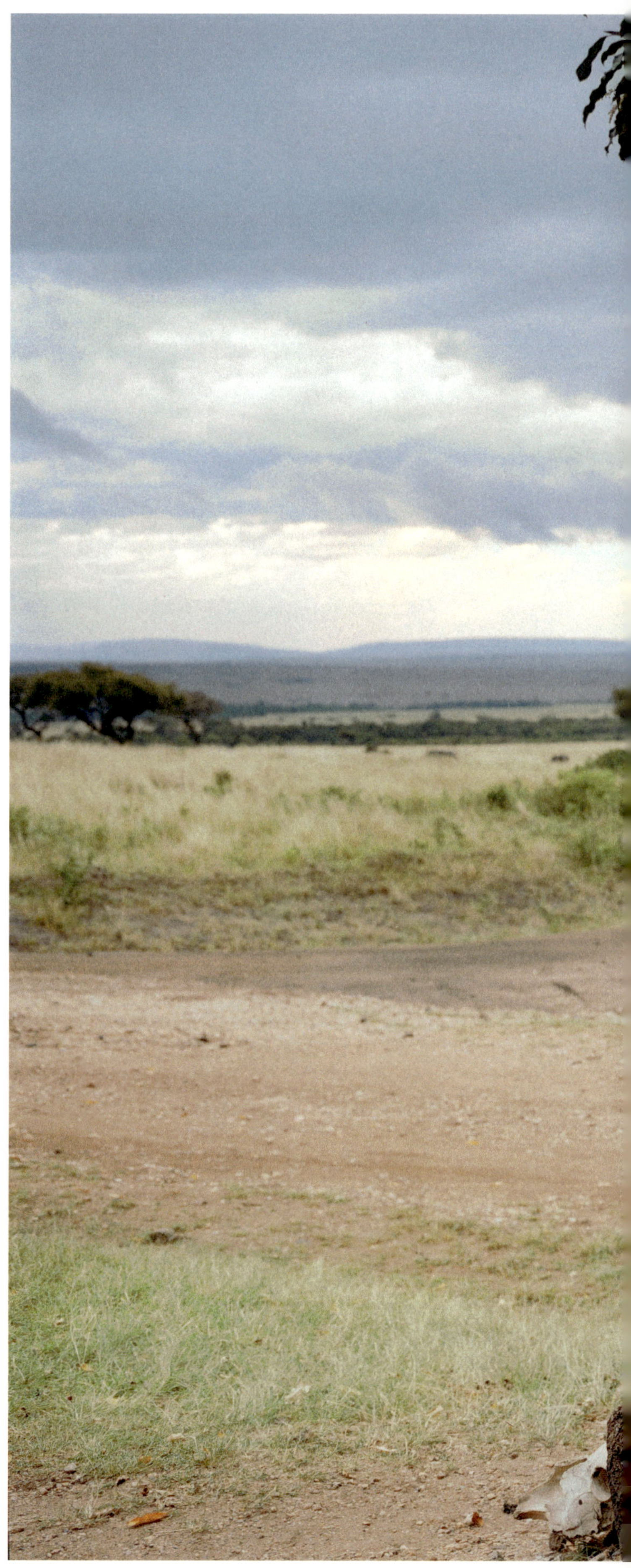

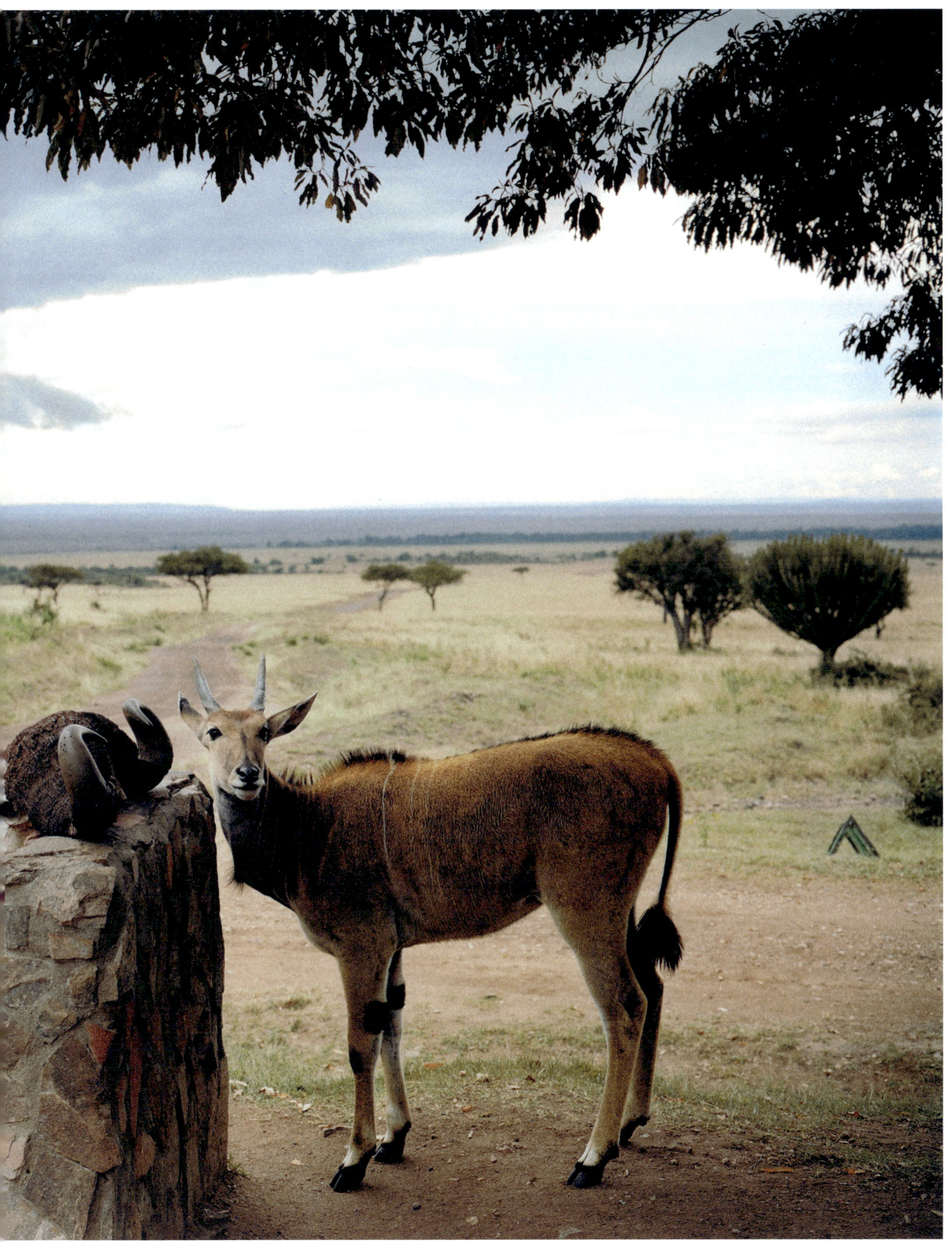

WAR
RIORS

Humans risking their lives for wildlife conservation

While researching the issue of human-wildlife conflict in Kenya, I stumbled upon a narrative that offers a refreshing perspective amidst the prevalent tales of wildlife and habitat destruction.

The distressing frequency of elephants and rhinos falling prey to poachers for their tusks and horns is extensively documented. Despite concerted global efforts, the situation remains precarious. The reality is more intricate than commonly perceived, constituting a resource-driven struggle involving both marginalized and privileged sectors of society.

Impoverished individuals, whose families have coexisted with wildlife for generations, resort to poaching to sustain their households. Inadvertently, they contribute to the demand for horns and tusks among affluent Asians.

Through my research, I discovered that privately owned and managed game reserves and sanctuaries exhibit more effective wildlife protection than government-run national parks. Surprisingly, the anti-poaching efforts in places like Borana and Ol-Pejata conservancies have adopted a highly militarized approach, resembling an army deployment. This transformation commenced with the translocation of Rhinos to these areas, making them prime targets.

Now, well-trained rangers are adequately equipped to confront and combat organized international crime rings. Regrettably, the news for them is less optimistic; their already perilous work has intensified as their adversaries have also become better funded and armed. Approximately 150 rangers worldwide lose their lives annually while safeguarding wildlife and habitat.

To honor their courage and dedication, I decided to capture these rangers in a distinct light—isolated from their familiar surroundings and photographed against a white backdrop in full gear, sometimes just moments before embarking on their patrols.

This approach not only highlights their attire, ranging from camouflage gear to tree branches, but also underscores the creative process behind achieving invisibility for self-preservation.

In a sense, the photographs strip away the camouflage, emphasizing the significance of the clothes worn by these individuals. This shedding of camouflage illuminates those who intentionally seek obscurity and are prepared to pay the ultimate price.

Some of the photographs were also taken in Garamba National Park in Congo-DRC, portraying a grimmer outcome compared to the private fenced conservancies in Kenya. In the latter, a significantly higher number of rangers are killed in action, and the entire rhino population has been eradicated. Garamba Park, a vast area bordered by two conflict-ridden countries, South Sudan and the Central African Republic, faces constant challenges. Rangers here confront rogue elements from both armies, uniformed gunmen on horseback, the janjaweed from Darfur in Sudan, armed cattle herders from Central Africa, and the brutal Lord's Resistance Army (L.R.A.).

Kenya and Congo DRC, despite being fundamentally different nations—one stable with more robust institutions, the other marred by perpetual conflict since 1997 with a corrupt and dysfunctional government—both contend with similar threats to their wildlife and habitat.

These threats are driven by a mix of corruption, poor governance, and the pursuit of control and profit from natural resources.

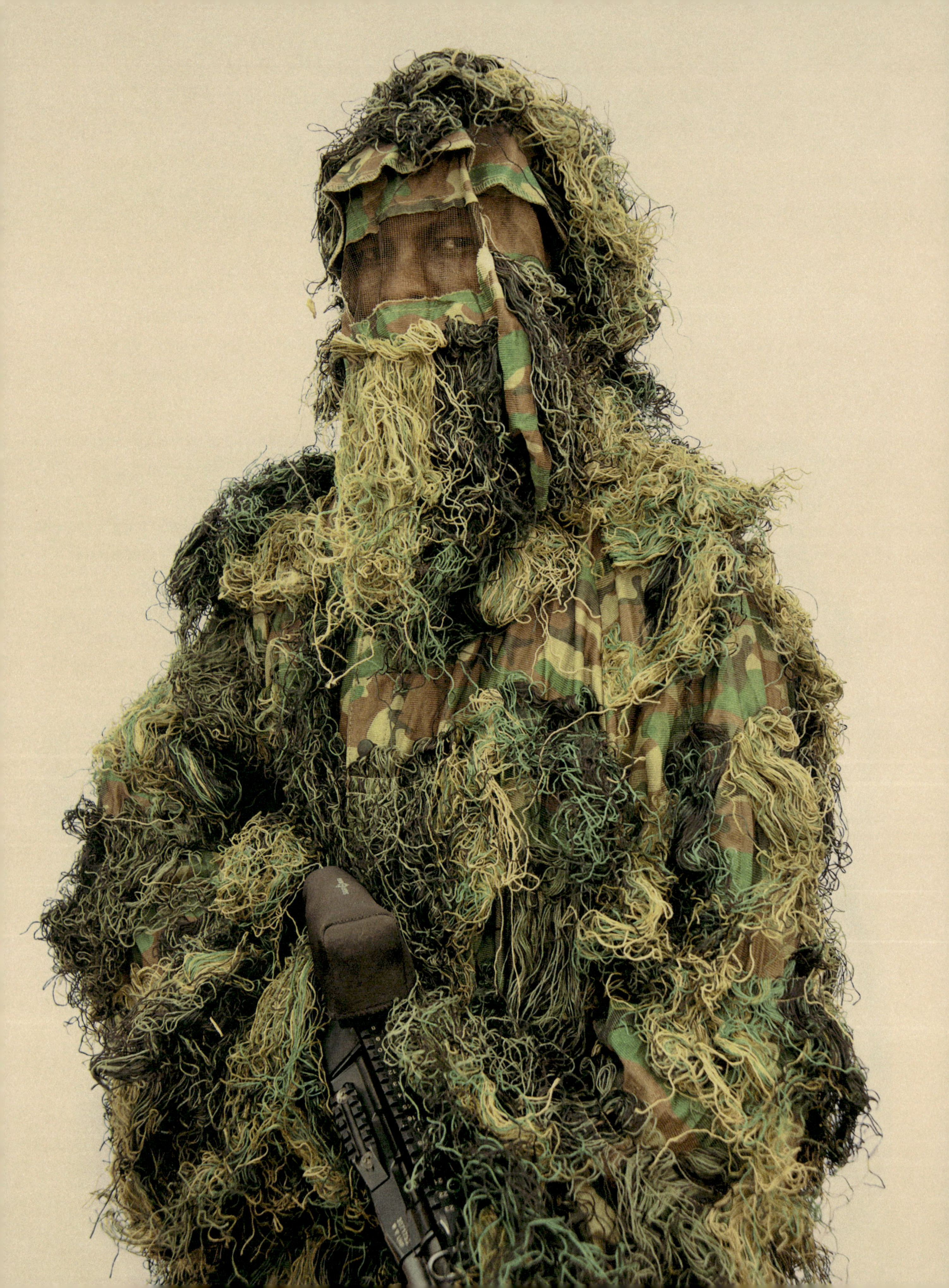

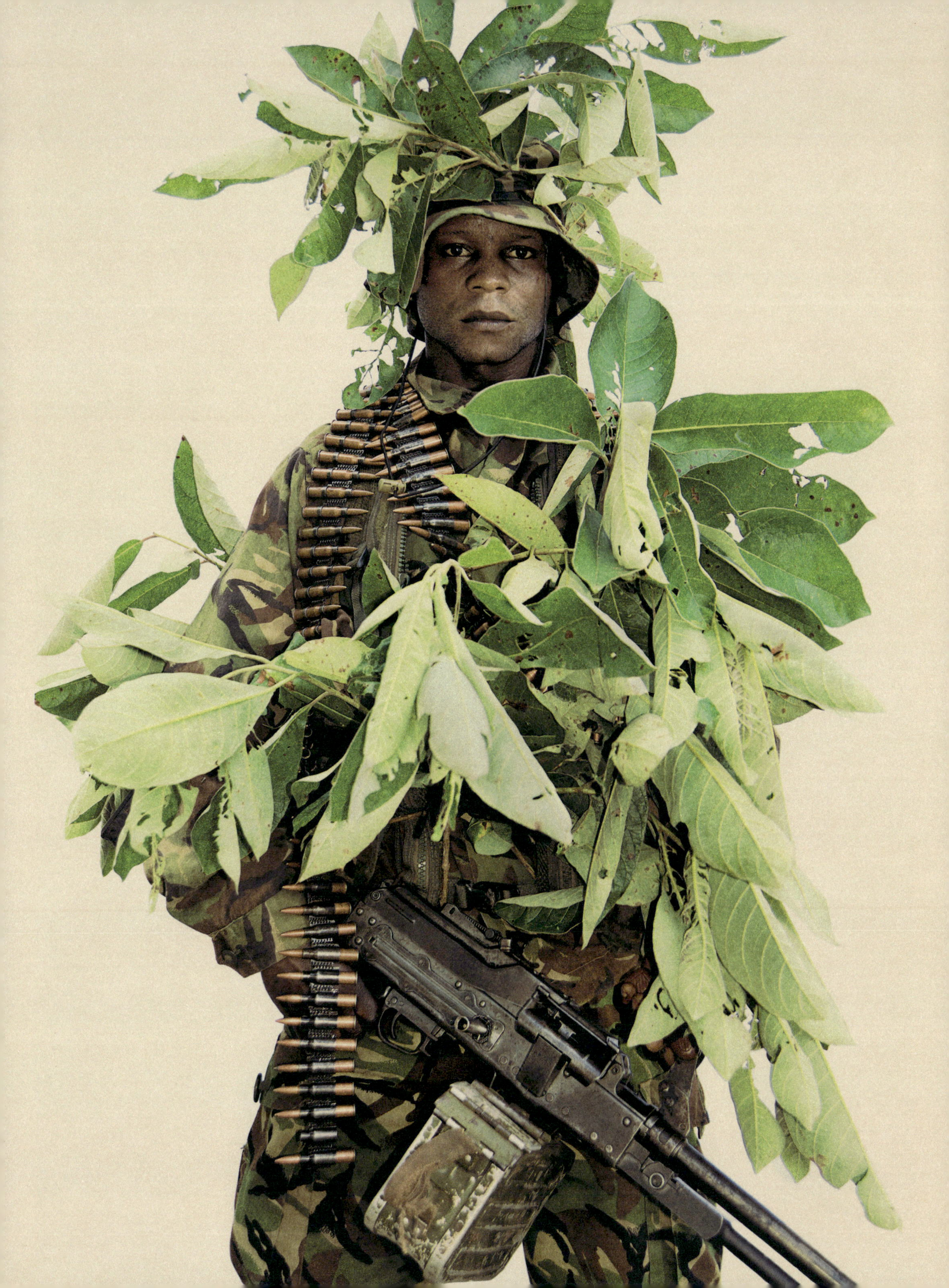

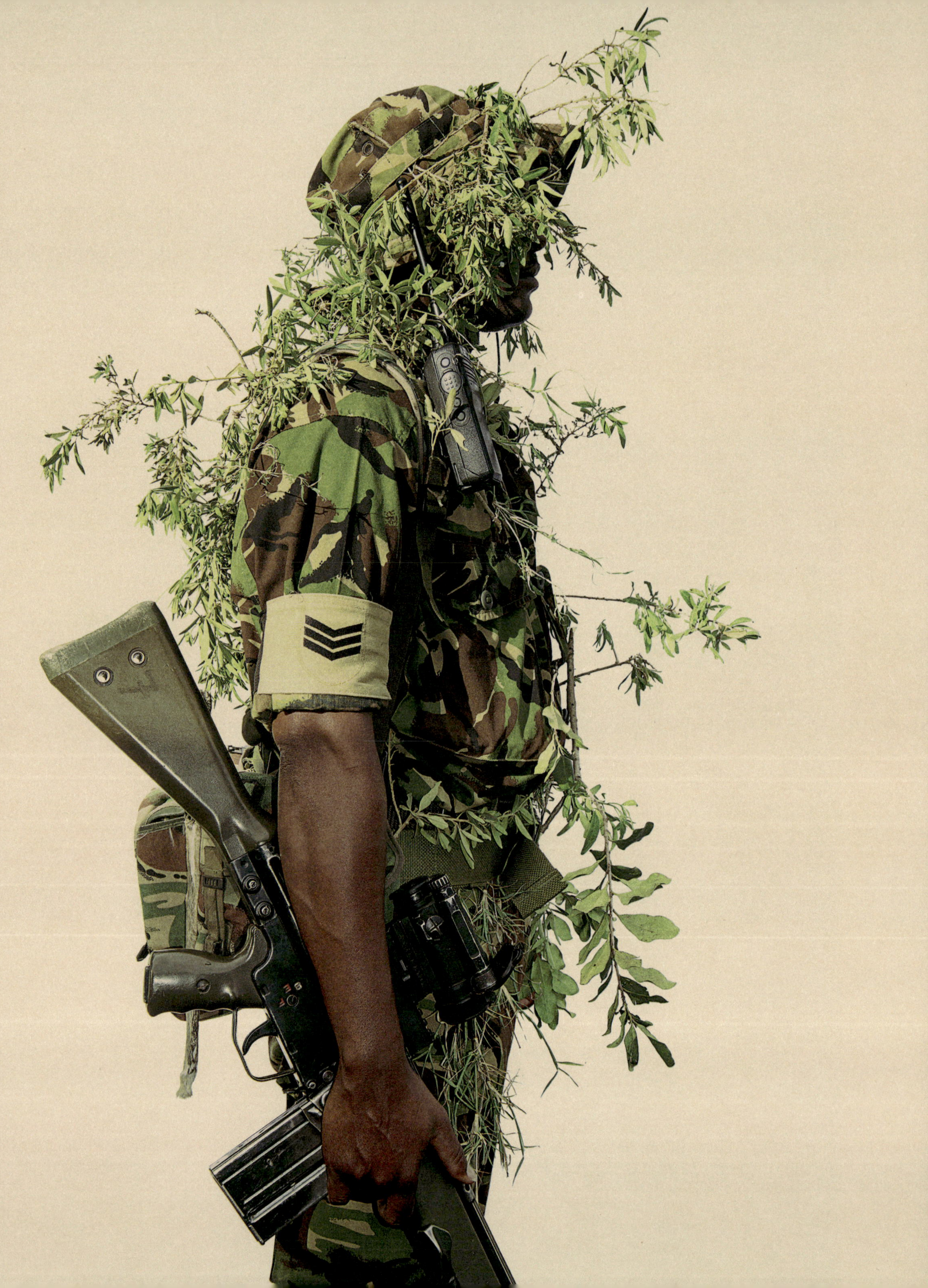

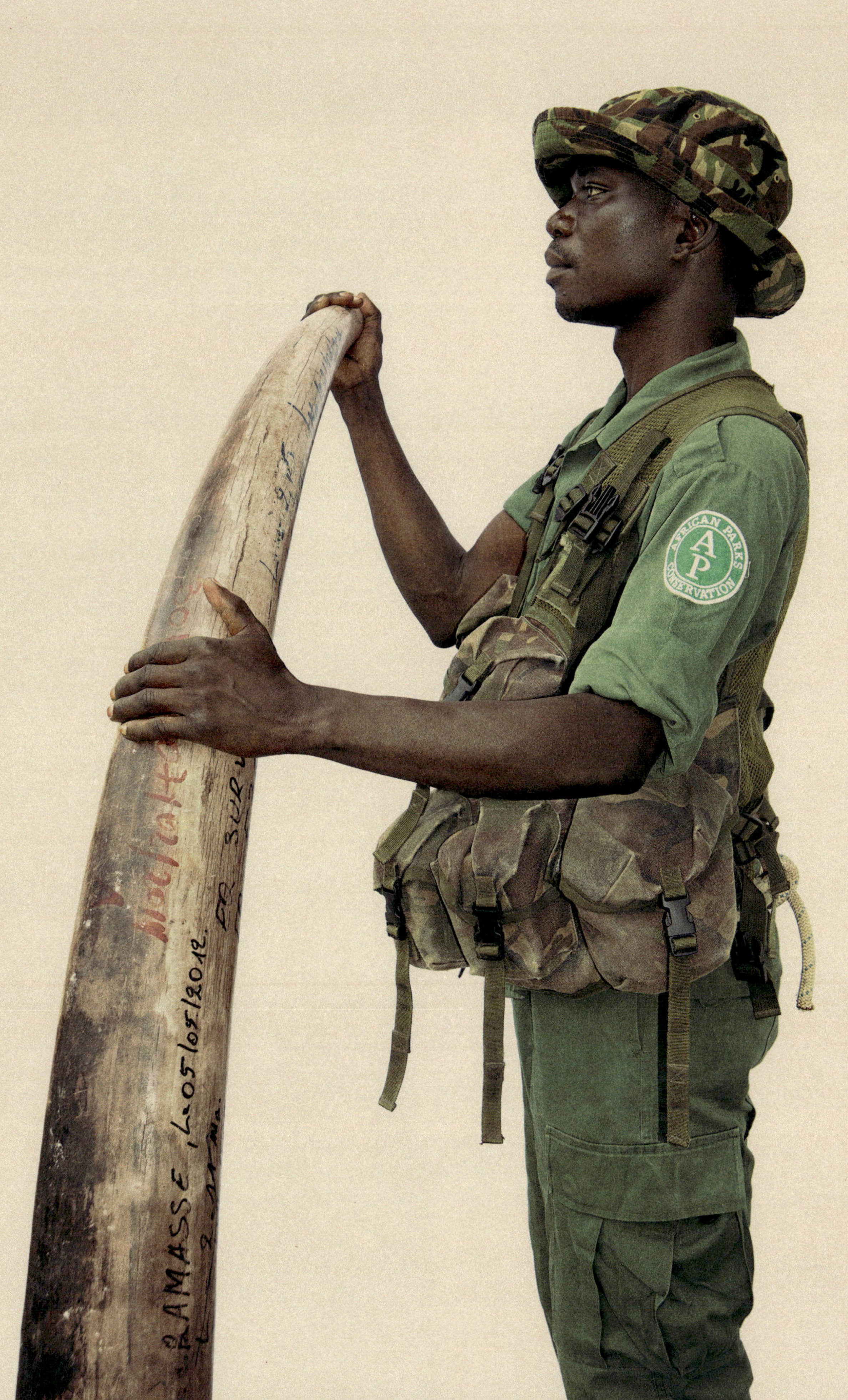
RAMASSE 405/05/2012
2. MAna

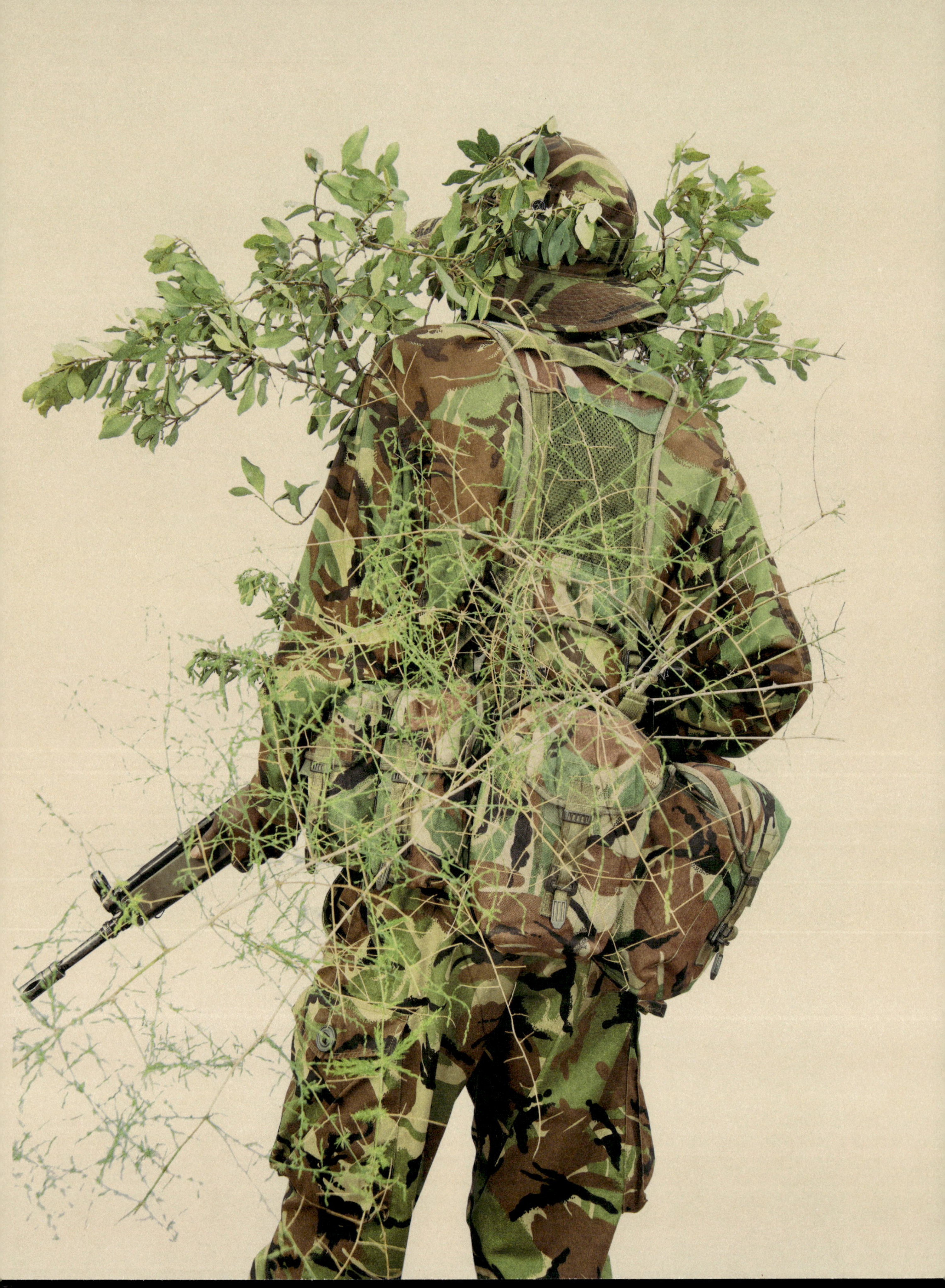

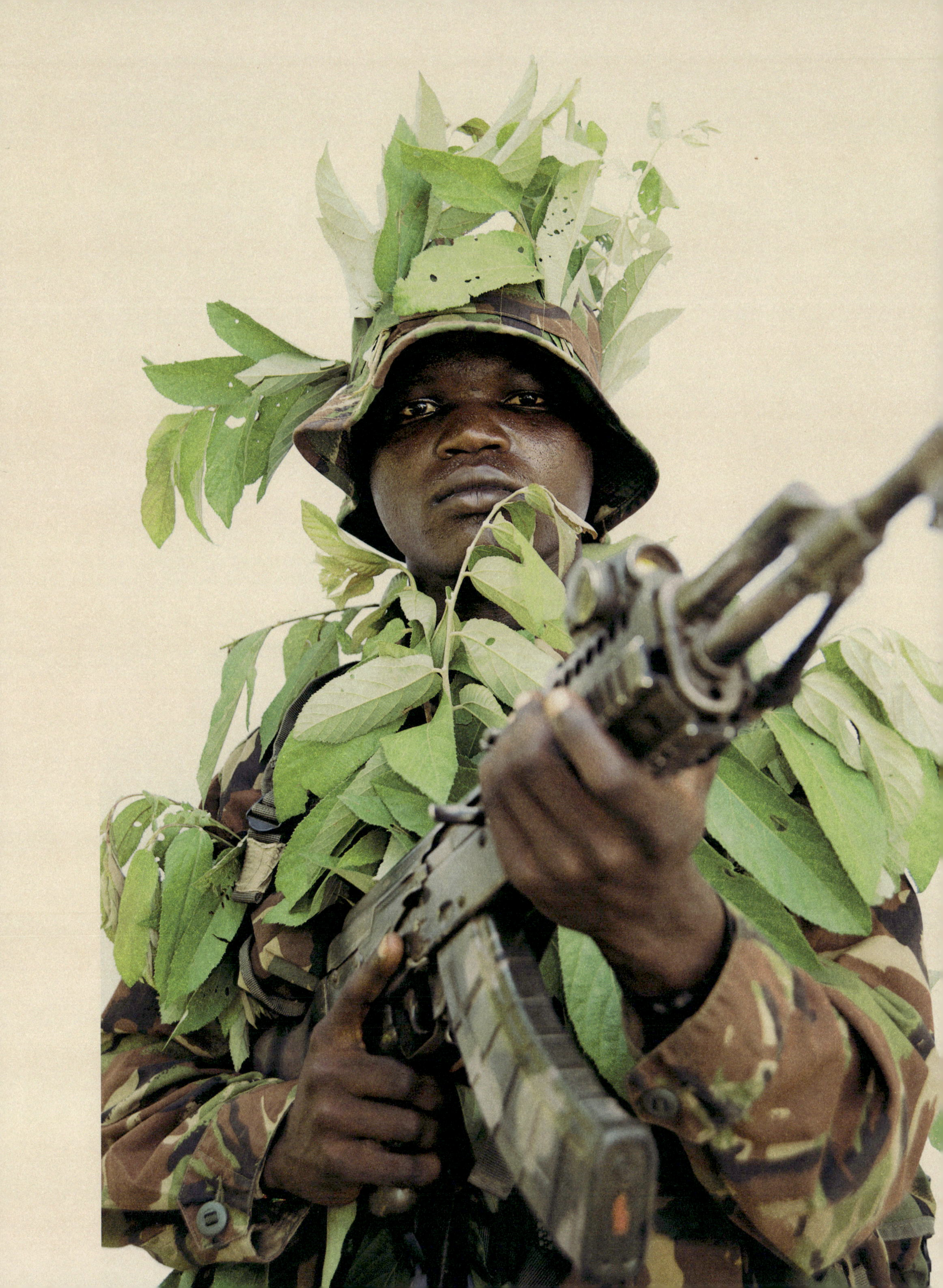

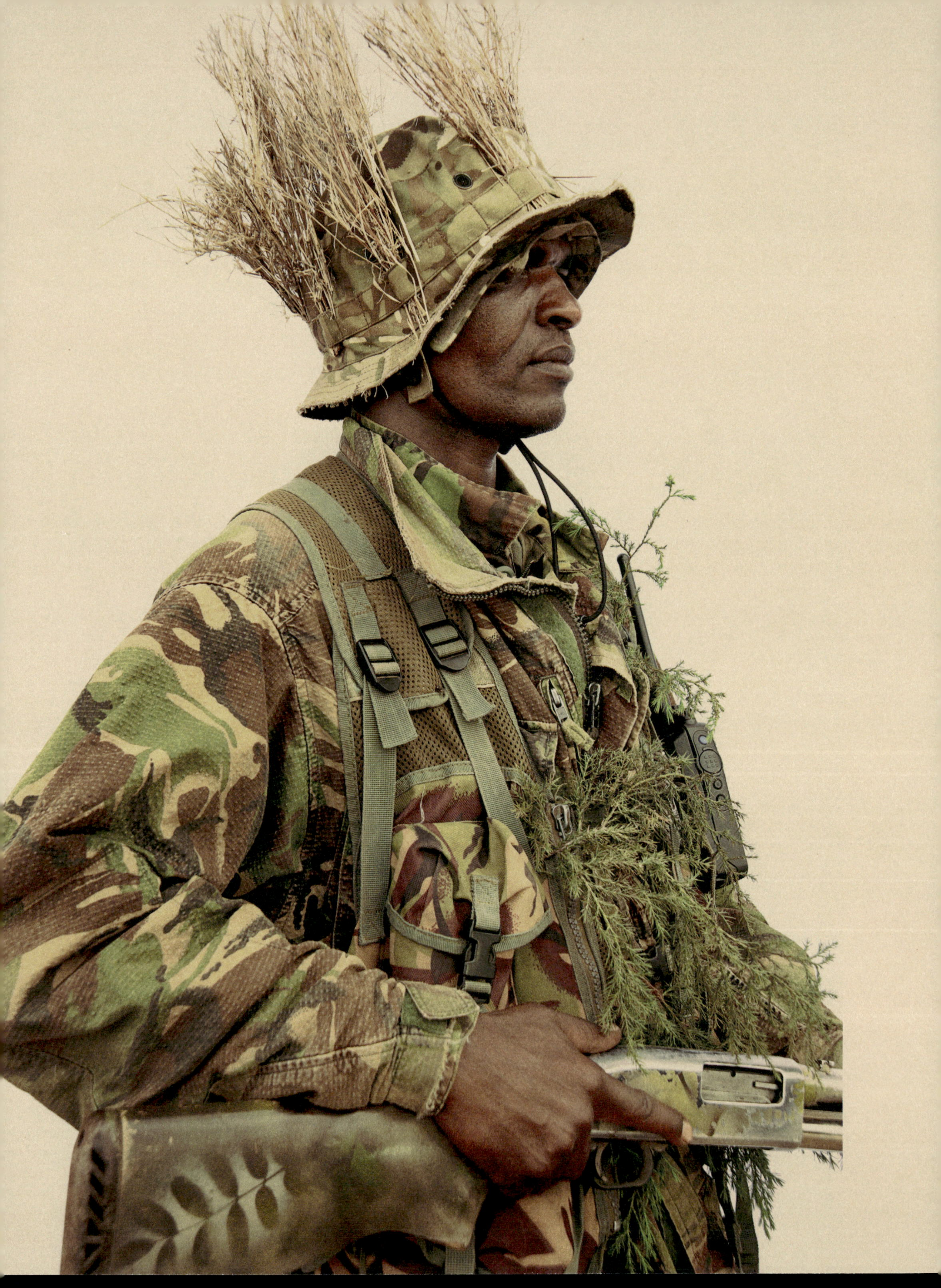

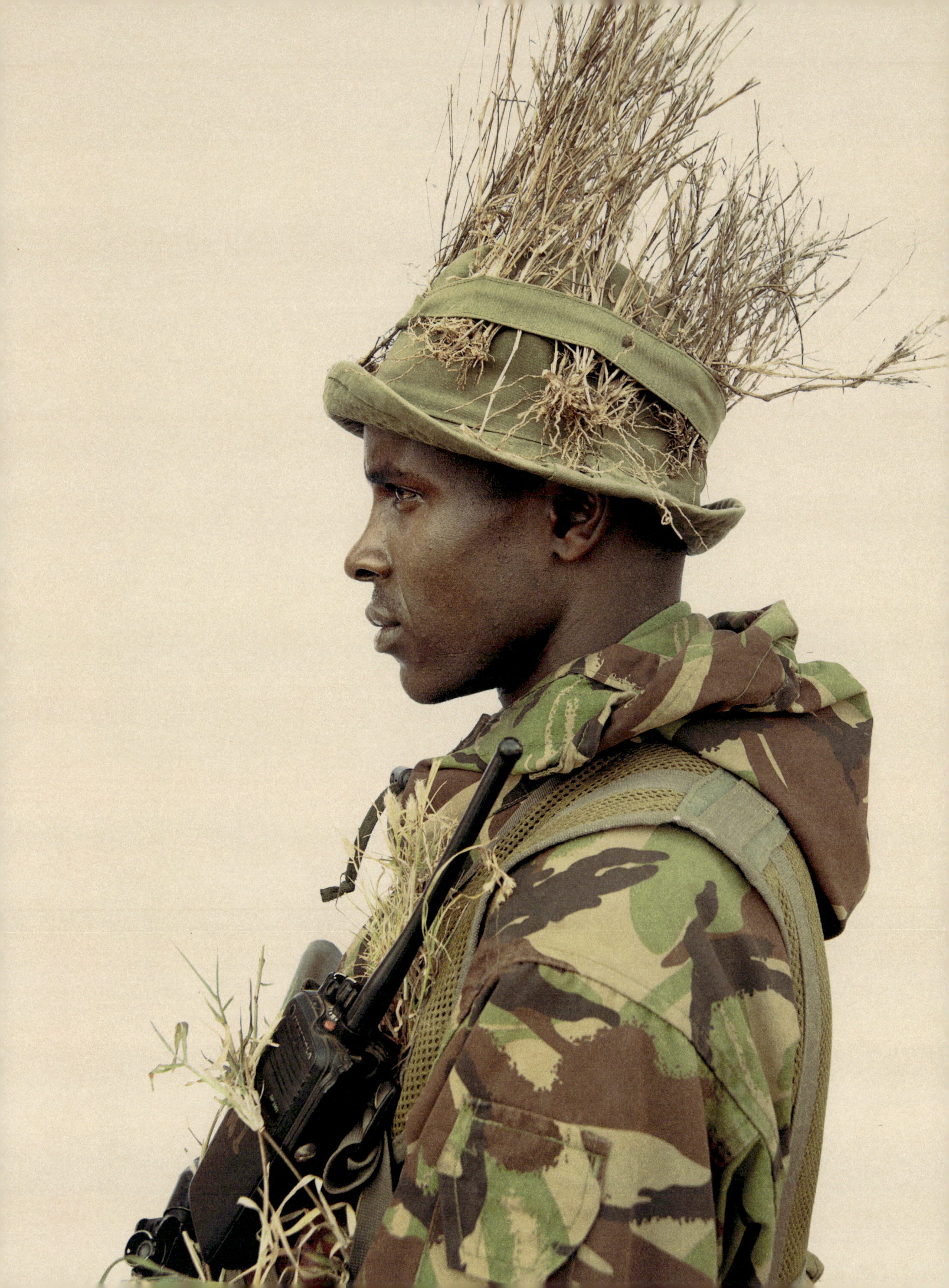

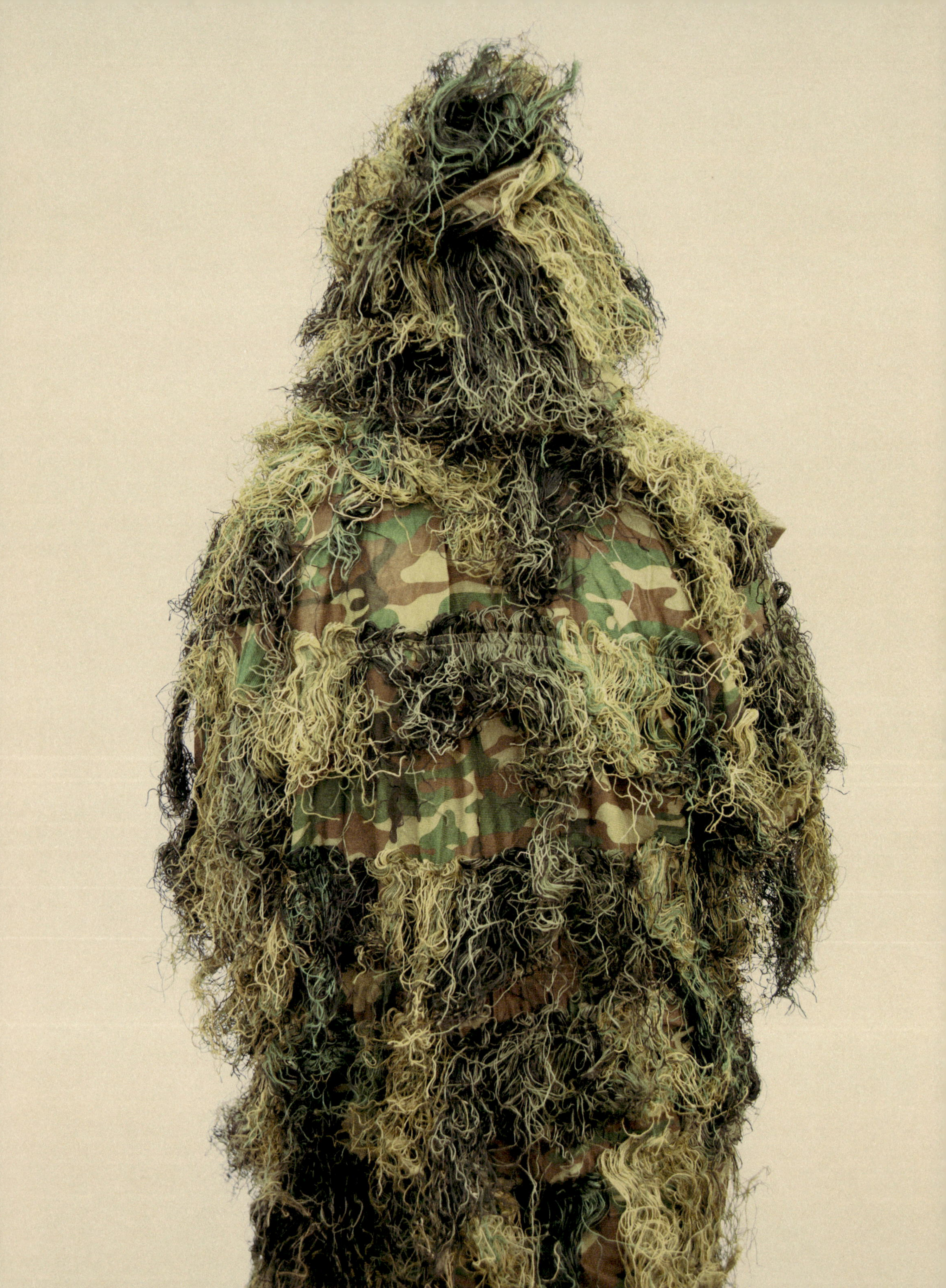

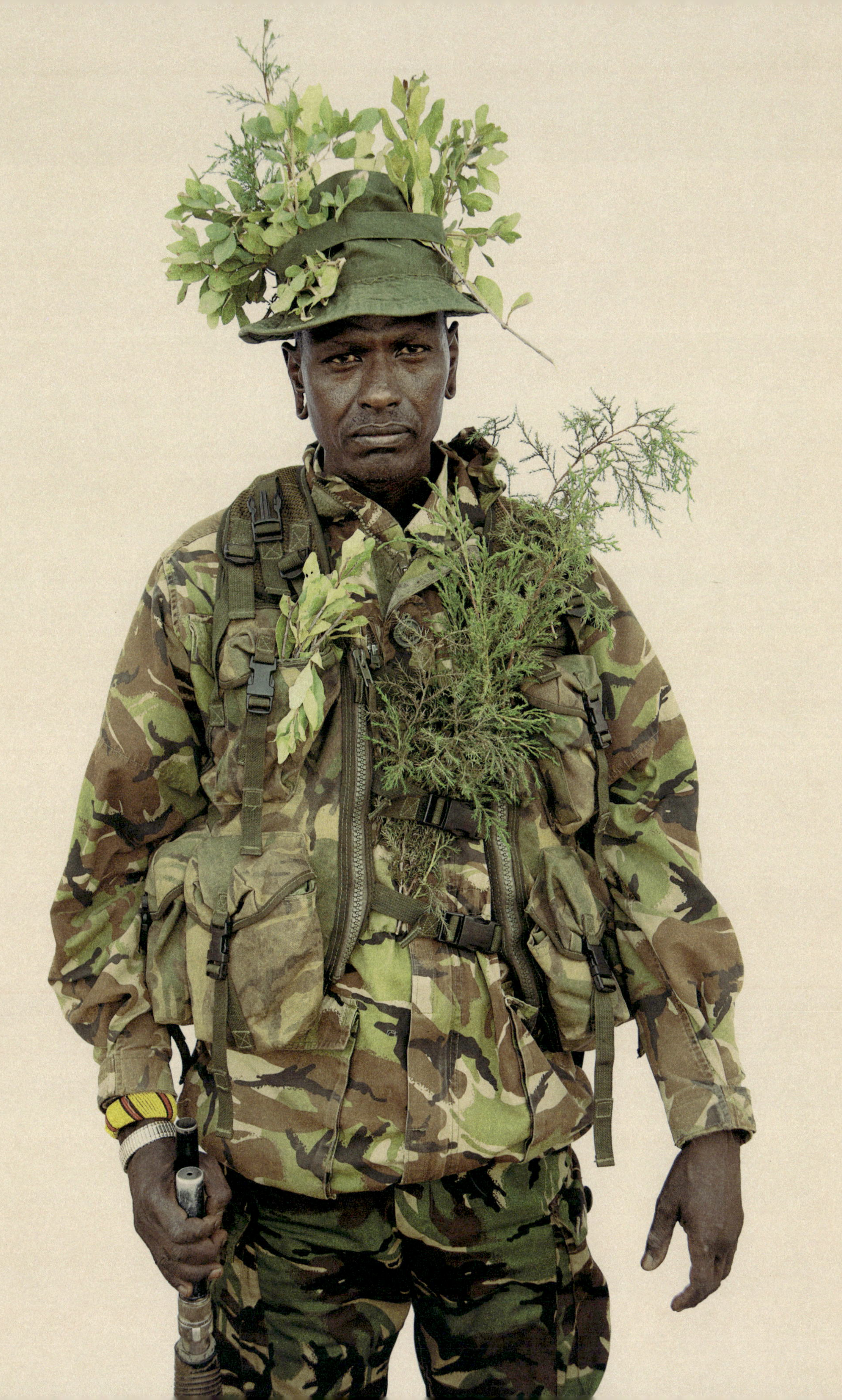

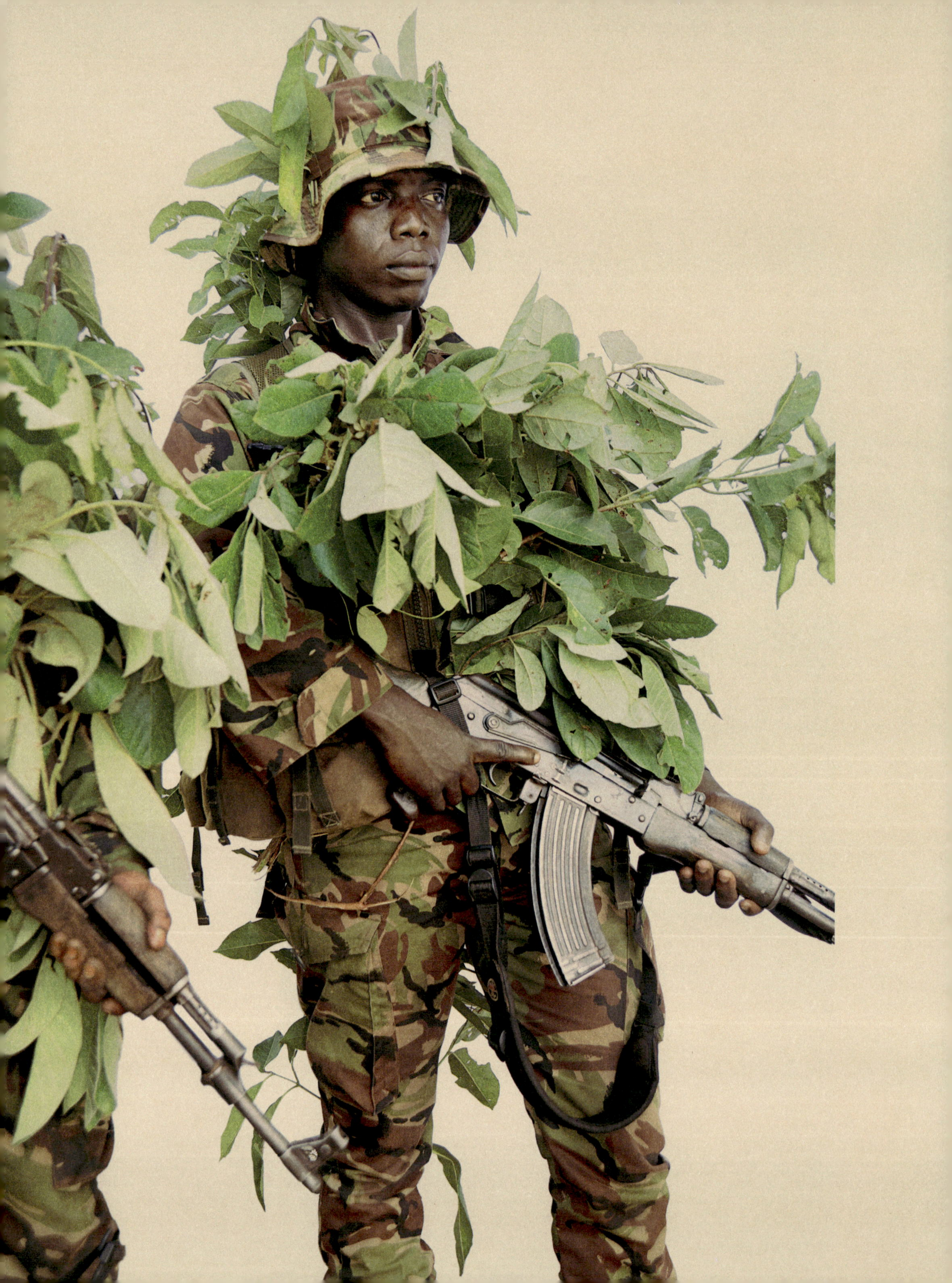

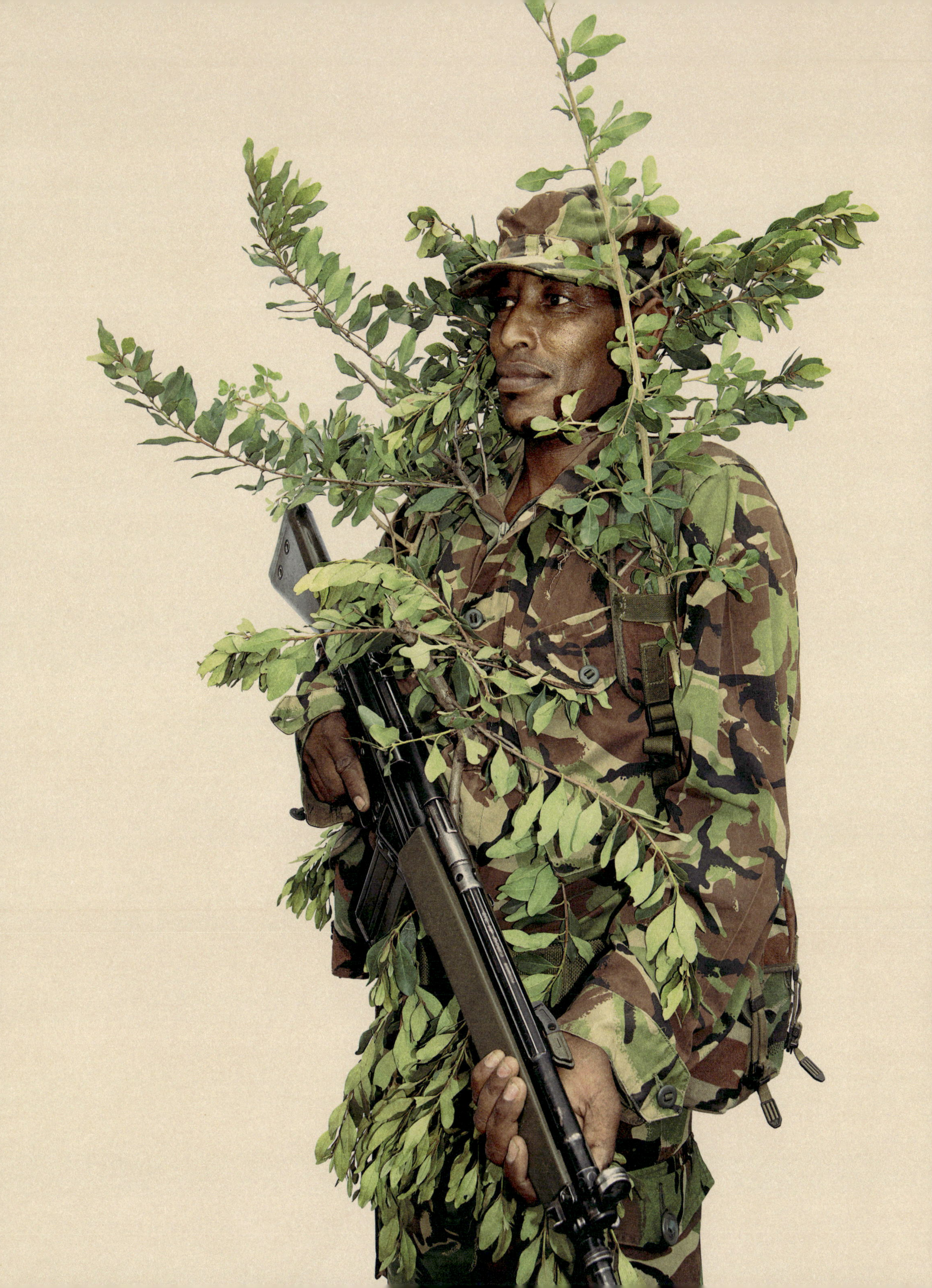

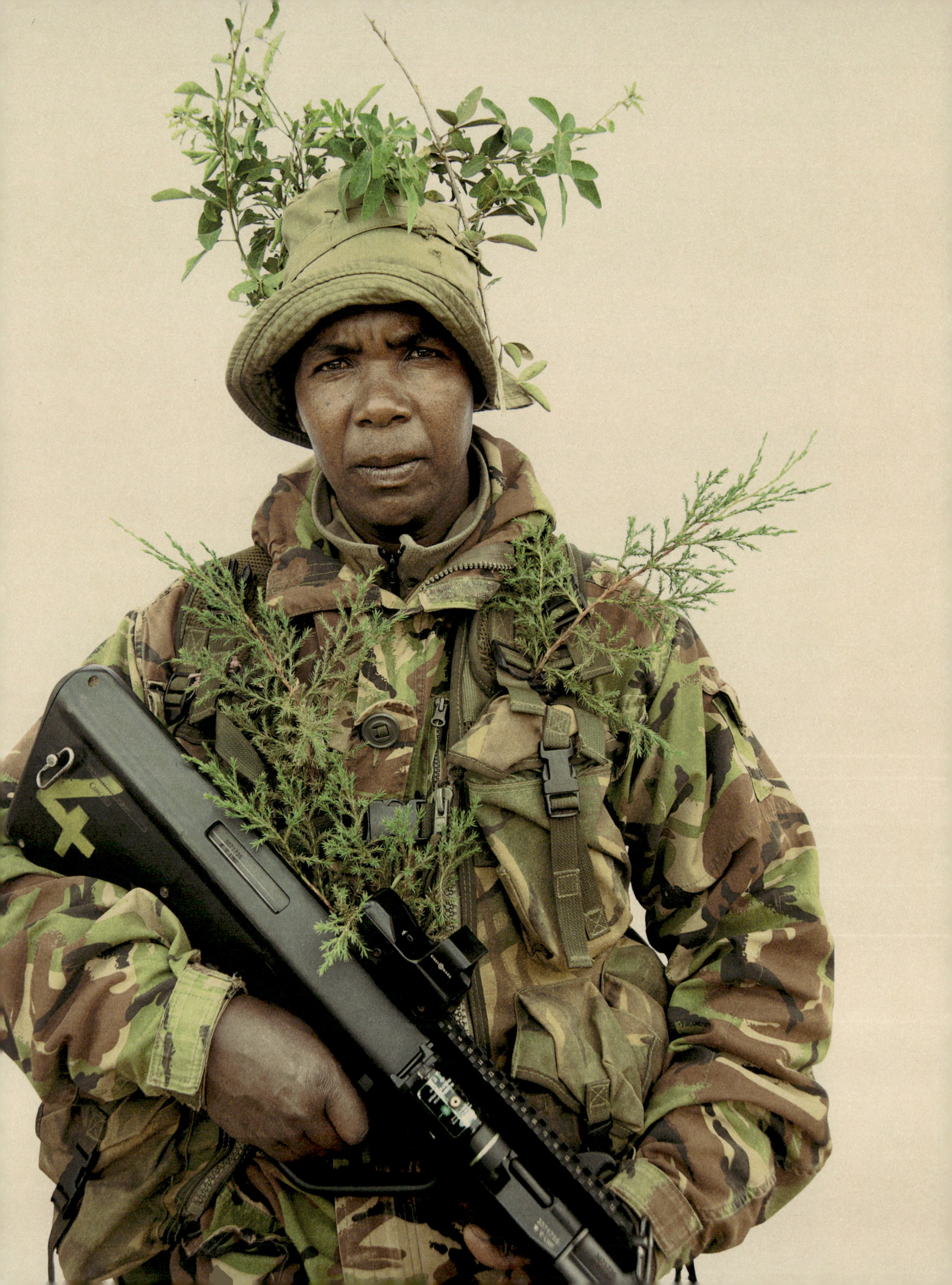

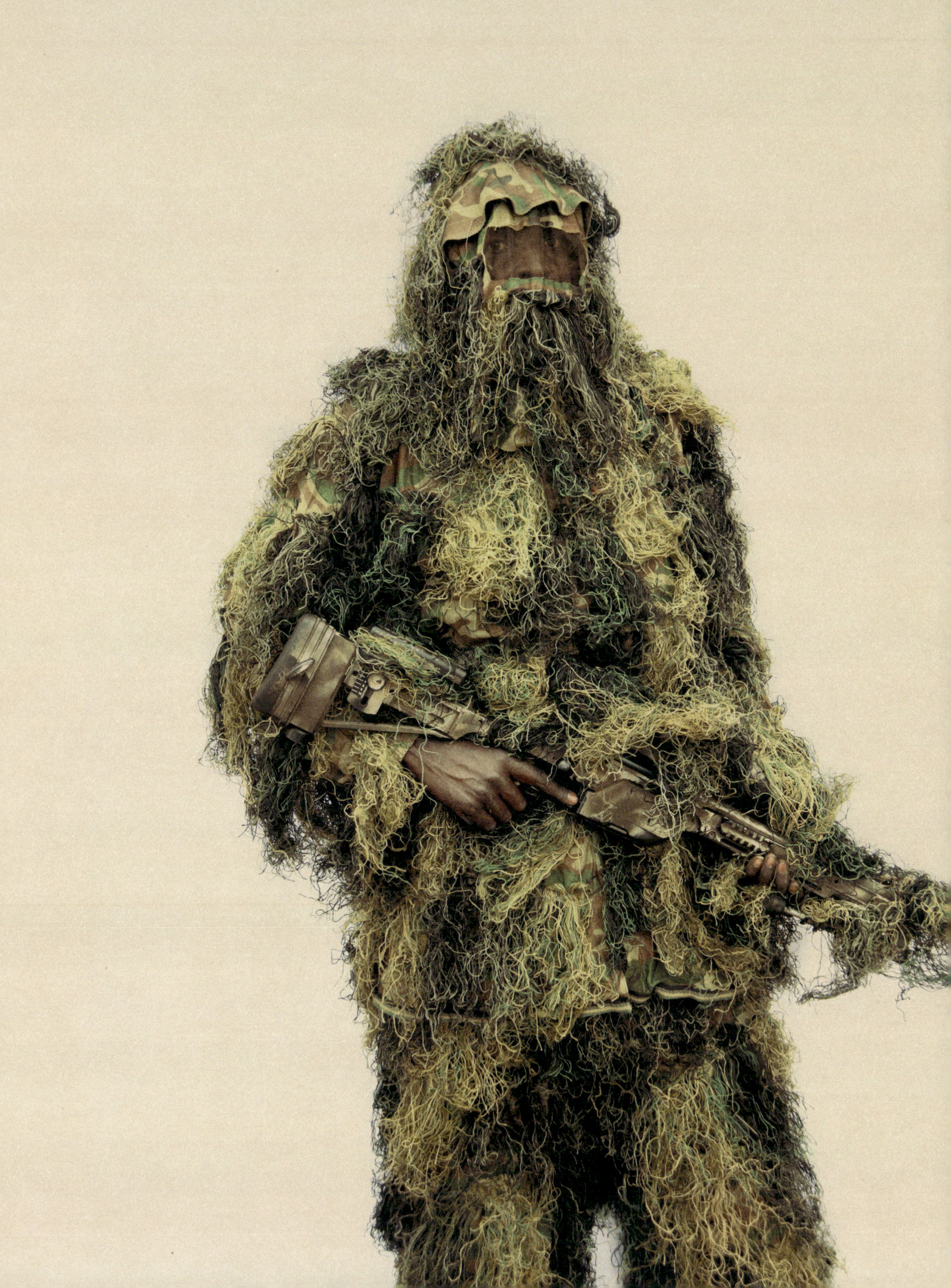

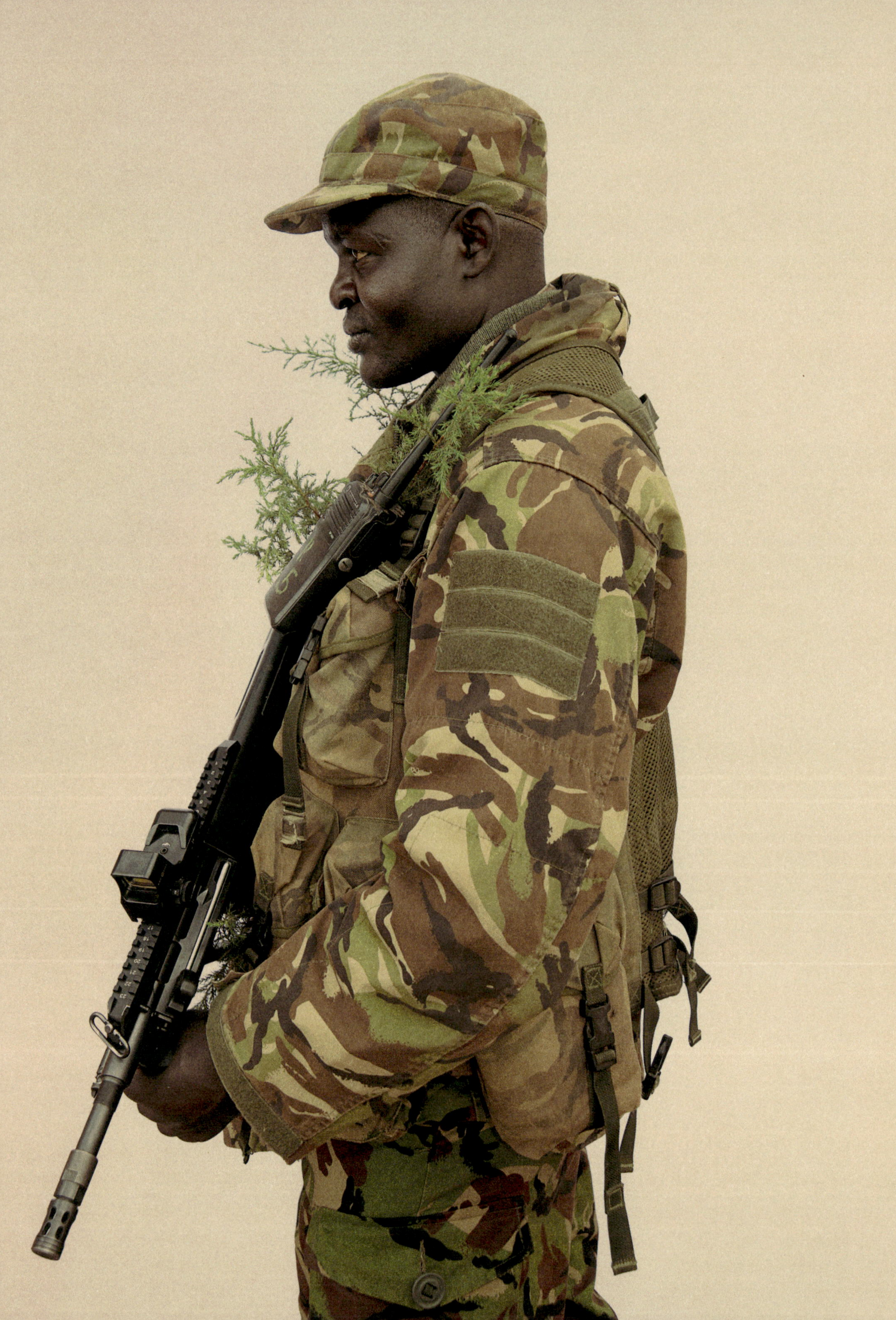

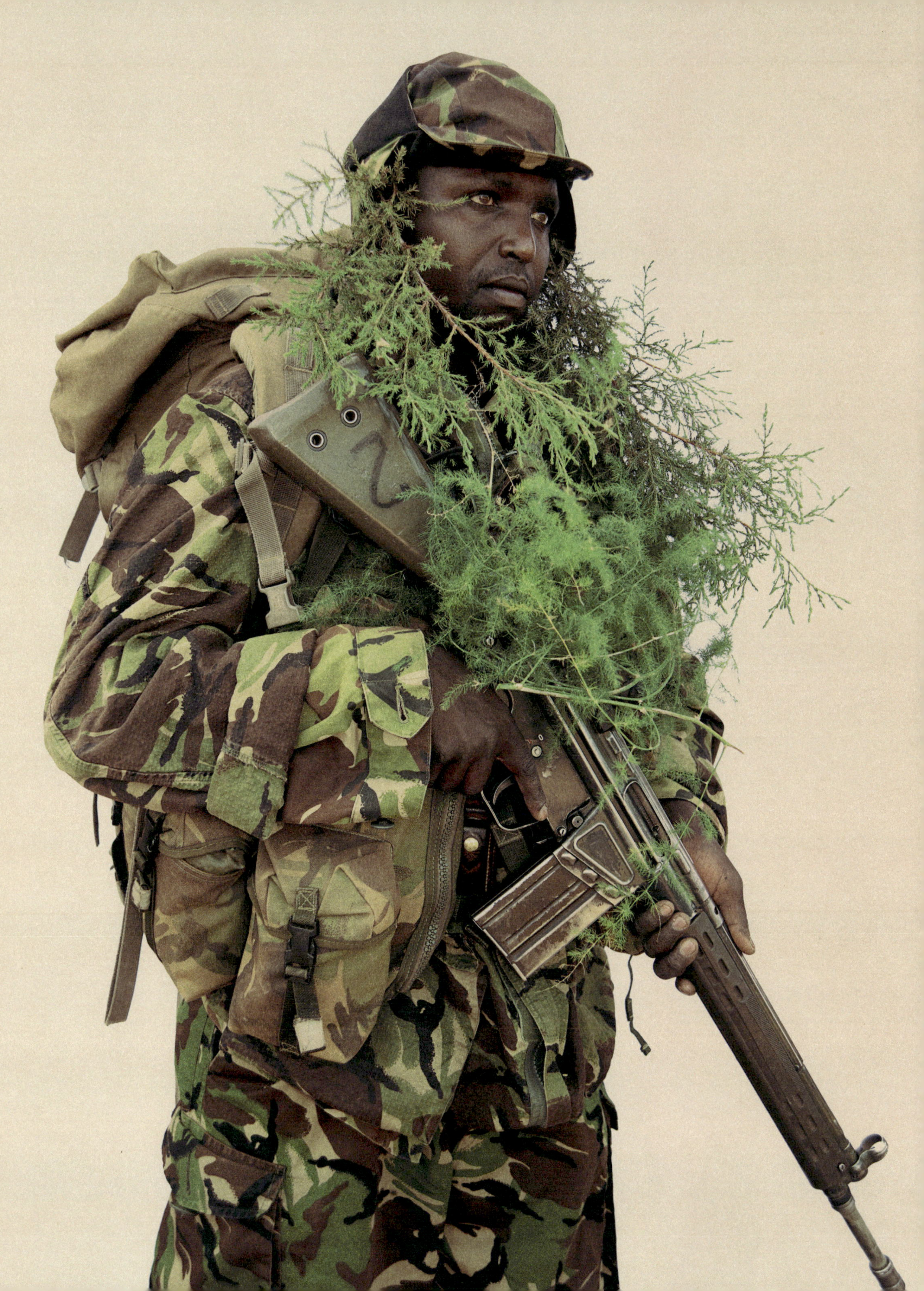

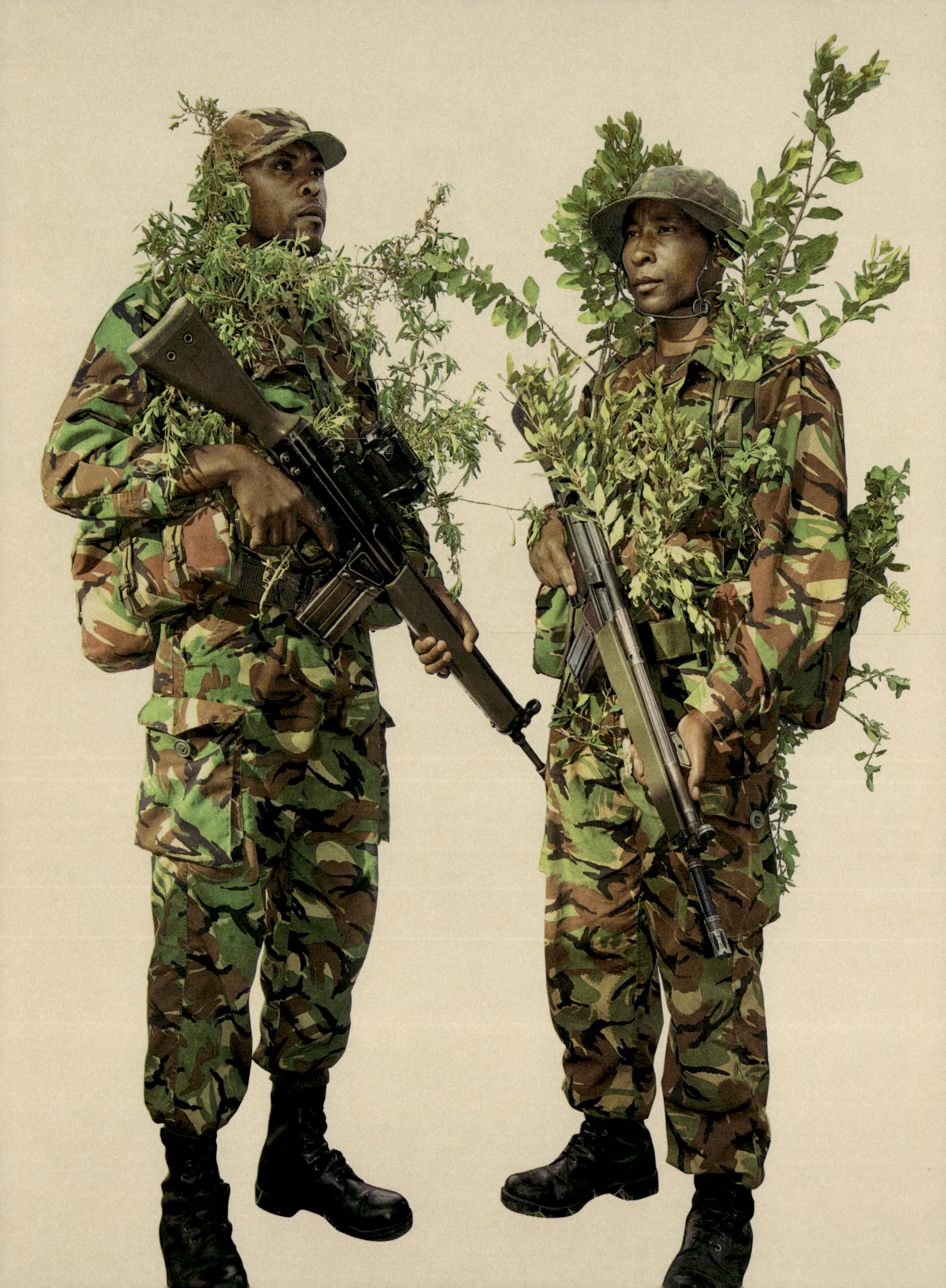

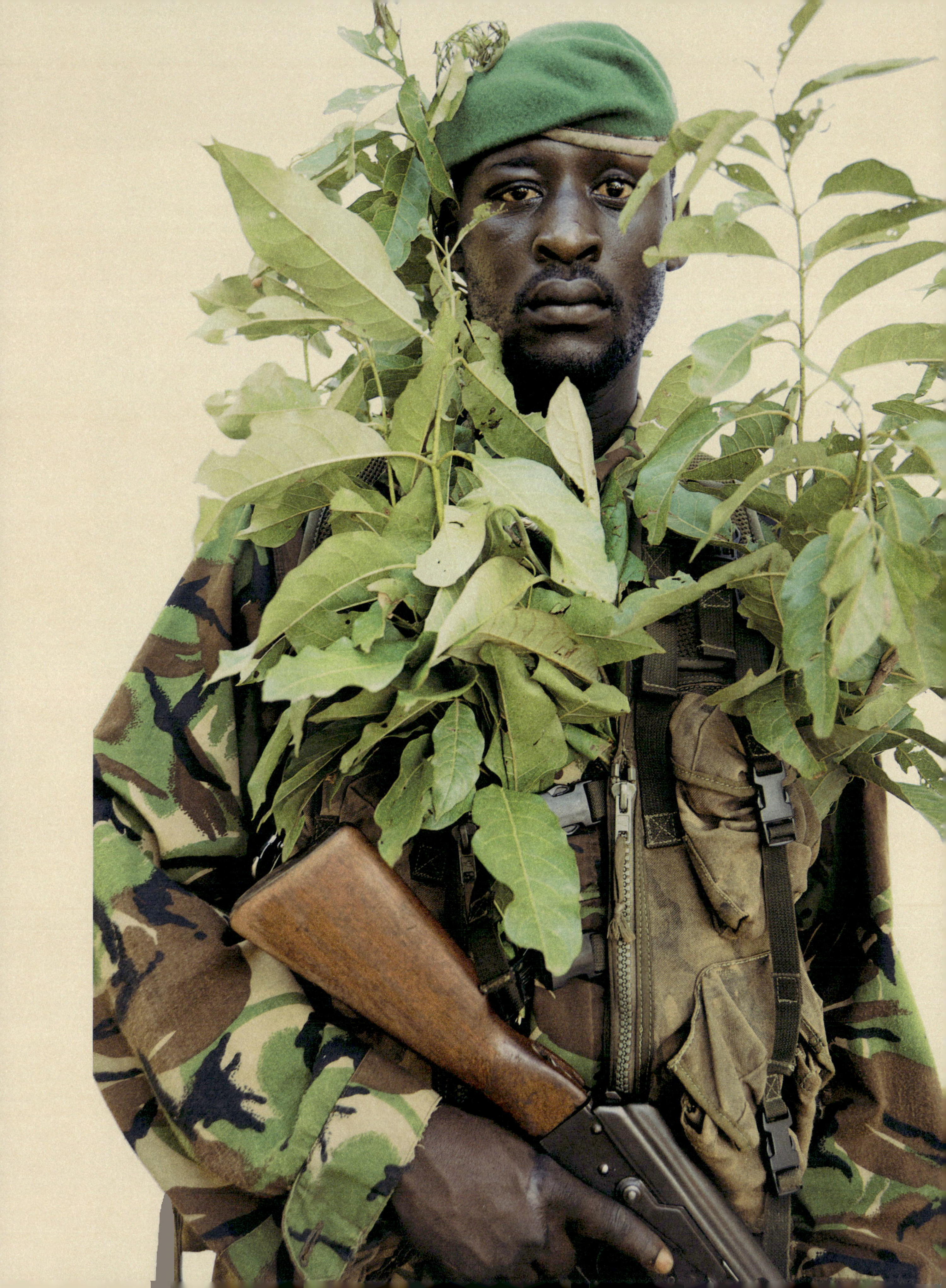

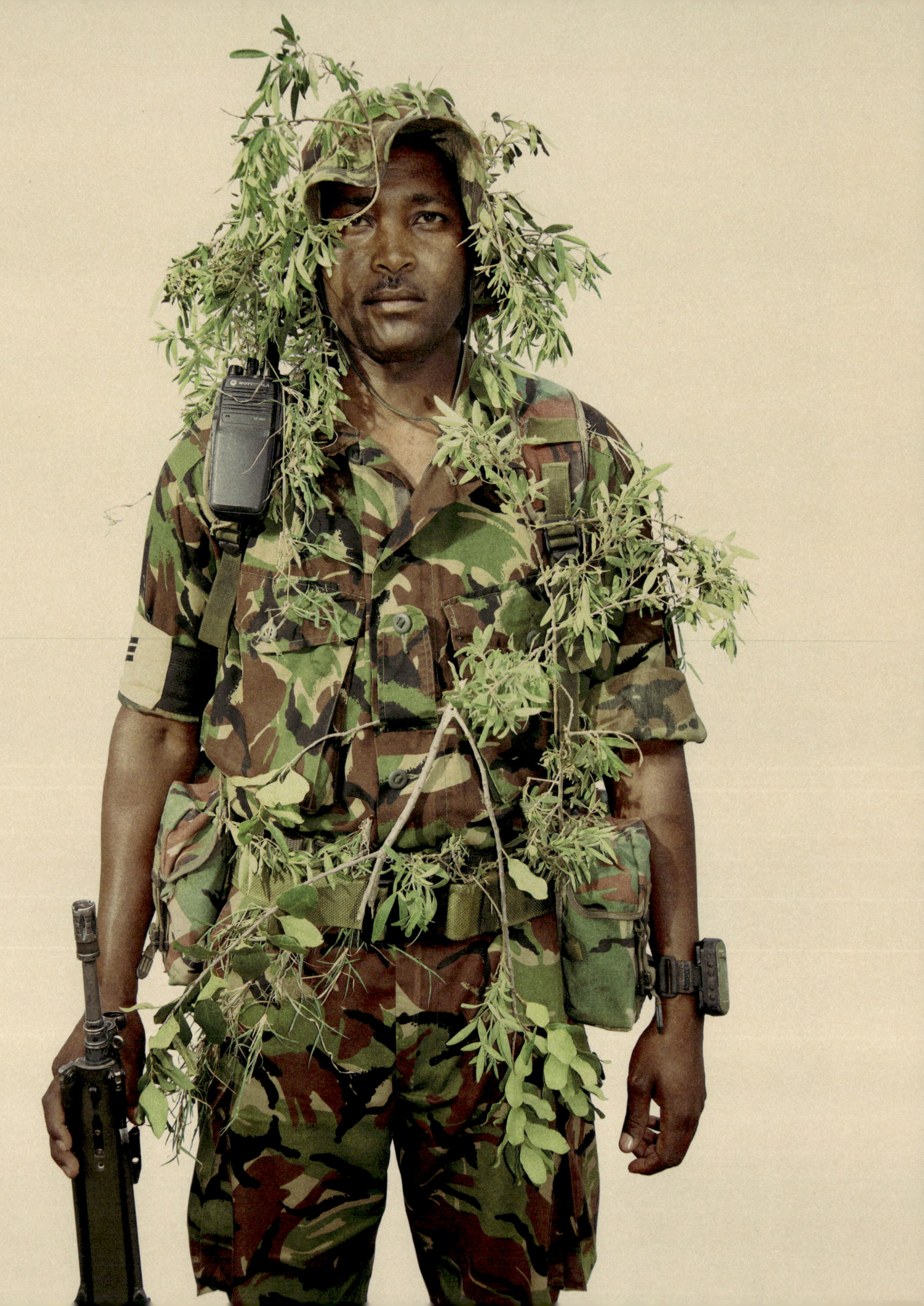

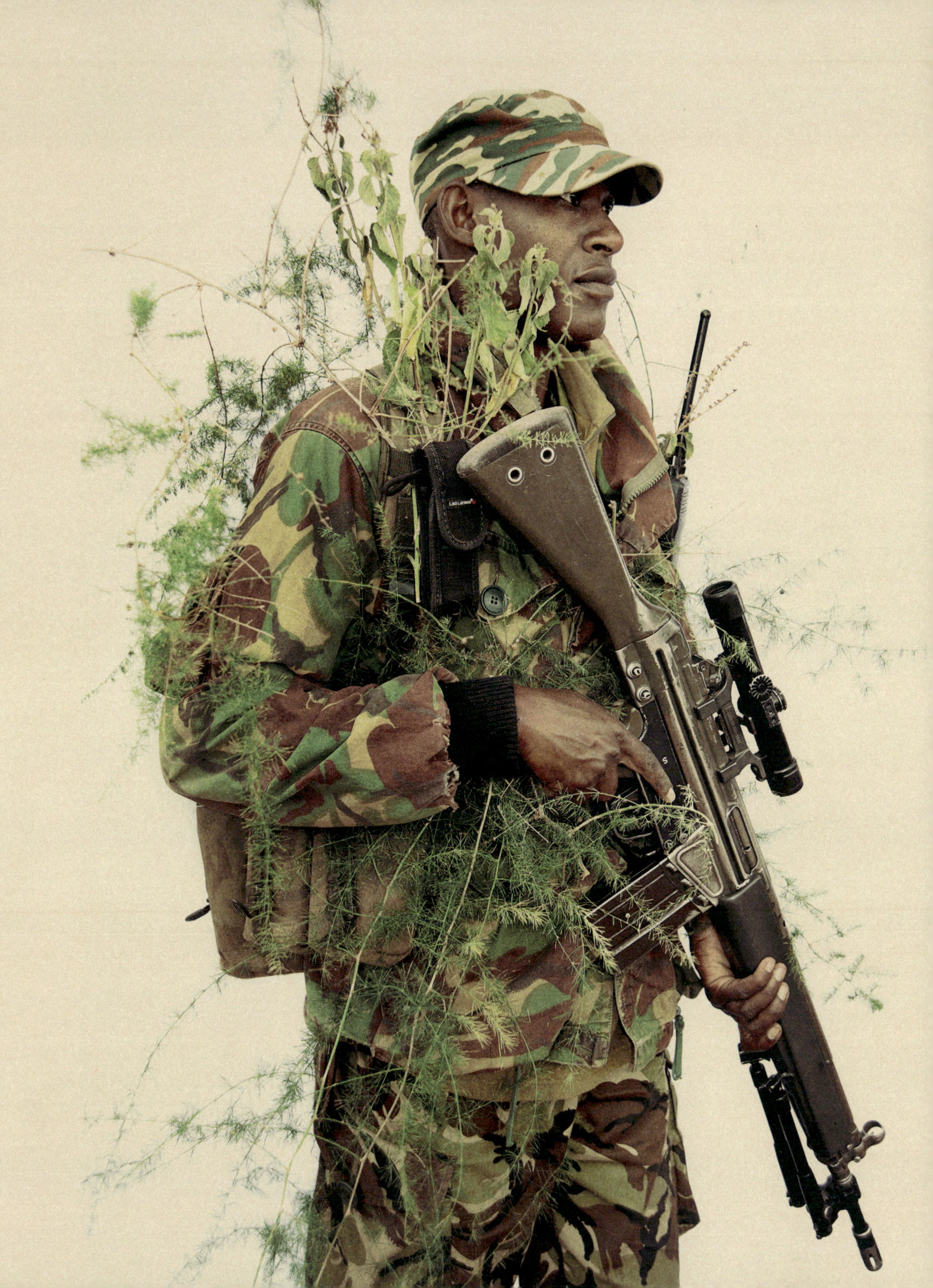

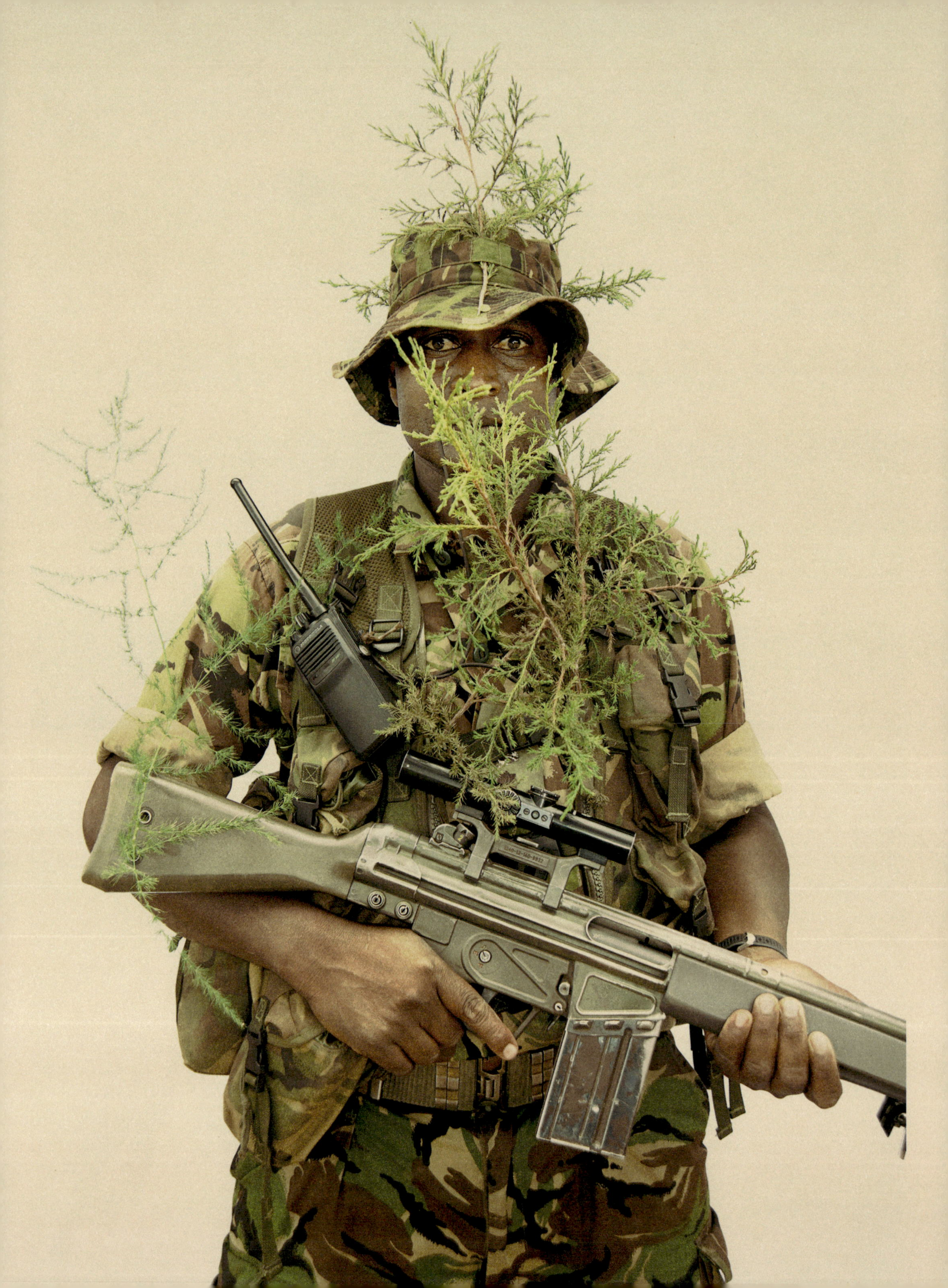

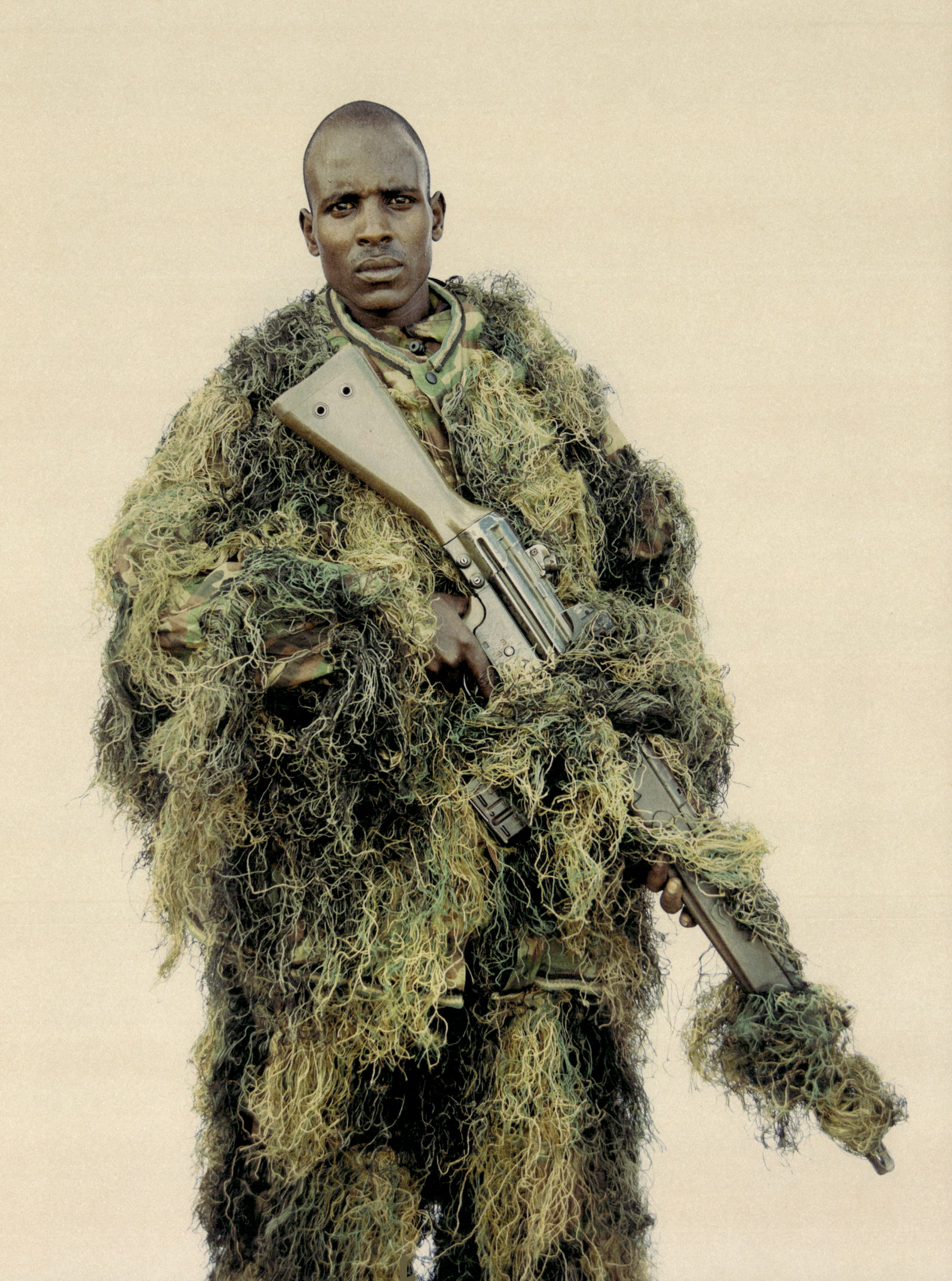

MEN VS WILDLIFE

Guide to Understanding Poaching, Wildlife Decline, and Conservation Methods

The true perpetrators behind the killing of African elephants are criminal enterprises endowed with the capability to establish and sustain supply chains that extend from the forests of Africa to the markets of Asia. They grease palms and pay off corrupt officials at every step of the way. To effectively curb poaching, the focus must be directed at the correct targets—corruption, criminals, and the purchasers of illegal ivory-employing appropriate law enforcement measures.

The tropical forests of the Congo Basin where this picture was taken, once deemed impenetrable, are now succumbing to the intrusion of logging roads, mines, and palm oil plantations, despite their remoteness.

The Central African Republic has been embroiled in a civil war since 2013, rendering it incapable of functioning properly and meeting the basic needs of its people.

Over a span of 36 years, the number of forest elephants has declined by more than 86%, and the population of African savanna elephants has decreased by at least 60% in the last 50 years. Additionally, between 2002 and 2011, the forest elephant saw a 30% reduction in its geographical range.

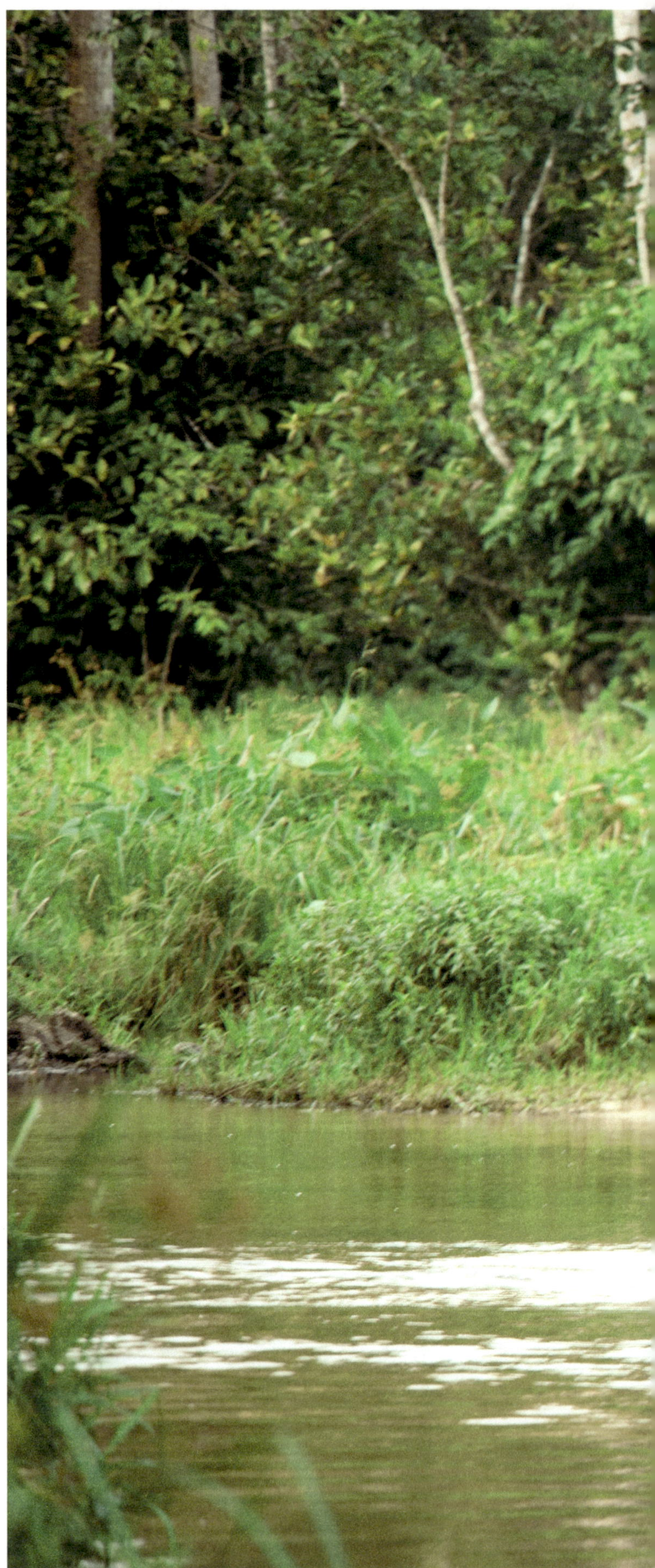

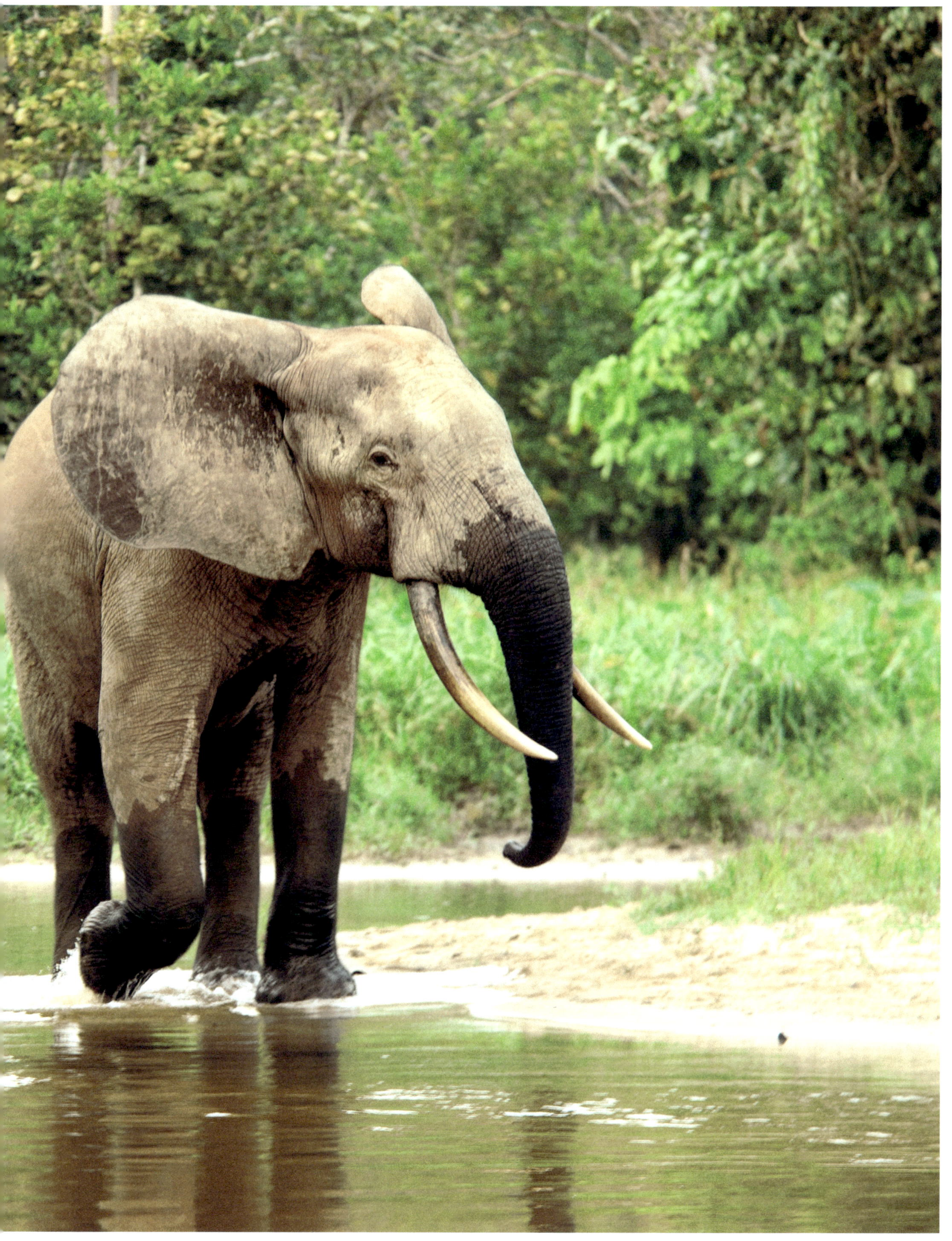

In the 1990s, when I was in my twenties, I remember coming across yet another foreign wildlife documentary crew in the Maasai Mara and thinking: I've seen this film before. Why are we repeating the same old theme: "The Serengeti Shall Not Die!"?

Why have we become fixated on the same kind of footage: a cute lost lion cub looking for its mother, baby elephants and wallowing hippos?

This genre of wildlife films has persisted for decades, excluding the complexities of the landscape they are trying to describe, editing out the humans, both those encroaching on these habitats and those trying to preserve them, and making it possible to believe, for the audience watching thousands of kilometers away, that this kind of scene is somehow 'natural' and that 'fortress conservation', is solving problems rather than creating new ones.

I still wonder why this kind of 'wilderness story' popularized by the gently stentorian tones of David Attenborough, (among others) is so dominant.

I suspect others share my frustration with this limited view, or at least I hope so. I worry that we are stuck in paradigms of left-over colonialism and white savior narratives from the last century. It was Europeans who decimated populations of large mammals as a matter of routine, regarded certain species as 'monsters', and glorified 'trophy hunting'. And it was Europeans too, who established modern conservation methods and continue to furnish the means to fund them.

I have witnessed these efforts over several decades and have come to see that the protection of nature and wild animals on the African continent is too often mired in vested interests, opportunism, and territorialism.

Money, profit, bribes, and influence peddling tend to dominate the field and there is a general contempt for the indigenous custodians who have sustained a close relationship with nature for millennia. I wonder if we can reflect on the errors that have been made and re-evaluate the systems of conservation, tourism, land development that are now elbowing for position.

It's a question that is becoming ever more urgent.

The effects of climate change are becoming clear and present. Many of us experienced temperatures in the 40sC in Europe over the past few summers and saw major rivers dry up. But it seems to me that mainstream media most often focuses on the Global South and on Africa as places that will be most directly affected; while at the same time assuming the solution will come from the wealthier countries of the Global North. Something is off kilter.

Where are the lessons and ideas and voices of the indigenous guardians of our world? How do we find these people who have been for so long repressed and ignored? What must we do to free ourselves from unviable conservation systems? What can we replace them with?

I am frustrated with the idea that the world assumes that funding is the only solution, that money alone can repair our relationship with nature.

Too often richer people and richer countries assume that their largesse gives them the right to dictate solutions to people on the ground. I think that charity, 'doing good', has become commodified and is too often condescending, allowing the 'giver' to retain a sense of superiority.

There is not enough consciousness or conscientiousness, not enough empathy, listening, humility, respect. There is little effort to engage with or try to understand the traditions and cultures that have sustained the ecological balance between man and wilderness.

The ideology that supports man's dominion over nature, is on its way out, but its exit is not without a struggle. And it's not yet clear what might emerge as a guiding philosophy for future conservation.

In the interim, the hangover of imperialism—cultural and economic—often condemns African nations to replicate old assumptions and mistakes. Conservation policies and laws in Kenya and Tanzania, for example, ride roughshod over the ethos and traditions of their pastoral populations.

The contest between large infrastructure projects and the preservation of ancient pasturelands is an ongoing dilemma in the region. Of course, there are many people doing good work on the ground, but I have often seen that much of their work, their innovations and ideas are disregarded or minimized or even appropriated. It is not only that Western-dominated institutions by-pass them, but their own governments and policy makers often blindly embrace foreign-designed conservation programs and structures.

I am just a photographer, an observer. I don't have an easy answer to these questions.

I hope that this book can become an atlas of exploration. I hope that it can show the scale of the problem and the hope of solutions through the hearts and minds of the many different people I have spent time with who are also grappling with these issues.

But I am also conflicted. What right do I have to weigh in on this debate? As a white man of European provenance, why should I claim a stake in Africa's future?

I am the son of three generations of a French family born in Madagascar. I grew up in the Comoros Islands, Djibouti, I lived many years in Kenya. I am now based in Lisbon, but I travel throughout the continent, working, meeting old friends, and making new ones, several months a year.

Most of my life has been spent roaming the African continent as a documentary photographer. As a white, Western male, living in Africa afforded me access and privileges which were not extended to my equally gifted non-Caucasian peers. I was commissioned by numerous western media organizations to take photos that have often, I must admit, conformed to certain African stereotypes.

I always sought to resist these tropes, as most of those of us who feel a sense of African belonging do, but sometimes the selection of certain images made me cringe. In my need to earn a crust in a field of diminishing opportunities, my resistances to such preferences were admittedly feeble.

I am conscious too, that inevitably, being white and working for Western institutions, my pictures may have carried a certain kind of bias. It had been a constant conundrum for me that while Africa is my birthplace and had been my home for so long, I remained an outsider. When my father, Yves Bonn, died in 2015, I went through all his old documents and I stumbled on something my family had kept secret for a hundred years.

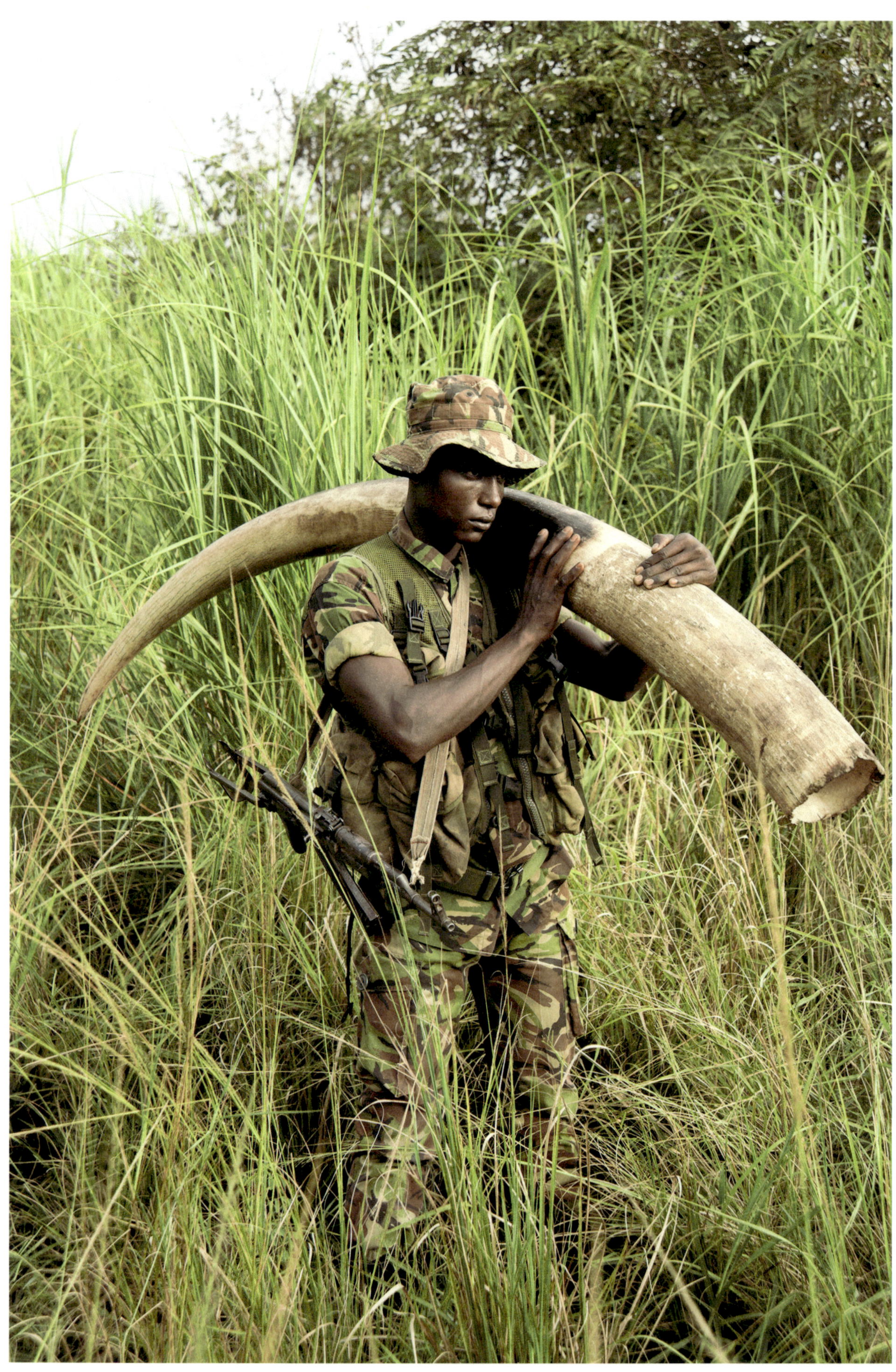

I found out that my great-grandfather, Albert Bonn, a French colonial army officer in Madagascar at the end of the 19th century, had married a Malagasy woman, named Razafindrafara, and had two children with her, including my grandfather born in 1901.

It's hard to imagine what the social consequences and context were like for a French colonial officer married to a Malagasy. I wish I could understand how it was to be a family in a time of colonial and racial division, dealing with the judgment, ostracism and imposed shame.

I wish I could ask my grandfather and father why this matter was kept hidden, as if it was an aberration.

Soon after my discovery, an editor at one American magazine I worked for subtly let me know that they would not consider me for African work again, basically because I was white. Of course, it stung, but I also understood.

Recently I found myself staring at a photo of my grandfather, a robust, light-skinned man sitting on the crocodile he had just shot. He is wearing a pith helmet and looks like the perfectly stereotypical white colonial male in Africa. But now I know the truth of his Malagasy mother behind his smile.

I feel very grateful to my Malagasy great-grandmother. Liberating her from the weight of a family secret has also liberated me, her descendant. I was also born in Madagascar and I feel I can inhabit my African heritage a little more easily because of her.

My father's work meant that our family moved every few years, from Madagascar to the Comoros Islands to north Yemen, Djibouti and finally Kenya. I grew up accustomed to planes and new homes.

I was fourteen when I first asked why, if we were French, we never lived in France. I had begun my lifelong quest to belong. Nairobi is cosmopolitan and international. Although I went to a French school, I interacted with young people from all over the world.

Nairobi was a fascinating paradoxical swirl of different cultures and religions, sophistication and suffering, fear and desire, where the veil between life and death was so very thin. Coming of age in Kenya was idyllic for me.

I had a front seat to observe the changing face of Africa, as the old ways mingled with the impulse towards western-influenced growth and nation-building.

The changes did not sit easily with me. It was not that I wanted Africa to be frozen in time or correspond to a western exotic fantasy version of itself, but I was concerned where the great rush towards economic growth was leading. The colonial era had undermined so many life-sustaining worldviews and deprived local ways of managing natural resources.

But the new independent governments did not foster indigenous legacies or heed the lessons that had allowed their peoples to cohabit with different species. If they had, perhaps a different kind of relationship with the environment might have emerged and even become a template for other countries.

As a young rootless boy, I roamed Kenya's wild spaces and felt a sense of place and a sense of belonging in that place. I wanted to hold onto this feeling, be able to trust that it would not change.

But it did, and it does.

I grew up surrounded by my father's collection of photography books and magazines. I would pore over the stories of adventurers and explorers and wanted to grow up and travel the world and take pictures.

It was almost inevitable that I would choose photography as my career.

I became a documentary photographer based in Nairobi. I traveled the continent, documenting its transformation, its wars and coups, its dreams and restlessness, its beauty and generosity and its sufferings.

Along the way I would spend time in its wildernesses, where I found a kind of shelter and reassurance that helped me to frame my experiences and to form a perspective on how to communicate my understanding, disquiet and wonder at the Africa I loved. I realize now that this questioning informs so many of my photographs.

Nairobi has undergone rapid change. It is no longer the frontier town I grew up in, but a dazzling, dynamic metropolis with a population of about 5 million. However, along with its growth come challenges: annoying traffic jams, pollution haze, and a busy population striving to excel in technology or finance, embodying the same aspirations as any great city. Unfortunately, urban development has encroached upon wilderness areas, displacing not only large mammals but also many other animal species.

There are not as many butterflies, duikers or hedgehogs in the city's verges as I remember from my childhood. The ancestral codes and values that sustained the delicate balance and interconnectedness of ecosystems, have been replaced by the western ideology of 'progress', and a commodification of the natural world that is barely ameliorated by phrases like 'sustainability.' From time to time you can hear references to Kenyan heritage in the dialogue and conversations around conservation, but these are vestigial and few.

"What endures?" asks a character in the novel 'Dust', written by the Kenyan nature custodian, public thinker, author and my friend Yvonne Adhiambo Owuor. Indeed, what can endure? Nature's rebellion—climate change—is increasingly as evident in Kenya as it is elsewhere. Weather patterns have shifted, drought seasons have become brutal.

How can we ensure that there is enough space for the natural world to thrive in collaboration with human beings and our ambitions? Must the pursuit of wealth be so devastating to nature?

Is there another ethos that can reflect the desires of humanity without sacrificing the environment? Should we resign ourselves to the extinction of the large mammals—elephants, rhinos, giraffes, as happened before in Europe and America?

In my opinion, governments need to come together to rethink their conservation policies and stem the losses. But how can this hope be realized when so many politicians regard climate change as a hoax, when carbon emission targets are routinely stretched and so many corporations exploit opportunities in the regulatory loopholes to reap profits through cynical carbon credit trading? The emergence of a new multipolar world could bring hope of a new ideology for inter-species coexistence.

What might this look like? Who might it involve? What examples might we invoke?

This book is both a reflection and a quest. If there is a greater focus on Kenya, it is because it is the place I know best, and because, I believe, it remains a microcosm of the whole world.

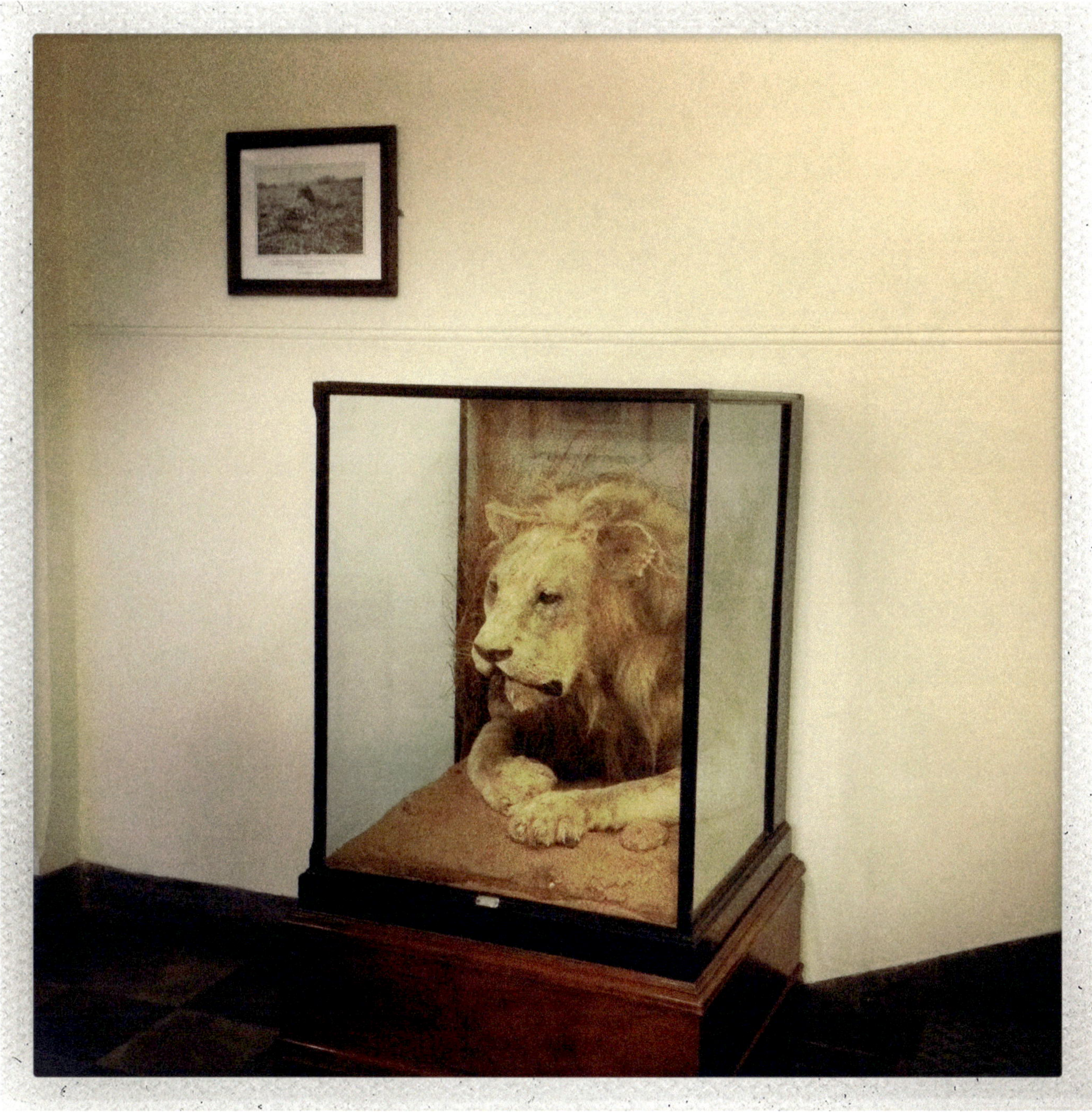

A lion trophy from the Colonial era is showcased in what once served as an exclusive club for only white members. It remains an affluent establishment today, frequented by the powerful elite of Nairobi.

For me, it serves as a metaphor underscoring the adage that the more things change, the more they stay the same. Post-Independence, a new generation of politicians assumed the roles vacated by the British. However, instead of serving the kingdom and the Queen, they persist in perpetuating the pillaging of the country for their own benefit, a practice that endures to this day.

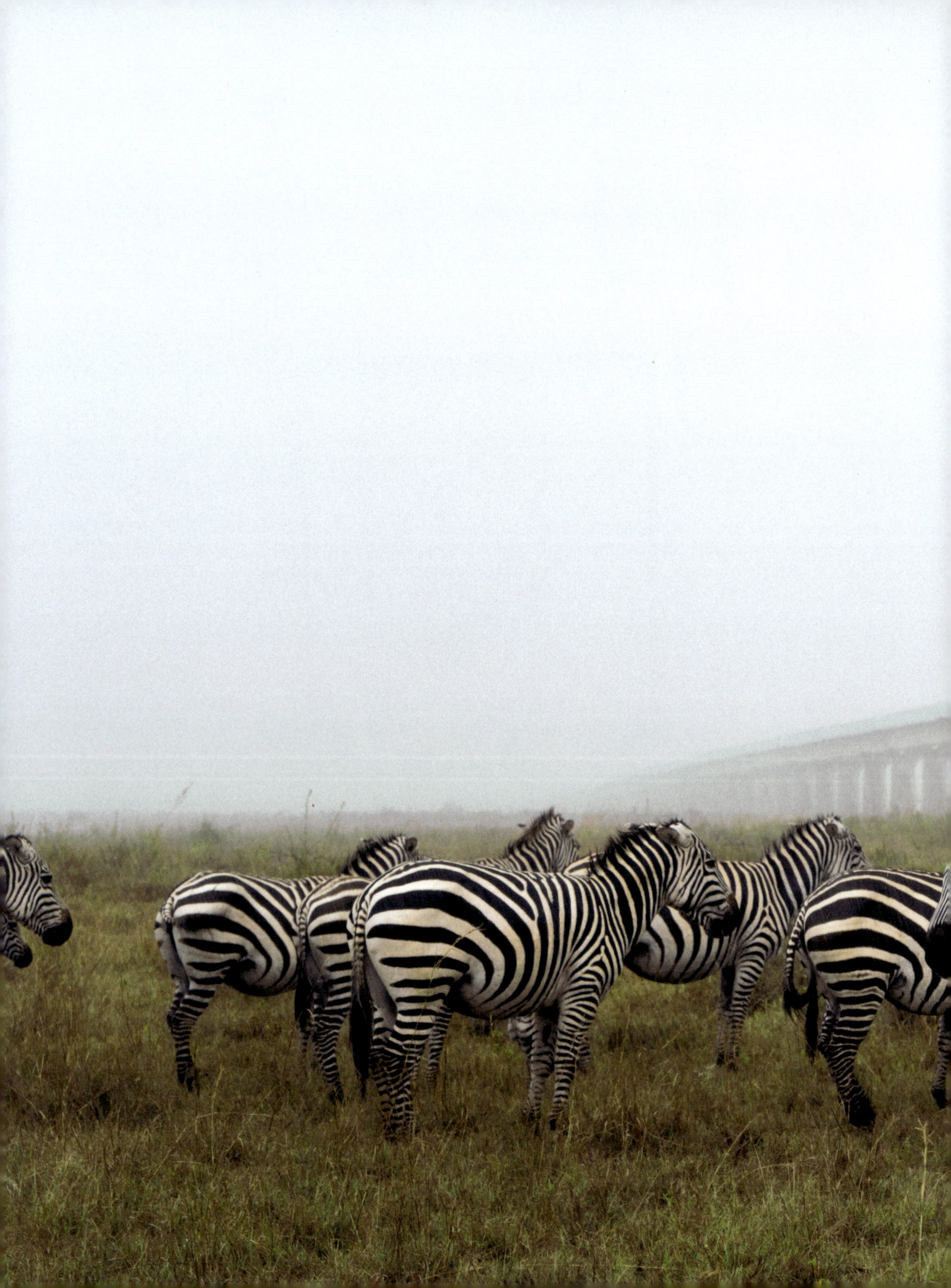

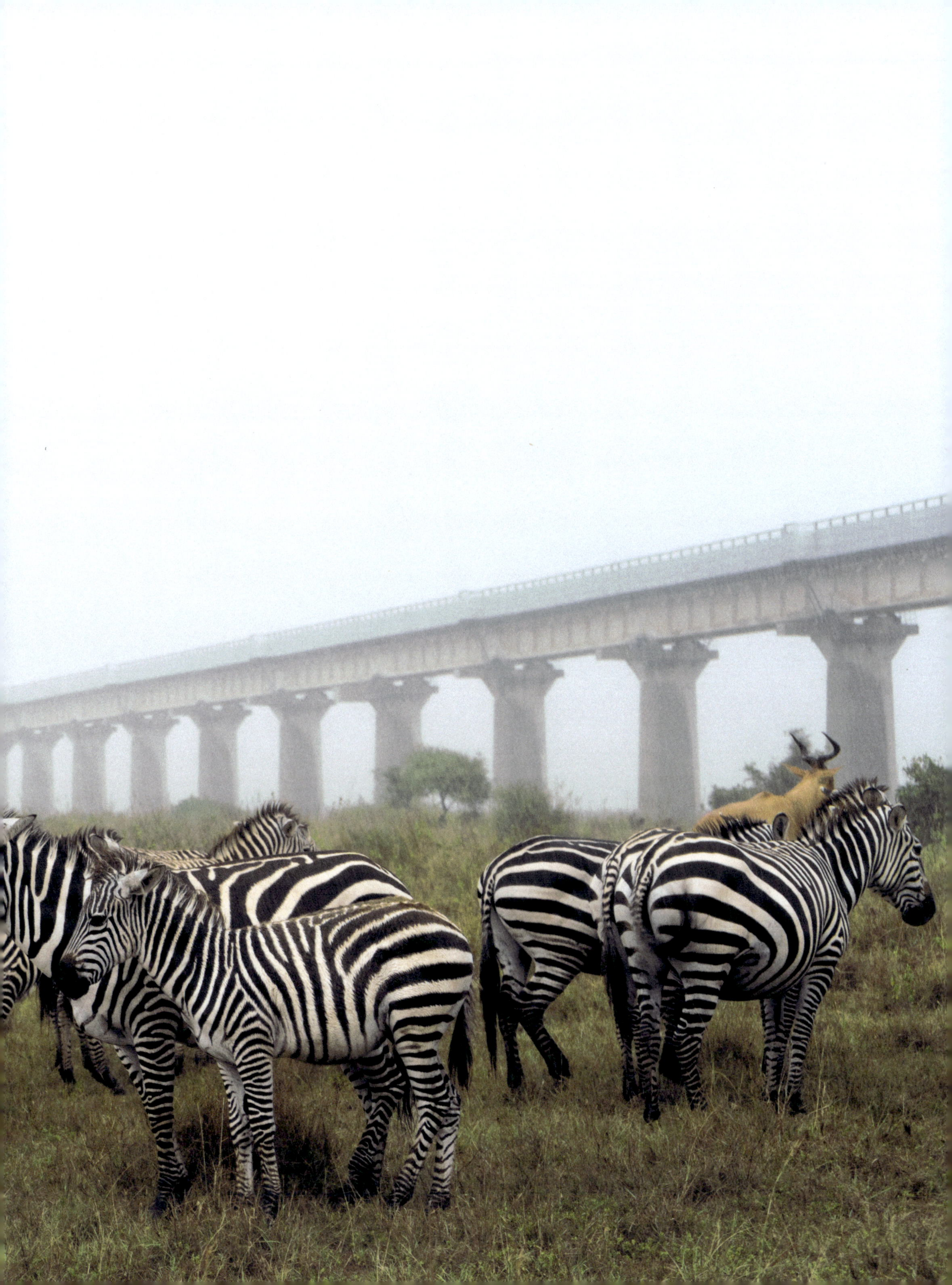

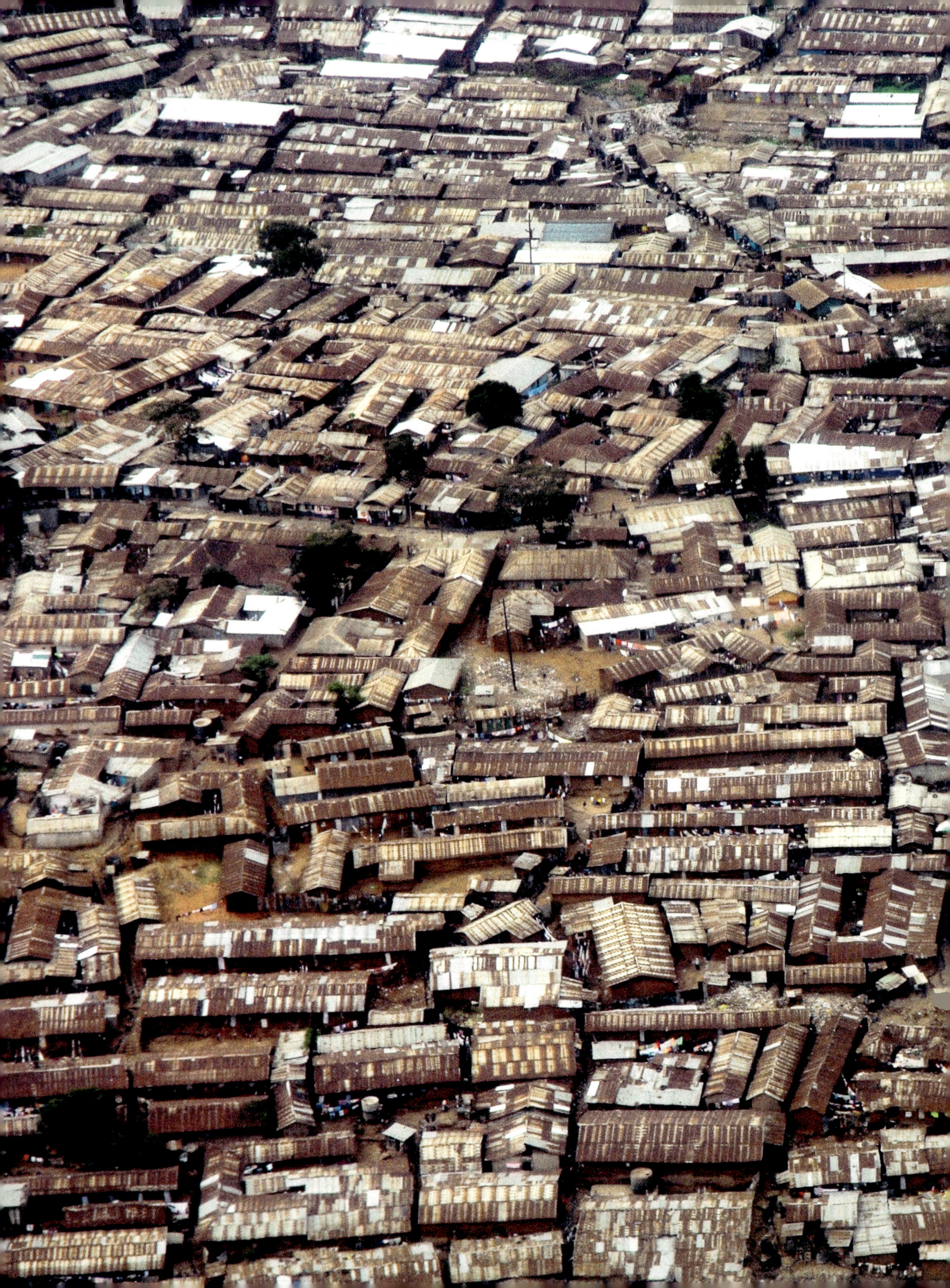

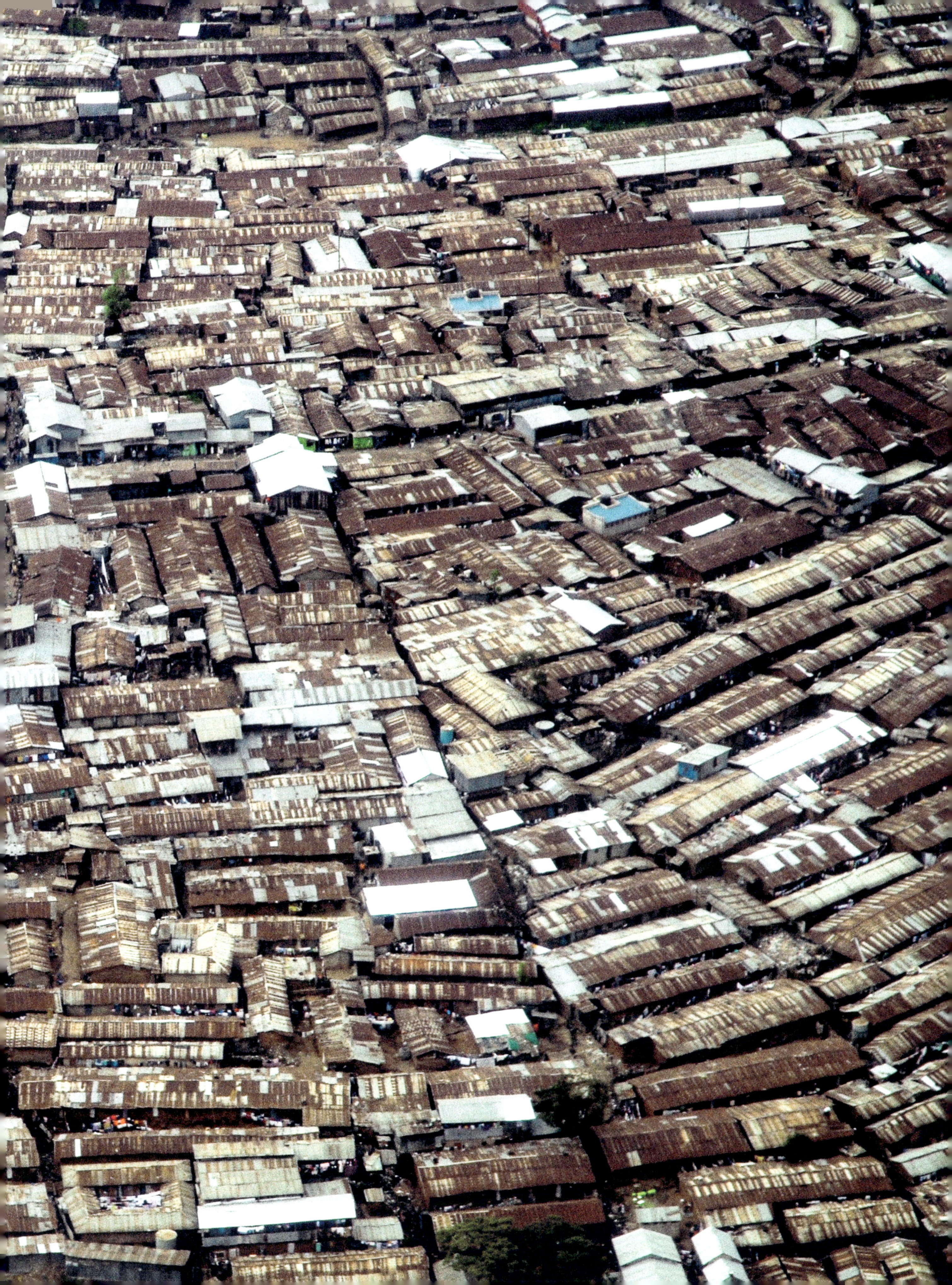

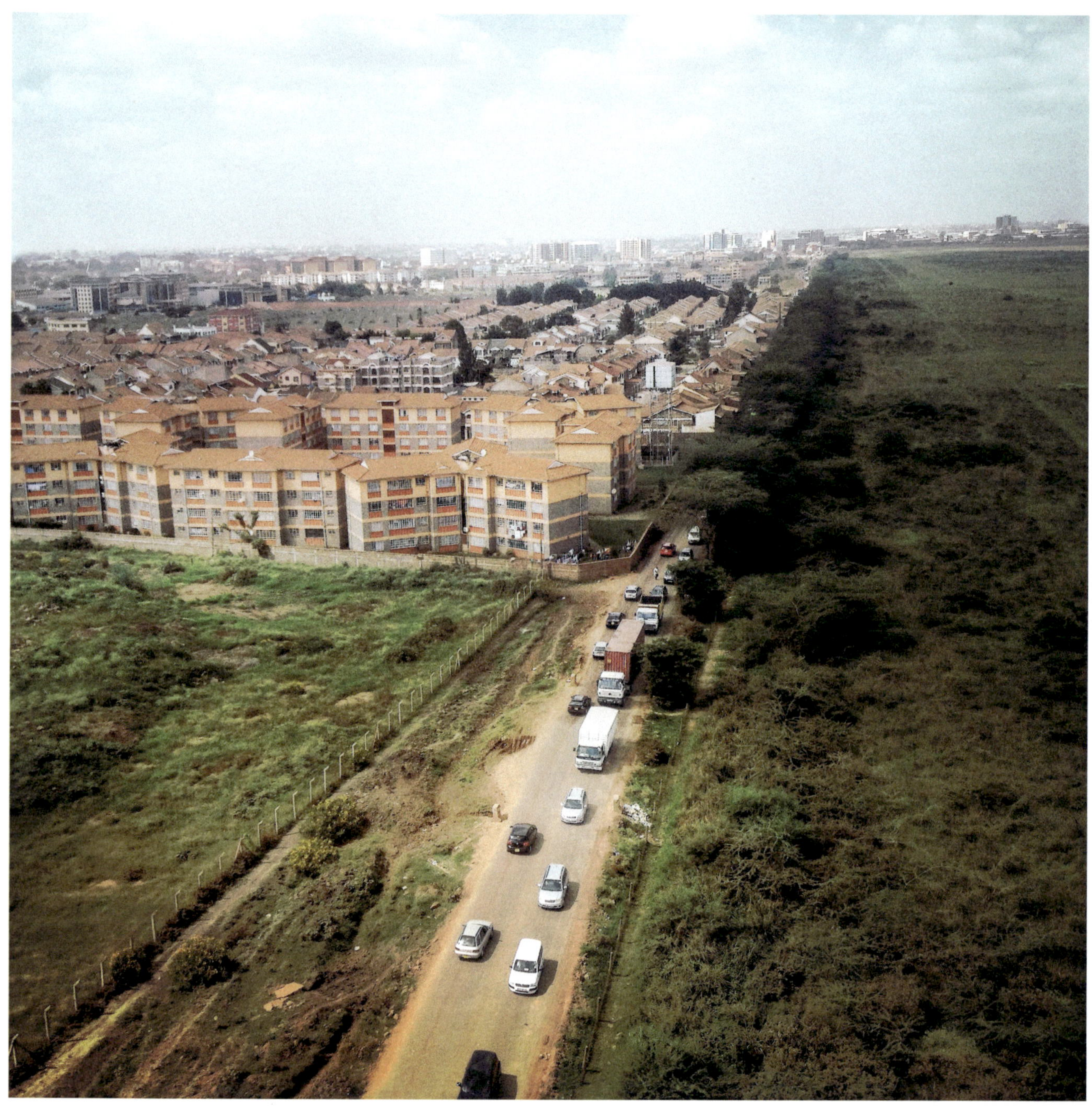

In this photograph lies Nairobi National Park, confronting the encroaching modern development of Nairobi city. Inaugurated in 1946, it stands as Kenya's first national park, situated just 7 kilometers to the south of Nairobi's bustling city center, the capital of Kenya. An electric fence demarcates its boundaries.

The paramount menace to the park and its wildlife emanates from the burgeoning population, infrastructure and human development—a shared challenge with every park and game reserve nationwide. Unsurprisingly, it contends with the pervasive issue of land encroachment, often fueled by corruption and ineffective governance, which exacerbates the threat faced by its wildlife and natural habitat.

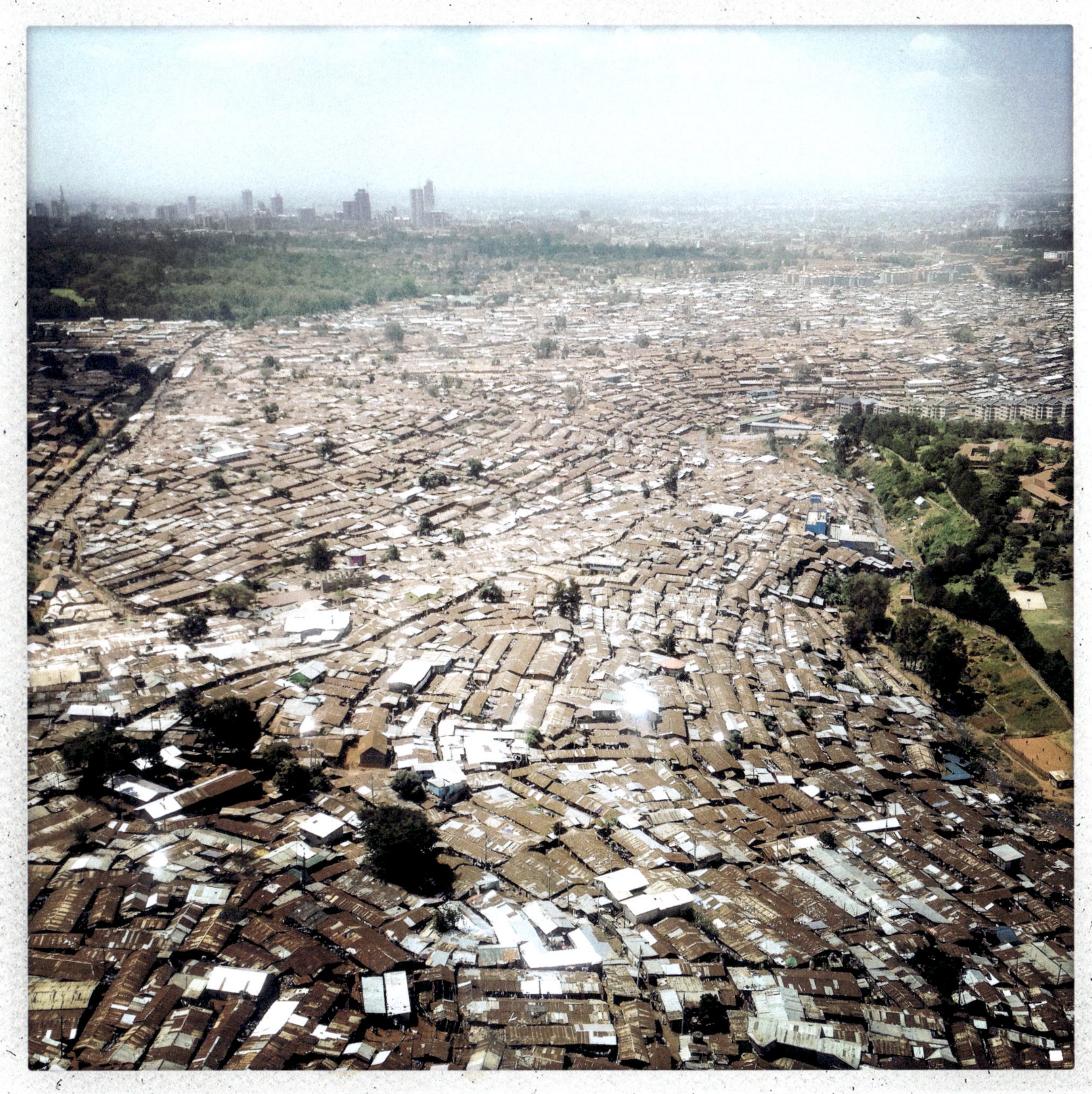

Kibera, prominently featured in the foreground and on the preceding page, stands as one of the largest urban slums in Africa. It sits a mere 6.6 kilometers away from the central business district, observable in the background with its towering skyscrapers. The majority of Kibera's inhabitants endure dire poverty, earning less than US$2 per day.

A significant portion of the slum's population lacks access to fundamental services, such as electricity, clean water, and medical care, resulting in the prevalence of diseases stemming from poor hygiene. Some estimates that the total population of Kibera ranges from 500,000 to well over 1,000,000.

When I look at this photograph taken in the city's central business district, I can't help but think that the menacing shadow of this leafless tree seems to be telling the begging child that its life has also been taken away.

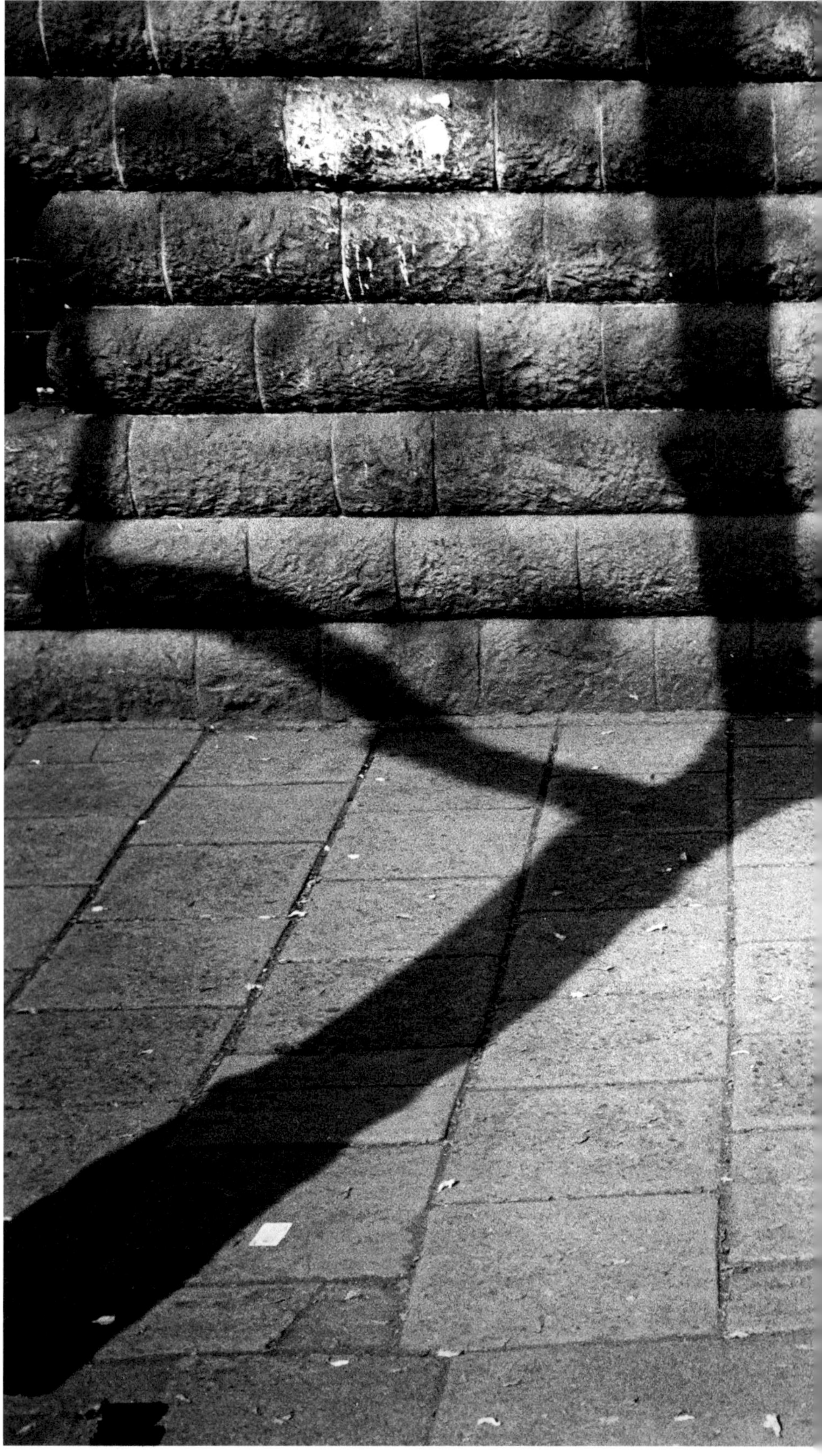

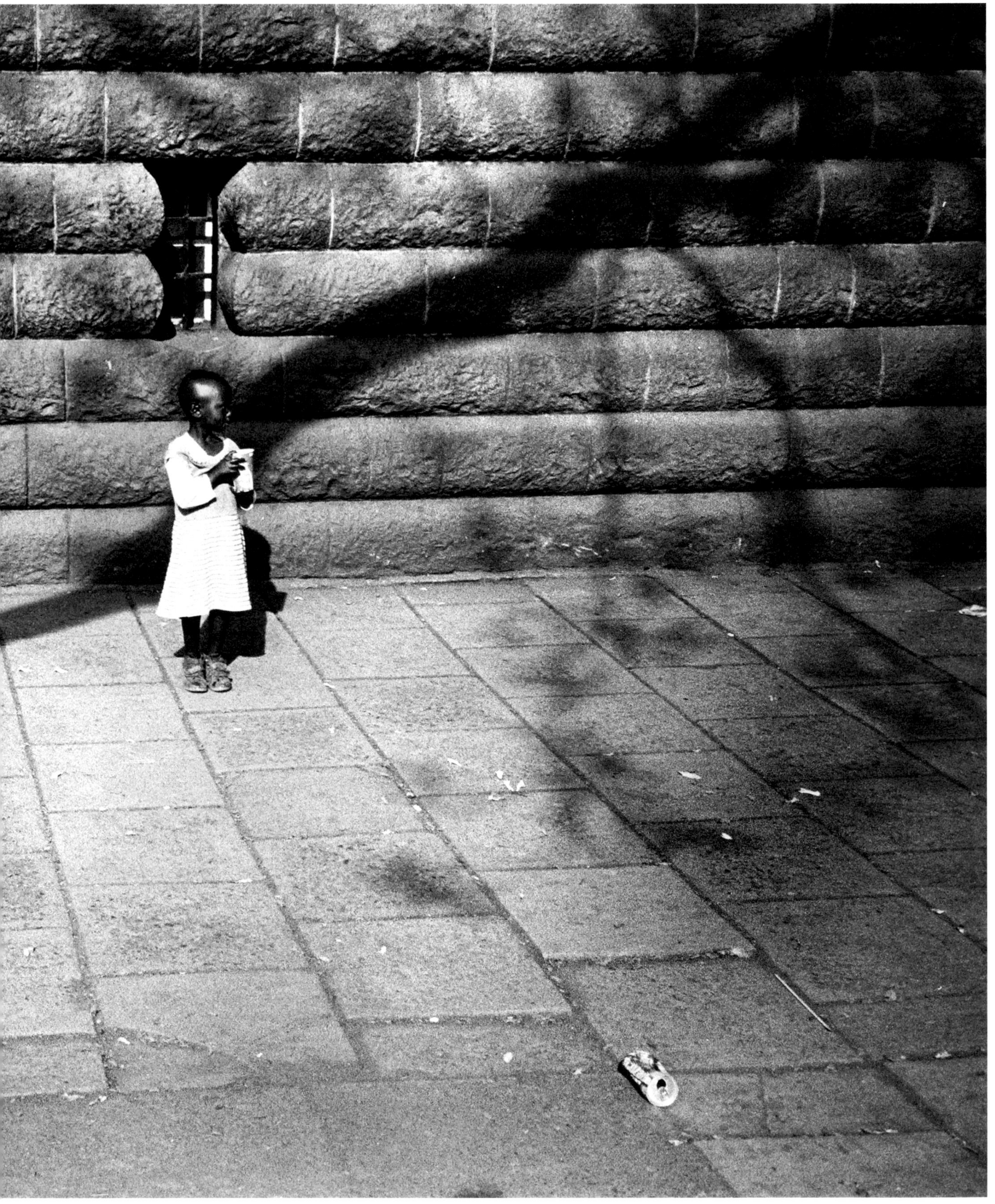

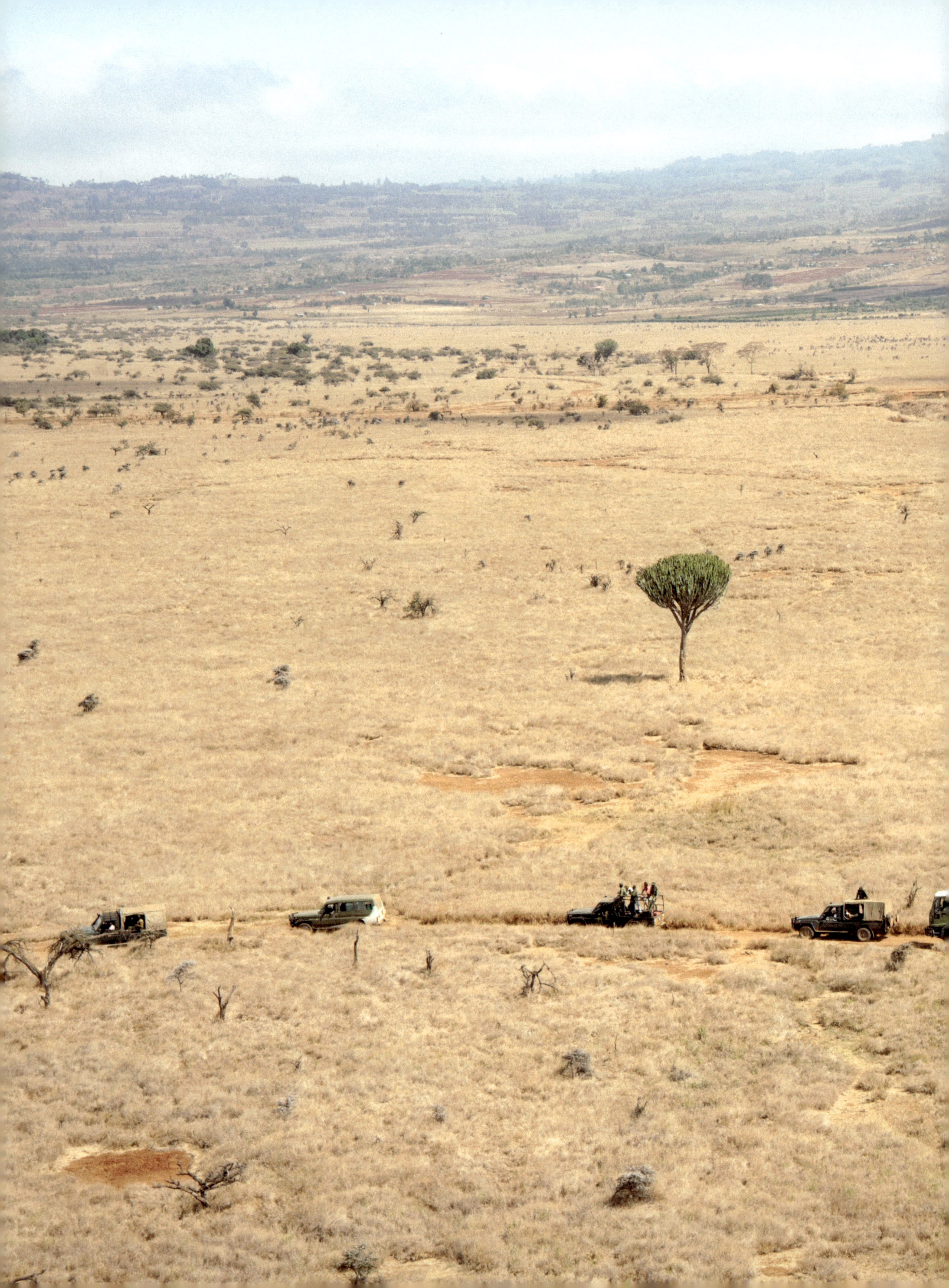

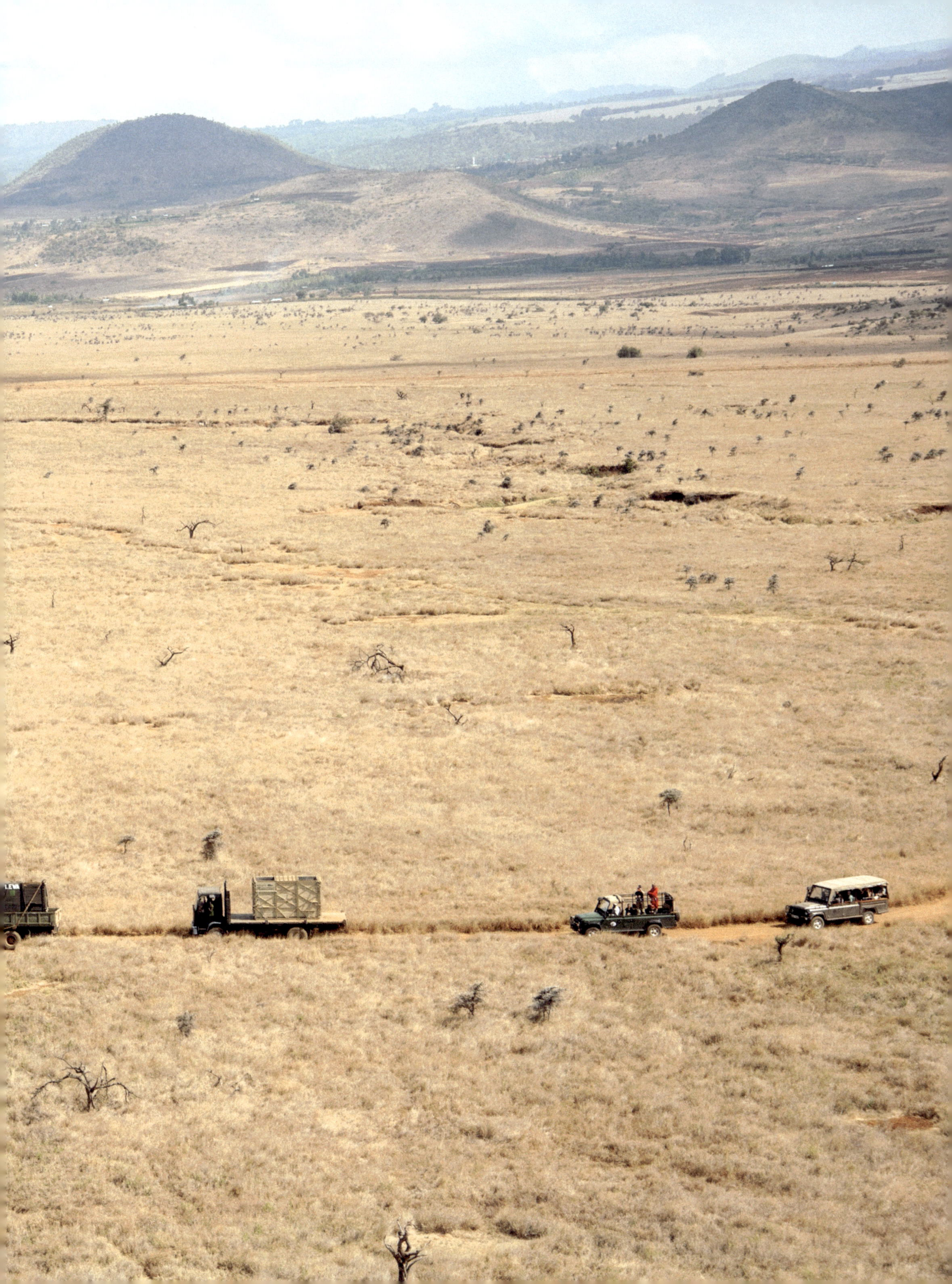

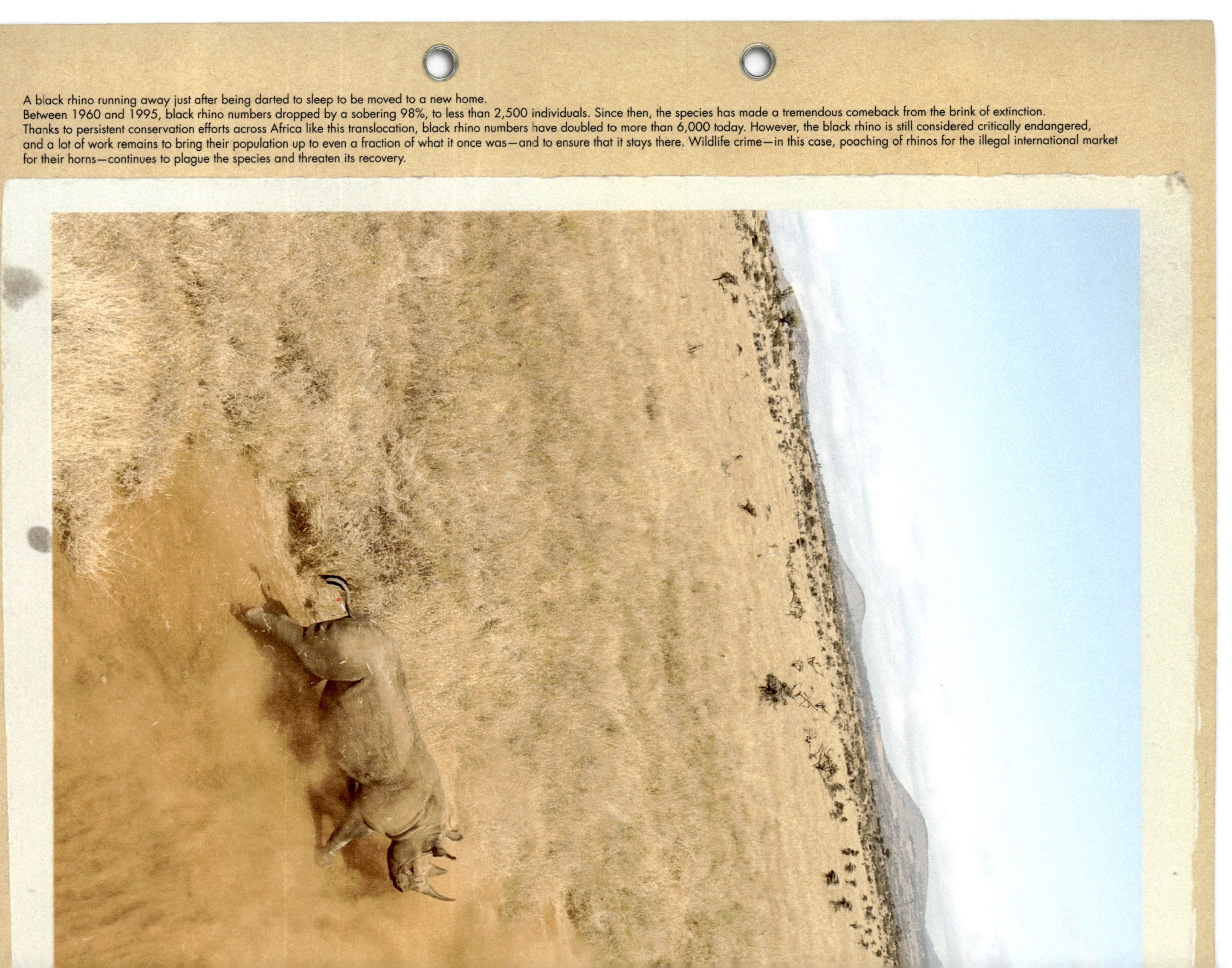

A black rhino running away just after being darted to sleep to be moved to a new home.
Between 1960 and 1995, black rhino numbers dropped by a sobering 98%, to less than 2,500 individuals. Since then, the species has made a tremendous comeback from the brink of extinction. Thanks to persistent conservation efforts across Africa like this translocation, black rhino numbers have doubled to more than 6,000 today. However, the black rhino is still considered critically endangered, and a lot of work remains to bring their population up to even a fraction of what it once was—and to ensure that it stays there. Wildlife crime—in this case, poaching of rhinos for the illegal international market for their horns—continues to plague the species and threaten its recovery.

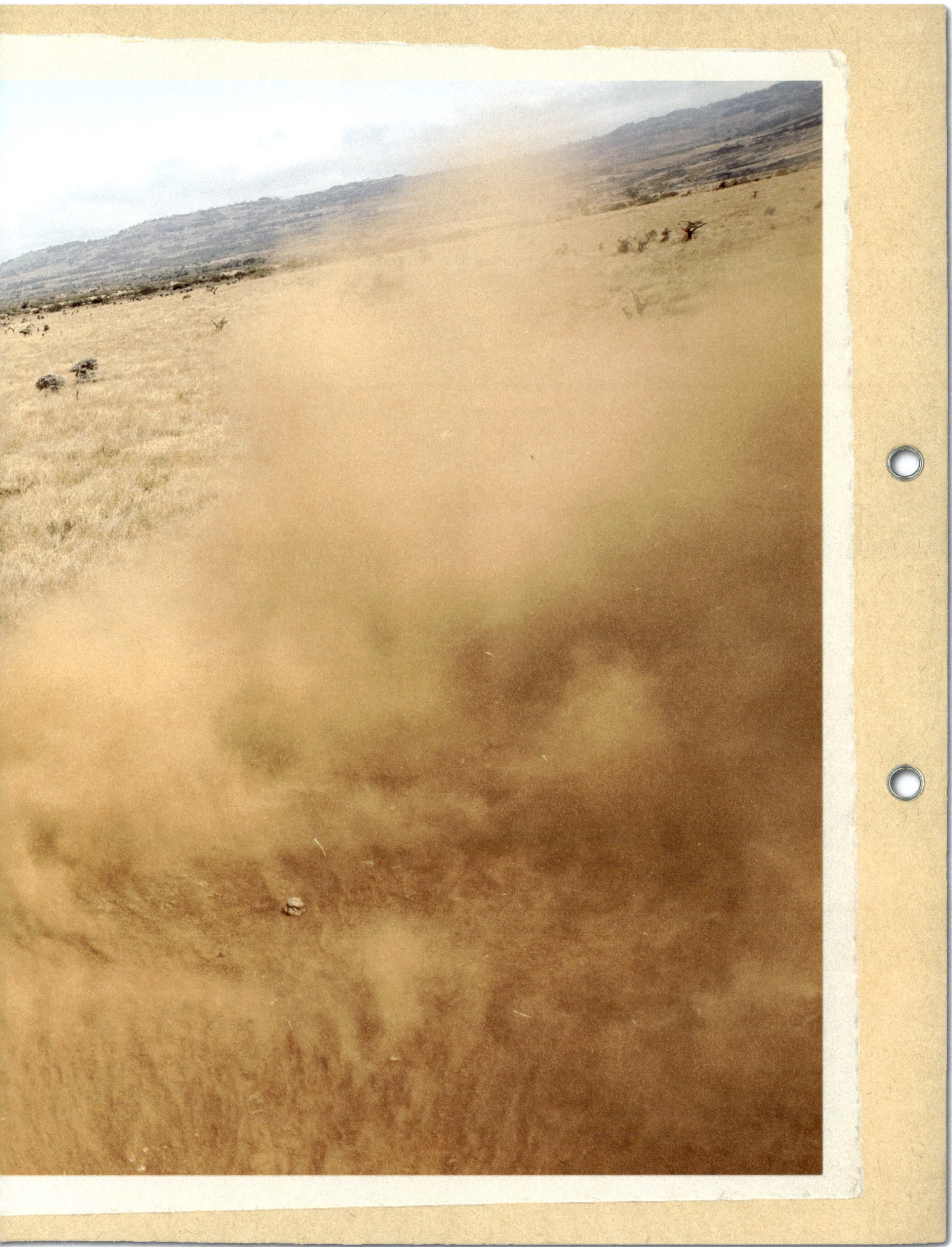

It took 15 years of meticulous planning for Borana Conservancy to be ready to welcome 21 black rhinos into its expansive 32,000-acre sanctuary. Lewa Conservancy, located adjacent to Borana, contributed 11 rhinos, while an additional 10 came from Nakuru National Park. This strategic translocation not only creates an expanded habitat for rhinos to traverse between the two conservancies but also reduces population pressure in Lewa and Nakuru. This is crucial, as rhinos require substantial territorial ranges for their well-being.

PREVIOUS PAGES:
The ground team eagerly awaits word from the Kenya Wildlife Service Vet on board the helicopter about the exact location of the rhino that has just been sedated with the tranquilizer.

Their task is then to begin the delicate procedure of horn removal and to install a transmitter in what's left of the horn, to track the animal's movements before it is relocated to its new habitat. At the time, the cost of this relocation amounted to $260,000, while the annual expenditure for the safety and conservation of a sustainable rhino population amounted to $500,000.

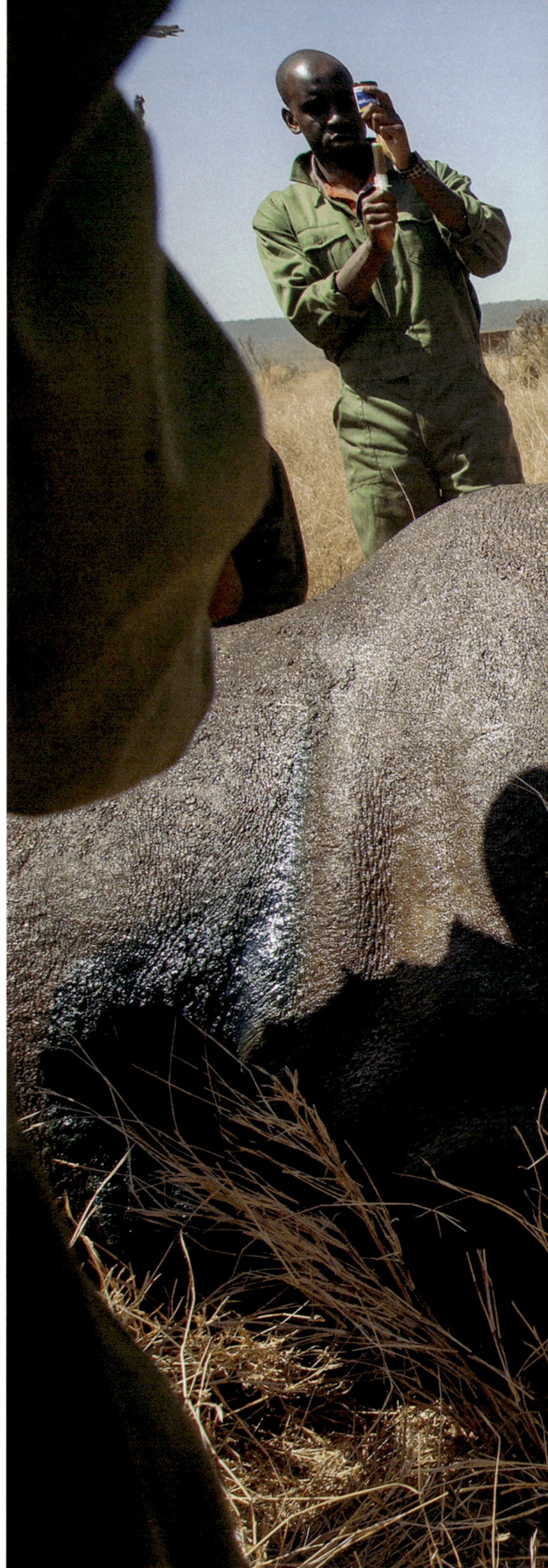

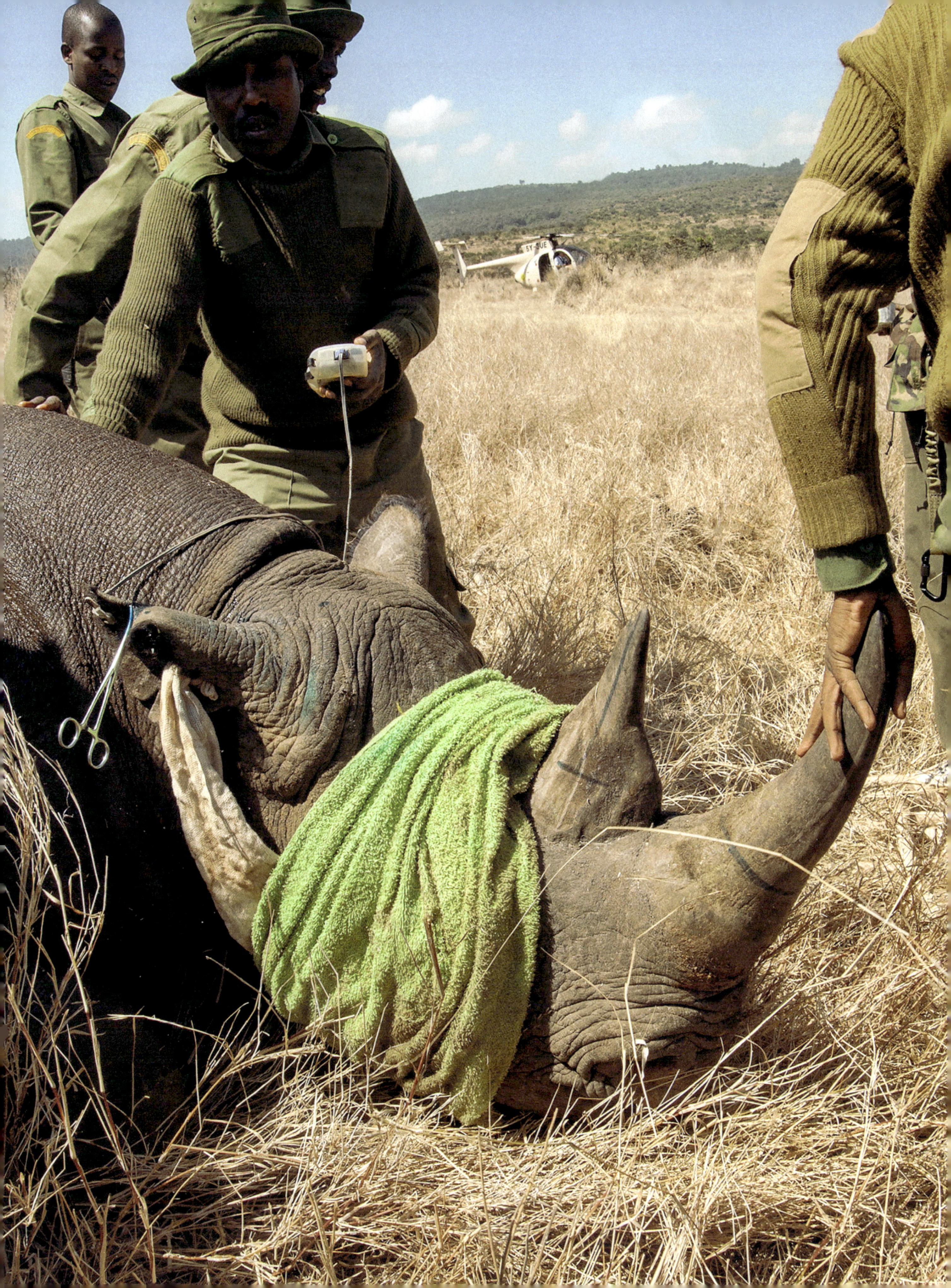

One of the 21 black rhinos being translocated to Borana Conservancy awaits release from the crate that transported the animal by road from Lewa Conservancy. It is believed that removing the majority of the horn will dissuade poachers from targeting the rhino. A microchip is subsequently inserted into the remaining portion of the horn to monitor its location on a 24-hour basis.

However, we now understand that this isn't a sustainable solution, as some rhinos were still killed, and whatever remained of the horn was still extracted.

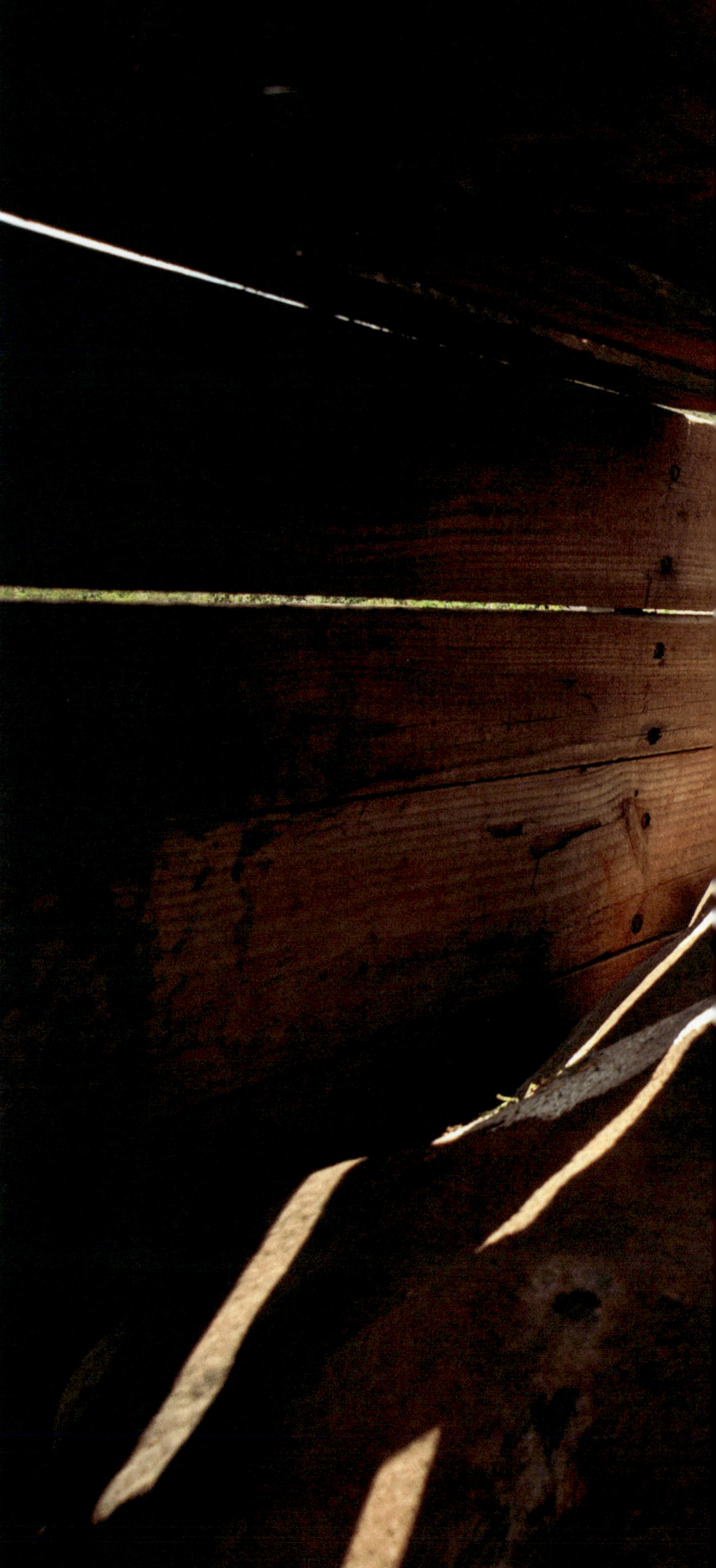

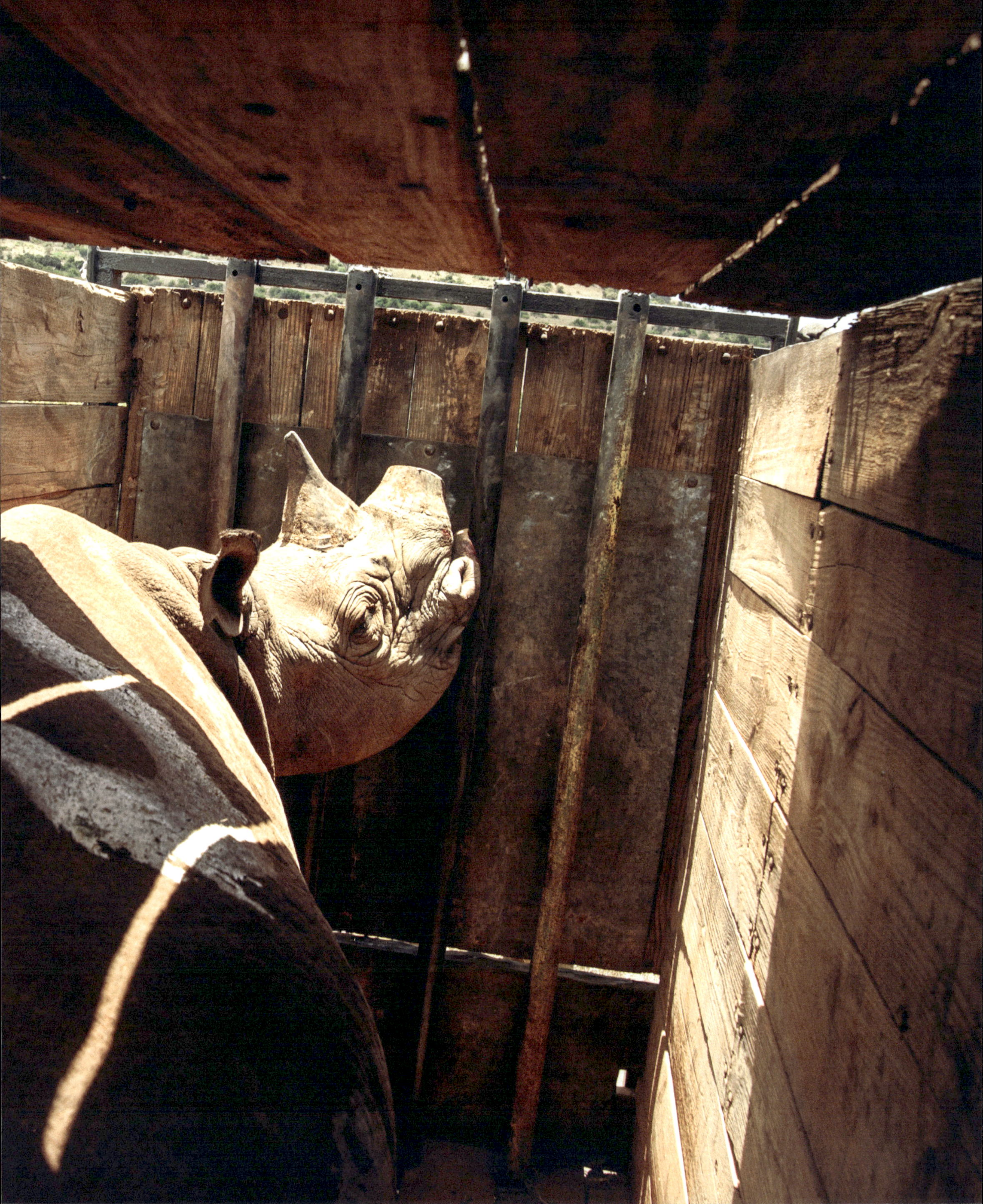

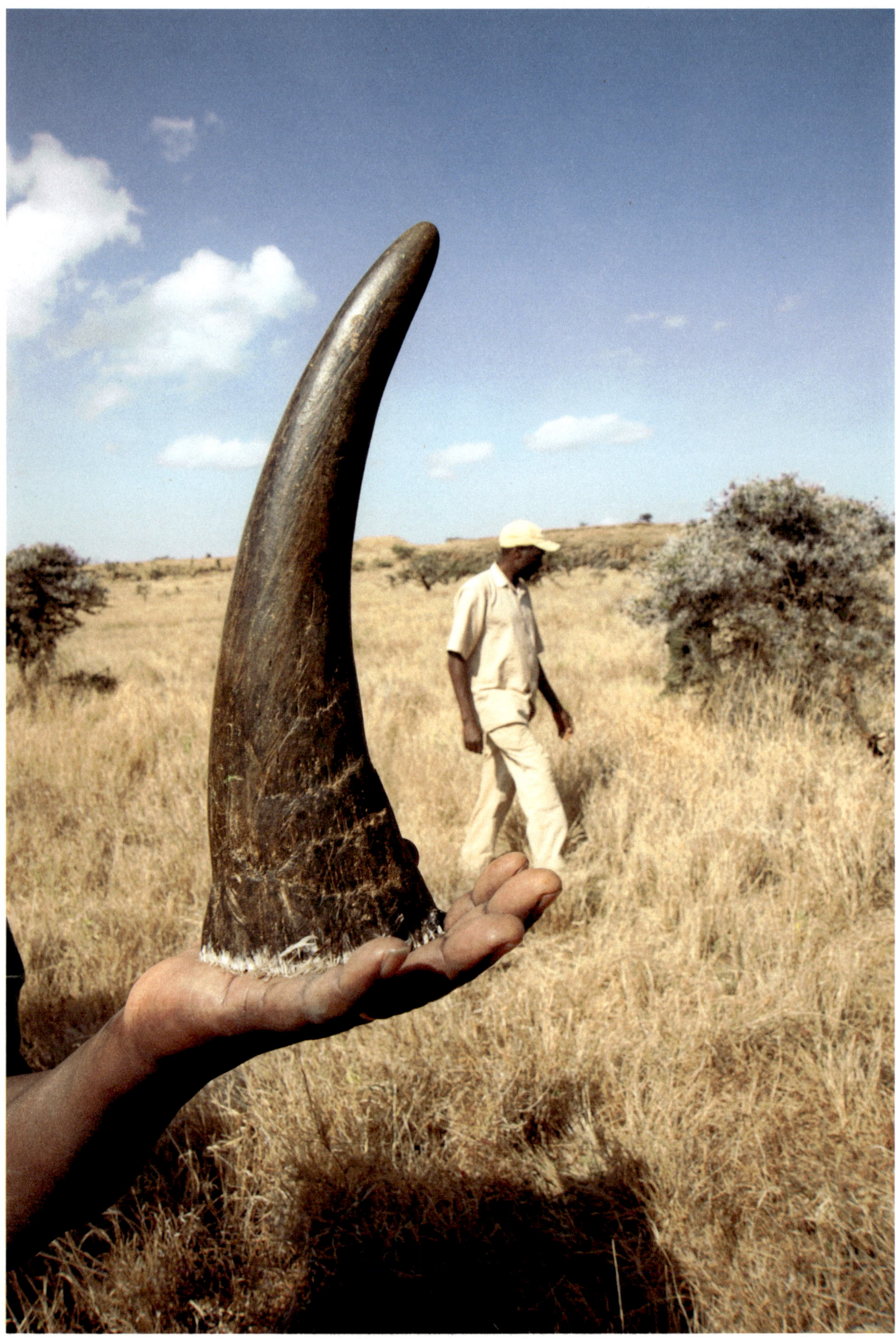

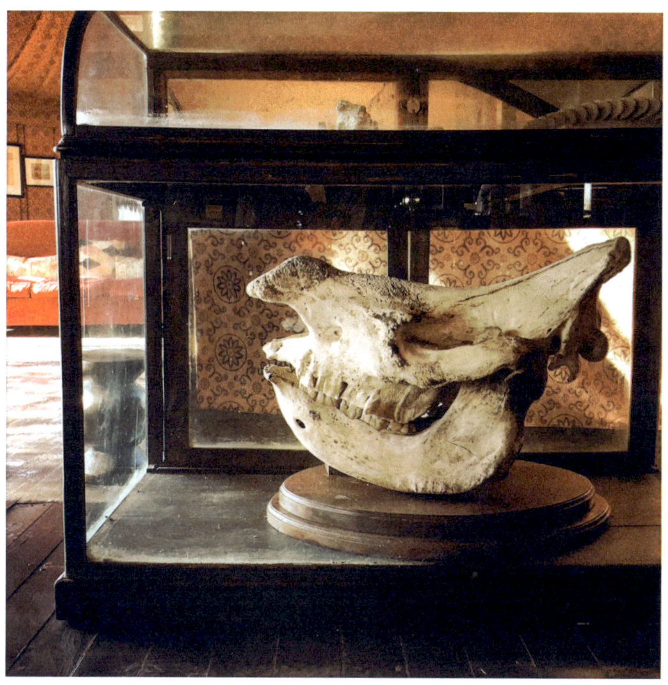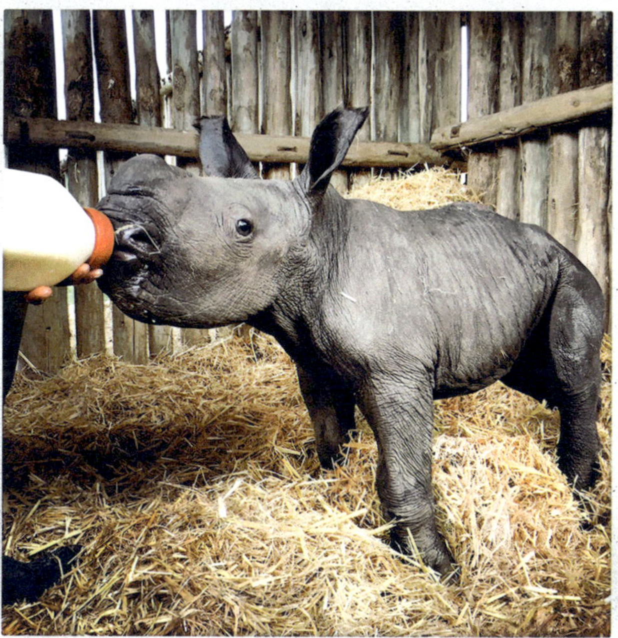

Above is a Rhino skull showcased at a tourist lodge in the Okavango Delta in Botswana. On the right is Ringo, a few months old Rhino who was abandoned by its mother and was cared for by the staff at Ol Pejeta Conservancy.

There is no doubt in my mind that homo sapiens now stand in direct competition to earth's other species.

Wildernesses are no longer limitless, but archipelagoes of shrinking enclaves. How can we find a sustainable balance that allows for human growth while also protecting animals and their habitats?

Does my photograph of a railway bridge cutting through Nairobi's National Park as zebras graze beneath its pillars offer a glimpse of an alternative future? What are the solutions to other issues like poaching, diminishing water supplies, desertification, the fencing of open communal lands traditionally owned by pastoralists?

Is the fencing of wilderness habitats the only way to preserve them? Should revenue generated through the sale of hunting licenses fund conservation efforts that could protect against construction and development?

Is it wrong to kill a certain number of animals to manage their populations?

Often solutions create new problems. Fencing off conservation areas can result in the overpopulation of animals, overgrazing, and desertification. And the consequences of colonial systems are not easily disentangled.

Big game hunting was a colonial pursuit; but as soon as Kenya was declared a British protectorate in 1895, it regulated all hunting and created game reserves to protect wildlife habitat. Indigenous tribes who had hunted for food, were denied their traditional means of livelihood and subsistence, were excluded from cordoned off hunting grounds and forced, under the new rules, to become poachers.

It's an old disenfranchisement that has fostered an ongoing resentment towards conservation systems and created a 'human vs wildlife' narrative that persists to this day. For example, in 1977, the Kenyan government banned hunting to try to control widespread poaching.

A year later it banned the sale of all forms of wildlife products. But the population was growing, cities sprawled into the country-side, development continued, poaching too. The system of conservation parks inherited from British rule, continued to alienate indigenous communities from their lands and way of life. Today tourist dollars maintain the parks.

But the tourist sector is dominated by elite companies and local communities do not benefit as much as they should. There needs to be a more integrated approach to the people versus animal question; fences just keep the issue in convenient silos of status quo. There are many organizations in Kenya and across Africa engaged in wildlife conservation, environmental sustainability and local community projects, but depressingly few are inclusive, regenerative and ethically run.

Over the last two decades, in my search for a better understanding of the complexities of conservation, I have observed the work of some very dedicated individuals trying their best to tackle the mounting cascade of human- wildlife conflicts. I have come to the conclusion that none of them have a miracle solution, but that each holds a piece of the puzzle.

Paula Kahumbu and Richard Bonham are Kenyans who have, in different ways, been fighting for conservation for a long time. Kahumbu is an ecologist and activist who turned to storytelling. She started the first African-produced wildlife television series, "Wildlife warriors," aimed at an African audience, in which she travels to wilderness areas and meets Kenyans working to save endangered animals.

She believes that most Kenyans don't see themselves as stakeholders in conservation efforts and she is trying to revive the connection between Africans and their natural heritage. As she explained, "As an African telling the story of Africa's elephants, I hope that it will get more Africans interested in elephants".

Richard Bonham was a professional hunter for many years before he turned to conservation to save the Amboseli-Tsavo-Kilimanjaro wildlife ecosystem. Bonham was living in the Chyulus in the 1980's, running a tourist lodge he had built, when he realized that if something drastic was not done, the entire population of lions in the region would disappear.

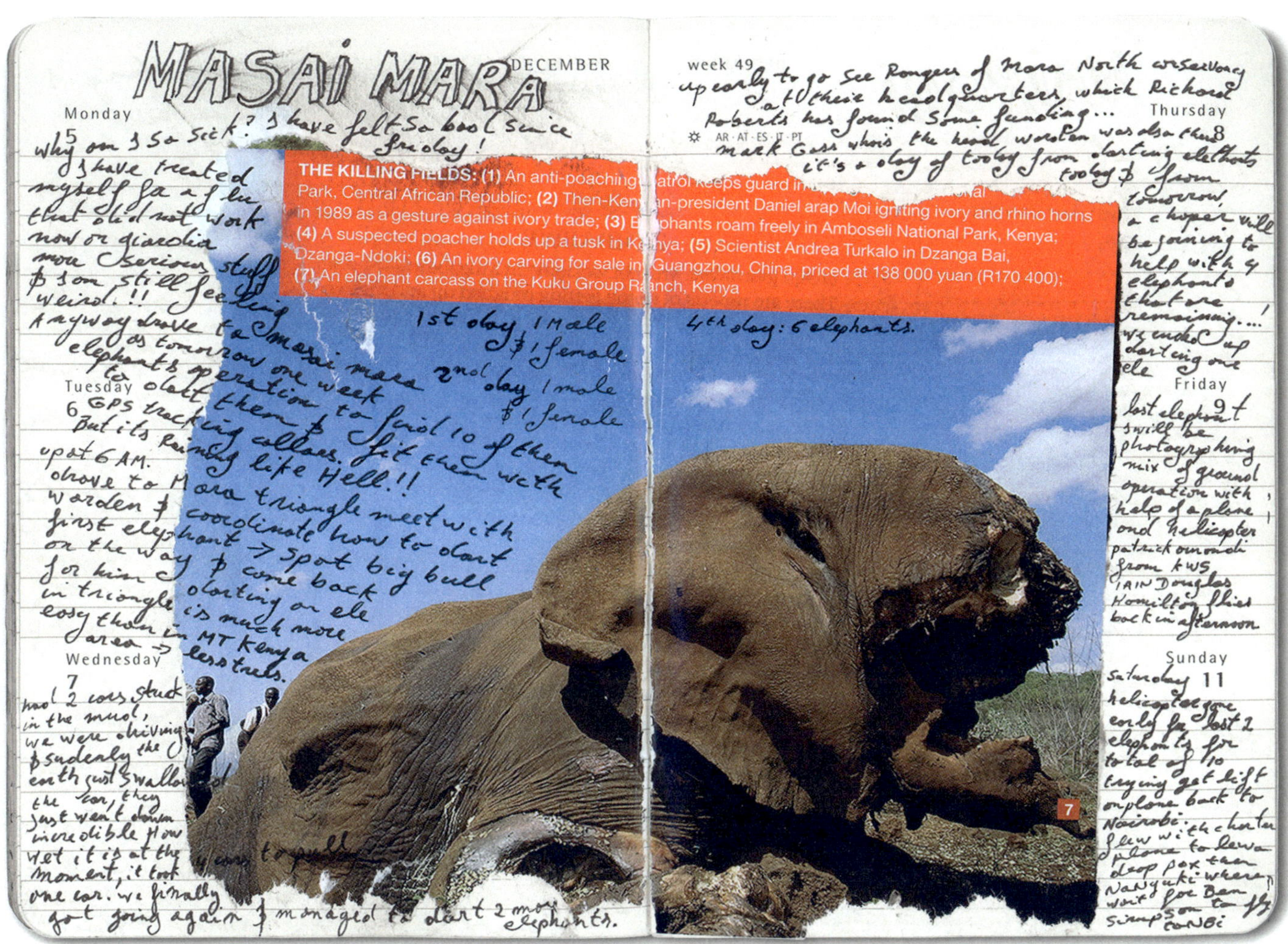

This elephant was slaughtered for its ivory in the Amboseli-Tsavo ecosystem, just outside Amboseli National Park. The poachers then concealed it with branches, giving them ample time to escape before the carcass was eventually detected by a plane.

He co-founded The Big Life Foundation and, in collaboration with the local Maasai community, initiated the first-of-its-kind 'predator financial compensation program'. This program aimed to compensate livestock owners when their animals were killed by lions or other predators, thereby reducing the likelihood of retaliation against the lions. Bonham aimed to foster tolerance for the lions and other predators among livestock owners. It became evident to Bonham that engaging local communities through incentive-based conservation projects, employment opportunities, and involving them in law enforcement was crucial.

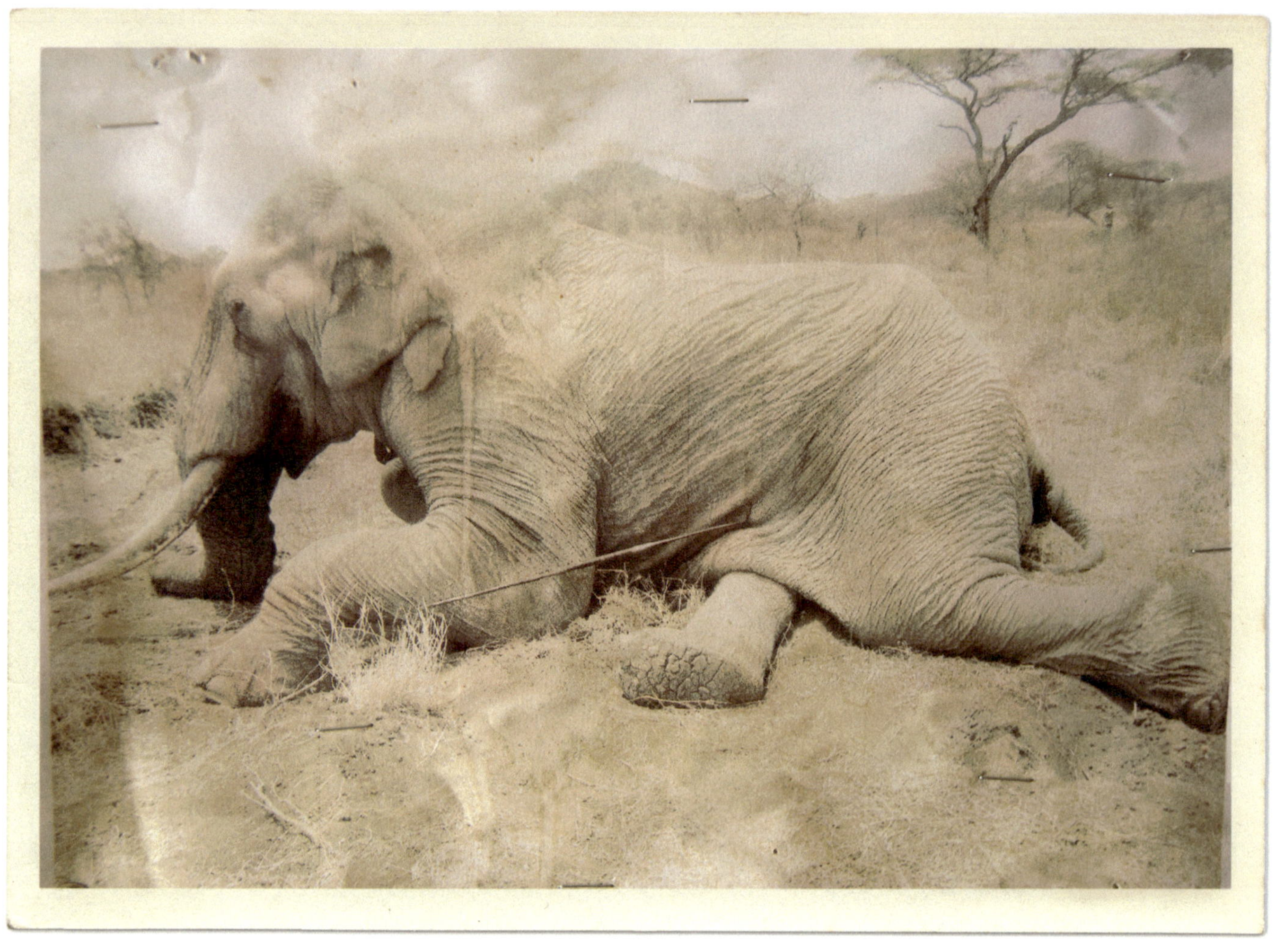

An elephant was killed by a spear, with its tusks left intact—a clear indication that the incident was not poaching-related but rather a retaliatory act due to the elephant invading and consuming the crops of a community member.

Without Bonham's program, the lions of Amboseli-Tsavo-Kilimanjaro would have disappeared by now. After this initial success, Bonham then launched the first Community Game Scout project, which employed local Maasai warriors to collect poachers' snares which had been appearing in frightening quantities. The organization now employs over 100 game scouts operating over an area of 1.6 million acres, with 36 outposts. Poaching is now under control. But the challenge remains to establish a dialogue with indigenous communities whose faith in conservation efforts has been eroded.

The difficulty lies in convincing them that tourism and eco-business can be as lucrative as selling their land or leasing it to commercial farmers. In large parts of the area that Big Life oversees, housing and development has spread along roads as well as other infrastructure lines like fences that obstruct ancient wildlife migrations.

Nowhere is this phenomenon starker than in the Kimana Wildlife Corridor, which connects Amboseli National Park to the Kimana Sanctuary and beyond to the Chyulu Hills and Tsavo. These gateways that connect different conservation areas are the key to the ability of animals to move out of Amboseli National Park looking for food, because the park can no longer provide enough for all its wildlife. At one point, the corridor funnels through a narrow pinch point, only 85m wide and 800m long. If that small gap closes, the implications would be catastrophic; whole populations of animals would be unsustainable.

I have begun to appreciate that despite the efficacy of individual projects, no amount of funding can abate the greatest threat to wildlife: the growing human population. It is expected that the world's population will grow to ten billion by 2050. More people means more conflict with animals. Even when anti-poaching strategies are successful, a new set of problems emerges. People tend to believe that when poaching is reduced, there is no longer a threat to wildlife.

But this, sadly, is not the case. For example, in conservancies in northern Kenya, 103 elephants were killed for their ivory in 2012. By 2018, this number had decreased to 3 in the same area. However, while poaching was brought under control, even more elephants were being killed in retaliation for damaging crops and houses, and in some cases, for causing human fatalities. The increase in conflict between people and elephants is now one of the most serious threats to the survival of elephants.

Ultimately, overpopulation is choking the land where wildlife lives and roams. There is no simple solution but focusing on opportunities and benefits obtained from living with wildlife instead of apart from it, is the only thing that can develop a coexistence.

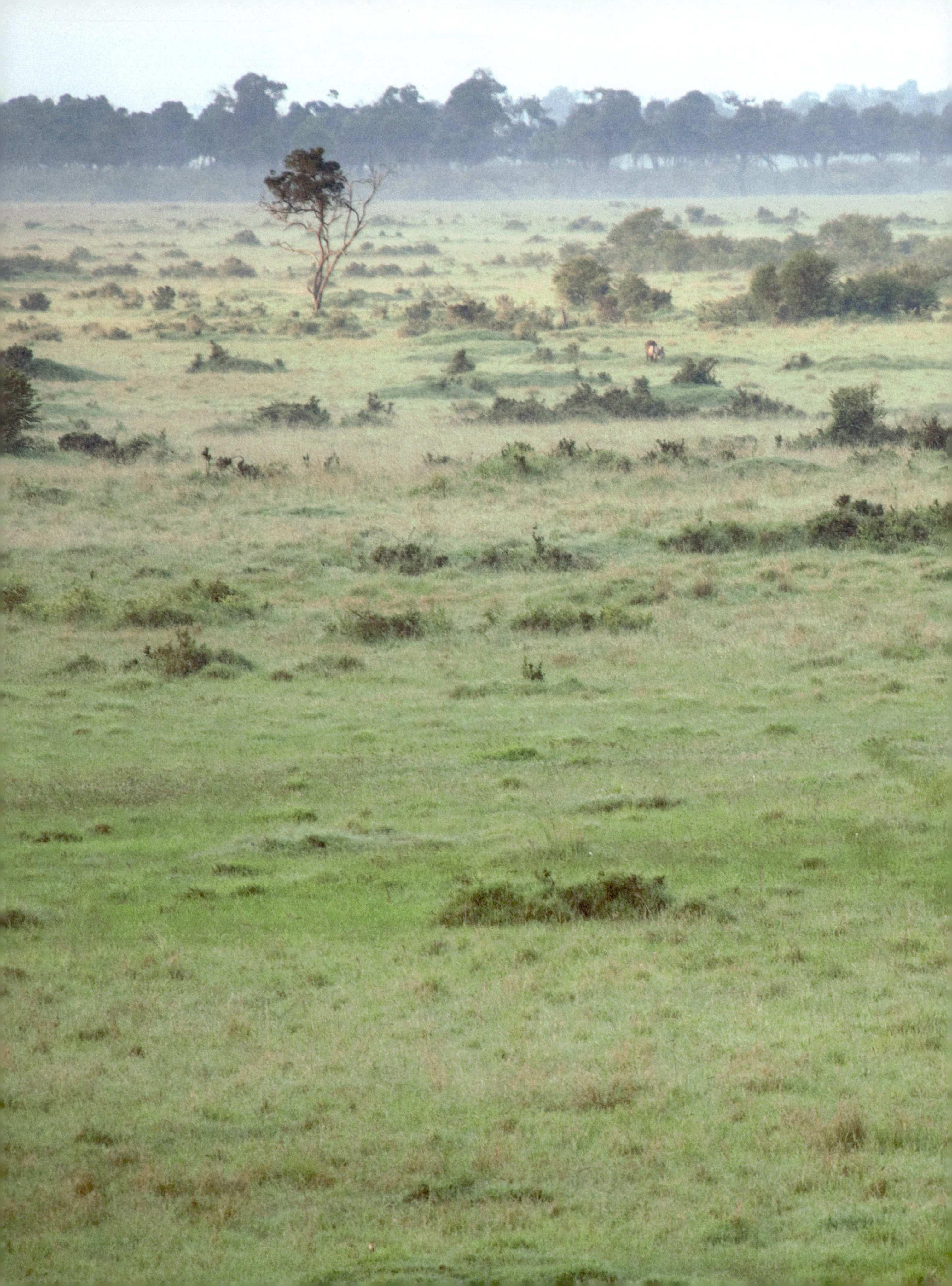

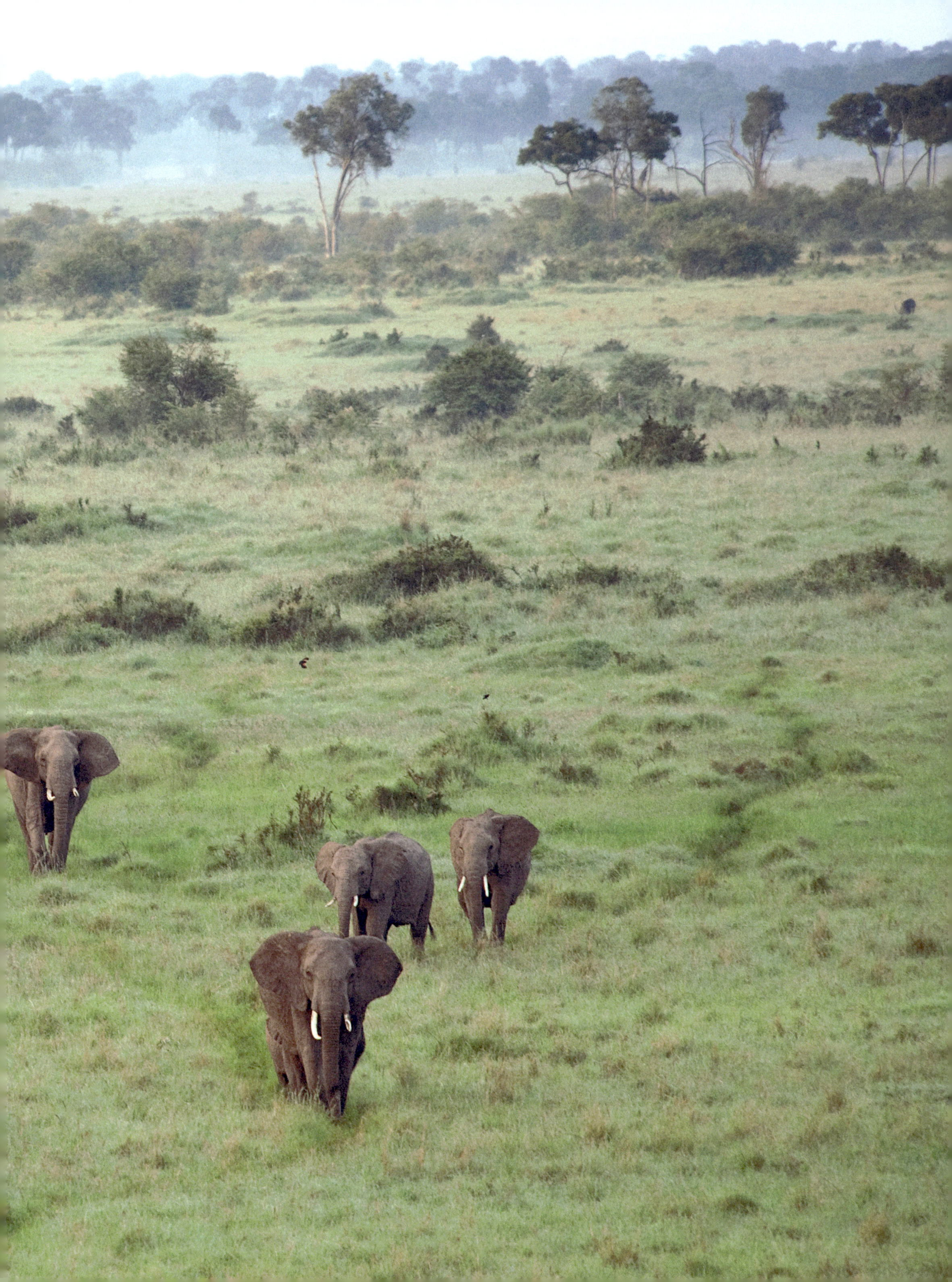

Ear notching involves tranquilizing the rhino to insert a unique ID marking into its ear, enabling researchers to accurately identify individual animals. Additionally, a microchip is fitted into the horn, allowing for tracking the animal via a GPS system. Throughout this procedure, horn shavings, skin samples, and measurements are collected for DNA analysis.

The population of black rhinos in Kenya has dwindled to around a thousand, a stark decline from the twenty thousand individuals recorded fifty years ago.

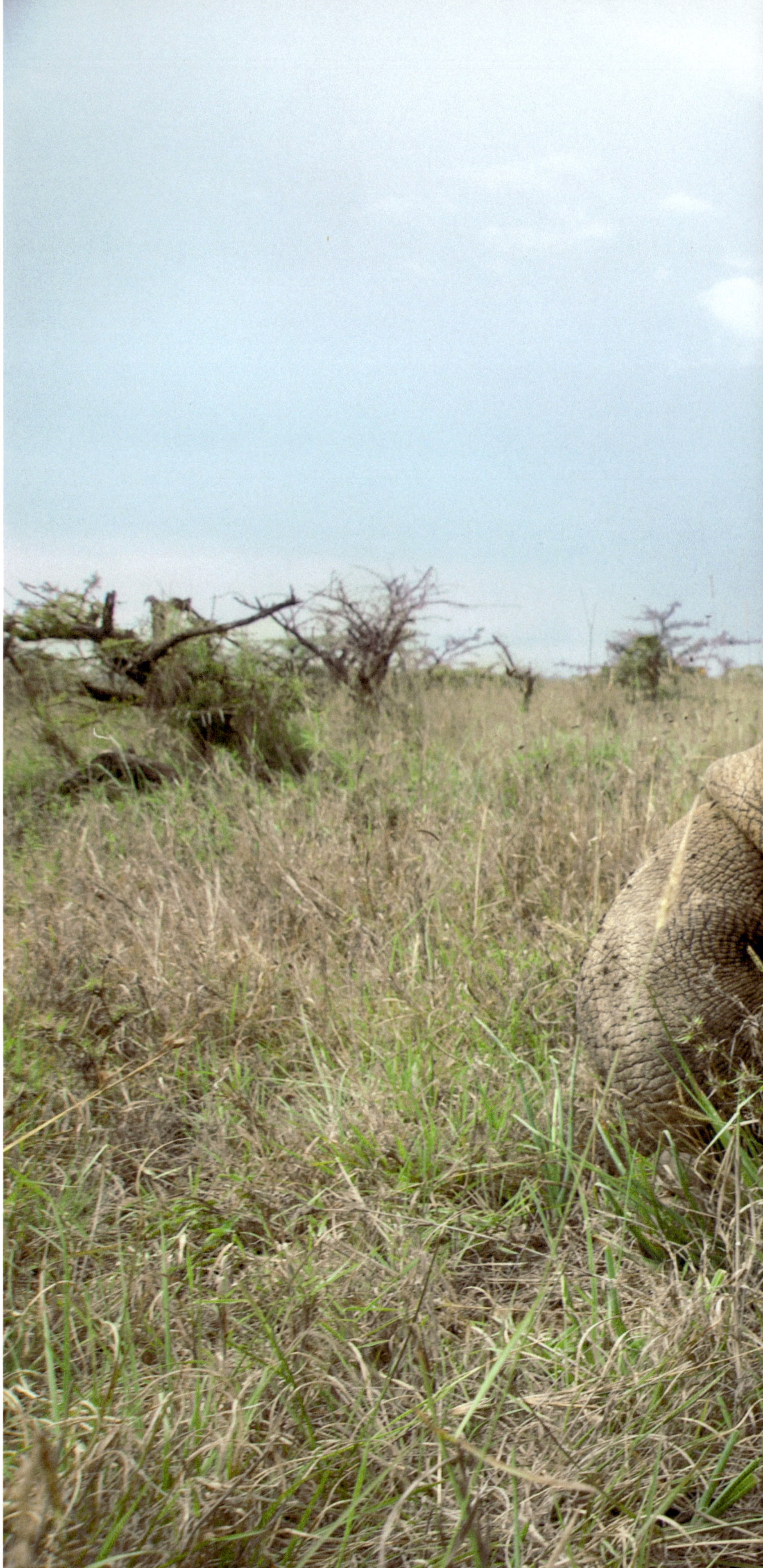

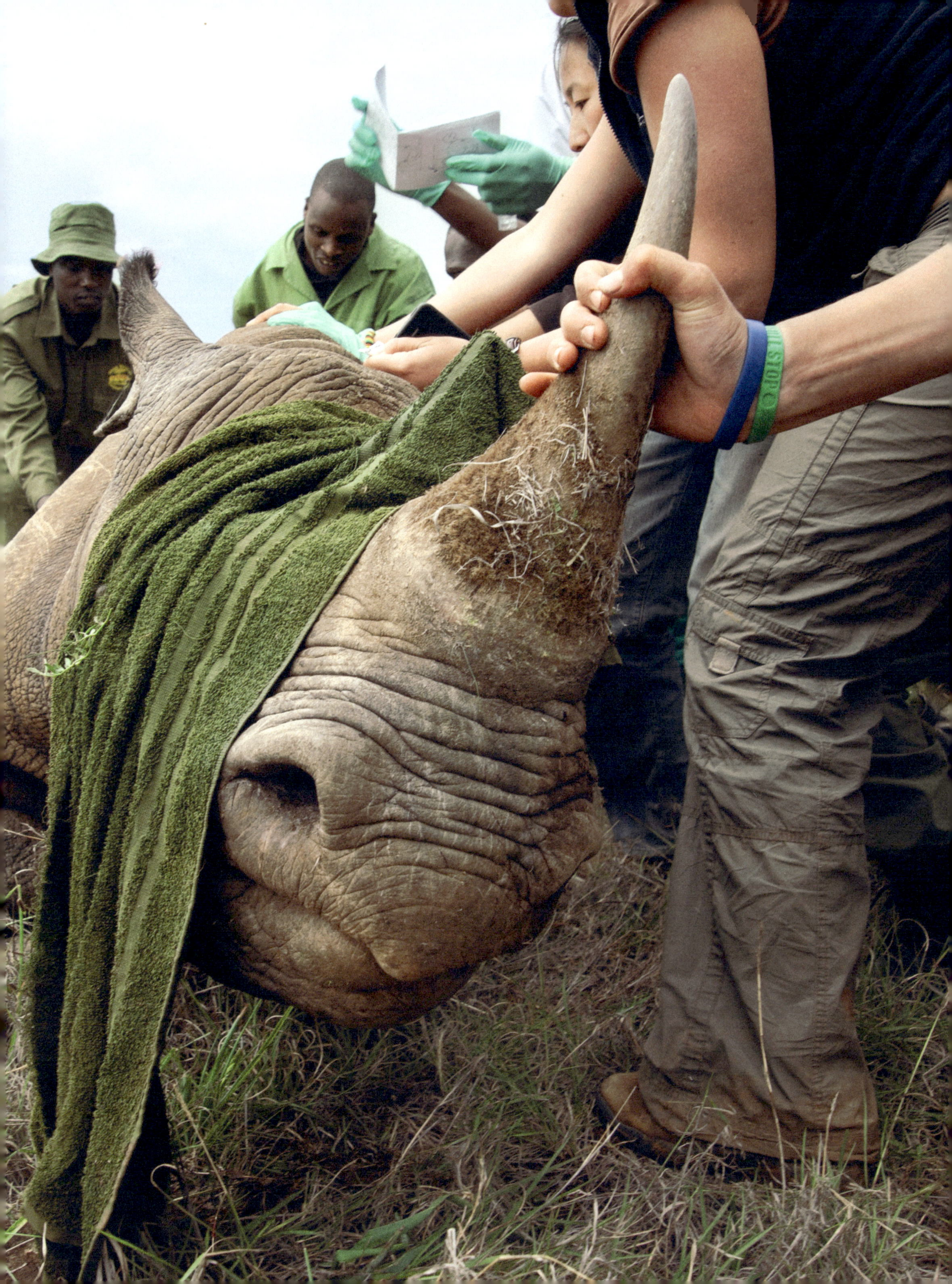

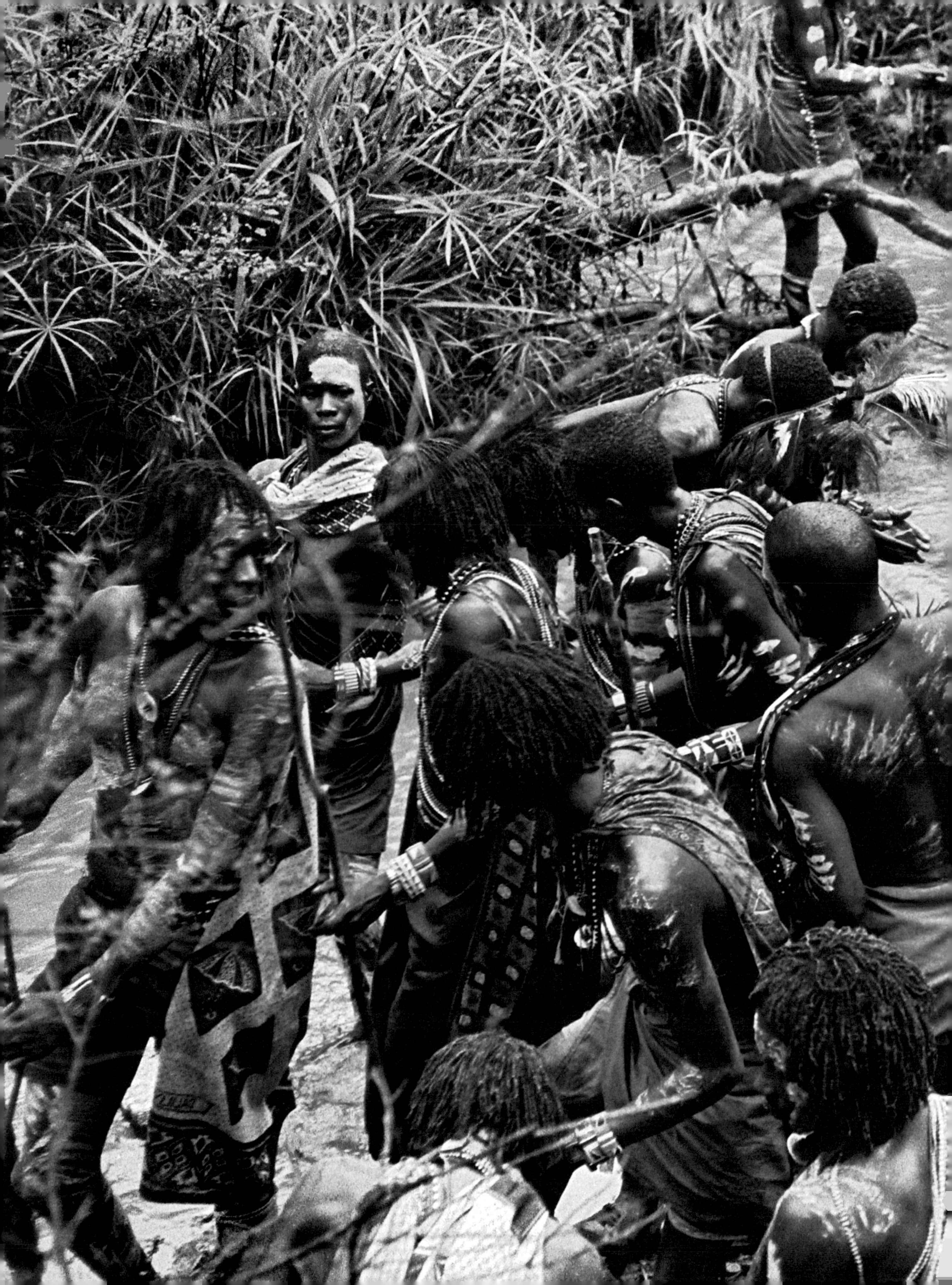

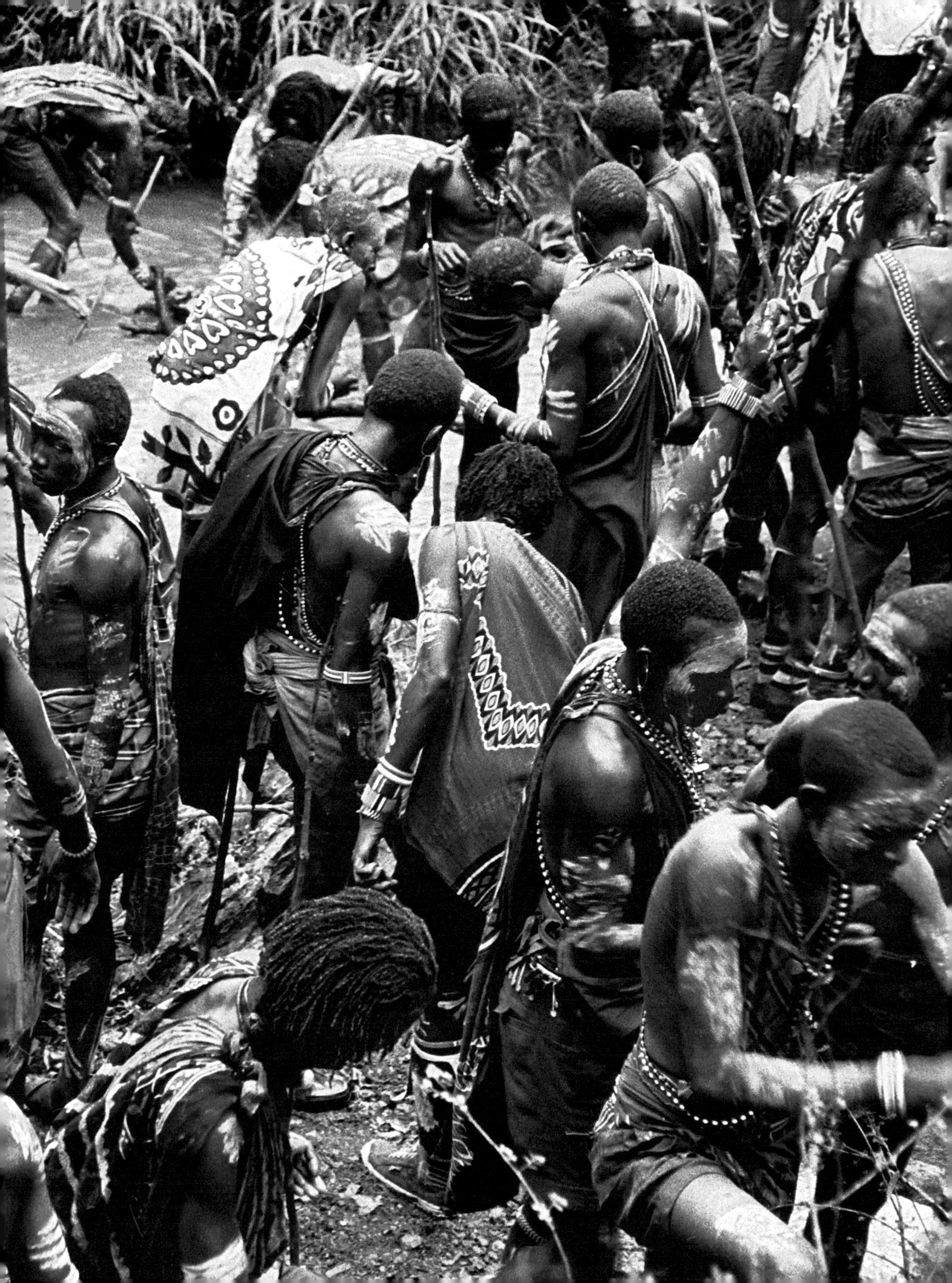

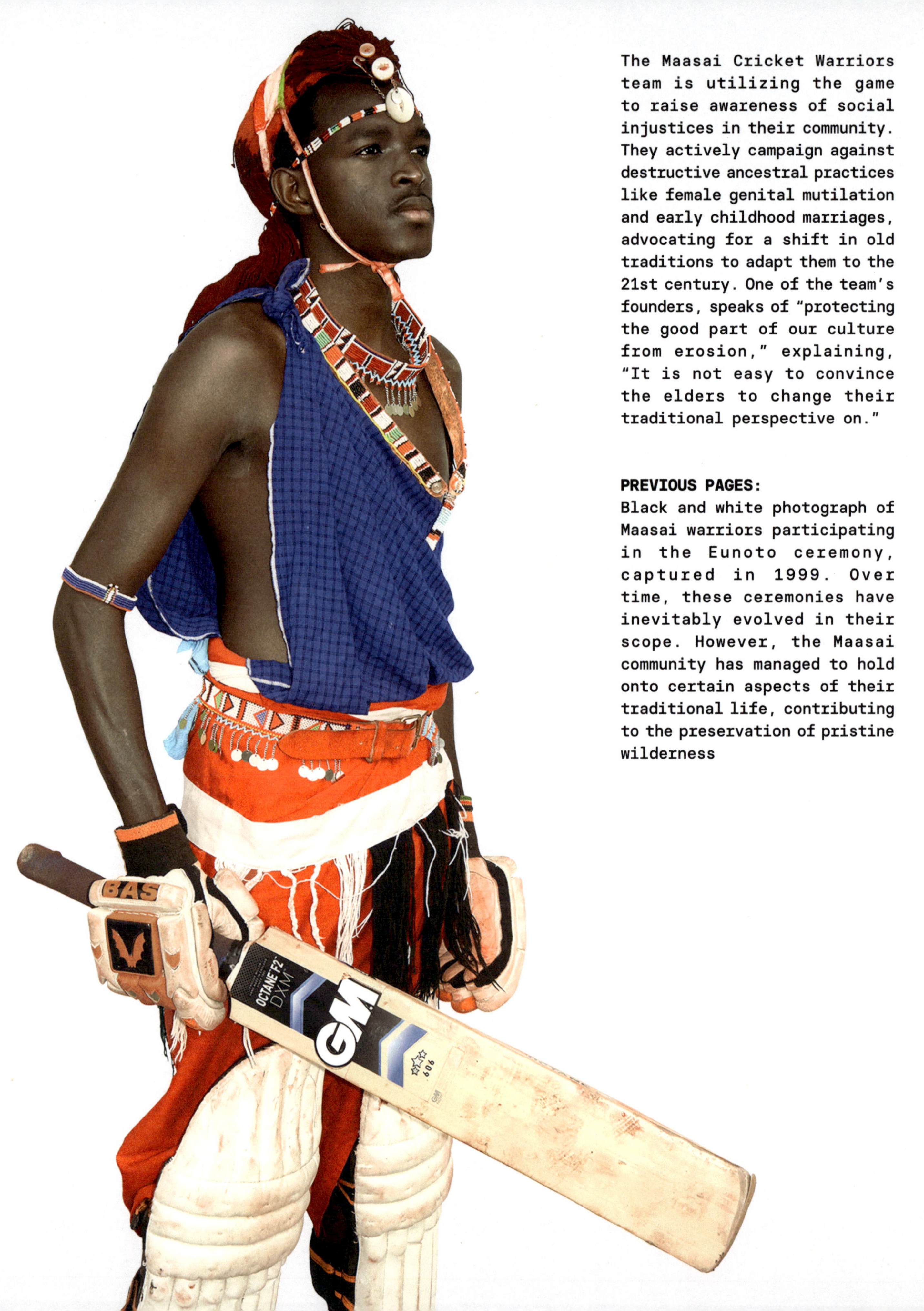

The Maasai Cricket Warriors team is utilizing the game to raise awareness of social injustices in their community. They actively campaign against destructive ancestral practices like female genital mutilation and early childhood marriages, advocating for a shift in old traditions to adapt them to the 21st century. One of the team's founders, speaks of "protecting the good part of our culture from erosion," explaining, "It is not easy to convince the elders to change their traditional perspective on."

PREVIOUS PAGES:
Black and white photograph of Maasai warriors participating in the Eunoto ceremony, captured in 1999. Over time, these ceremonies have inevitably evolved in their scope. However, the Maasai community has managed to hold onto certain aspects of their traditional life, contributing to the preservation of pristine wilderness

Some ancestral traditions on the continent have survived, often because tribes are protected by their remote locations or cut off by wars, but mostly they have vanished.

The Eunoto is the final rite of passage for a Maasai warrior, it takes place only every decade and at the end of the 90's, I was incredibly lucky to be invited to photograph it. In the two decades since I took those pictures, these kinds of ceremonies have either reduced in size and scope or ceased entirely but despite education, and western cultural influences, the Maasai people have clung to some traditional way of life.

In 1999, what I saw was hundreds of young men, from all over Kenya, who came together for the four-day event. They danced inside and around a traditional animal enclosure called a manyatta, and on the last day, very early in the morning, the "old" warriors gathered in a secret place where, washed of red ochre, symbolic of war, they painted themselves with white, the color of peace (as seen in previous pages). Witnessing something that felt right out of the Middle Ages was incredibly humbling, and I considere this experience as one of the highlights of my life.

Traditionally the life of a Maasai unfolded as a series of conquests overcoming fear and physical pain, marked by different ceremonies, which boys and men of the same age group would go through together, united in challenge and friendship.

Very early in their young lives, around the age of 12, boys were sent alone to look after herds of cattle, with only their father's blessing as protection. In this way they were taught to be fearless of the large buffalo and of the lurking lions.

Traditionally, both Maasai men and women had to undergo circumcision. For boys, the ceremony is conducted between the ages of 13 and 17, and for girls, between 11 and 13. This ritual, usually performed in the presence of Elders, marks the end of childhood and a new beginning.

Those who cried or flinched were often not allowed to participate in subsequent coming-of-age ceremonies, which meant they were forbidden from marrying and became outcasts for the rest of their lives.

More than a decade ago, a young generation of Maasai started questioning these rituals. They put down their warrior spears and took up cricket bats; playing sport instead of war, and women started to protest female genital mutilation which had been outlawed in Kenya in 2011. It's a complicated challenge to retain tradition while encouraging equality and social justice.

The Maasais, unlike many other tribes who have lost their ancestral tribal traditions entirely, are an example of adaptation. They have maintained a deep connection with nature, serving as custodians of the land they've used for cattle.

Their enduring traditions have played a crucial role in preserving certain enclaves as pristine wilderness. One of these places, Kenya's Loita Forest, overlooks the Masai Mara, and under the guidance of Oloiboni Mo-kompo ole Simel, the spiritual leader of more than a million Maasai who live in Kenya and Tanzania, has managed, at least for now, to keep eager developers and shady government officials at bay.

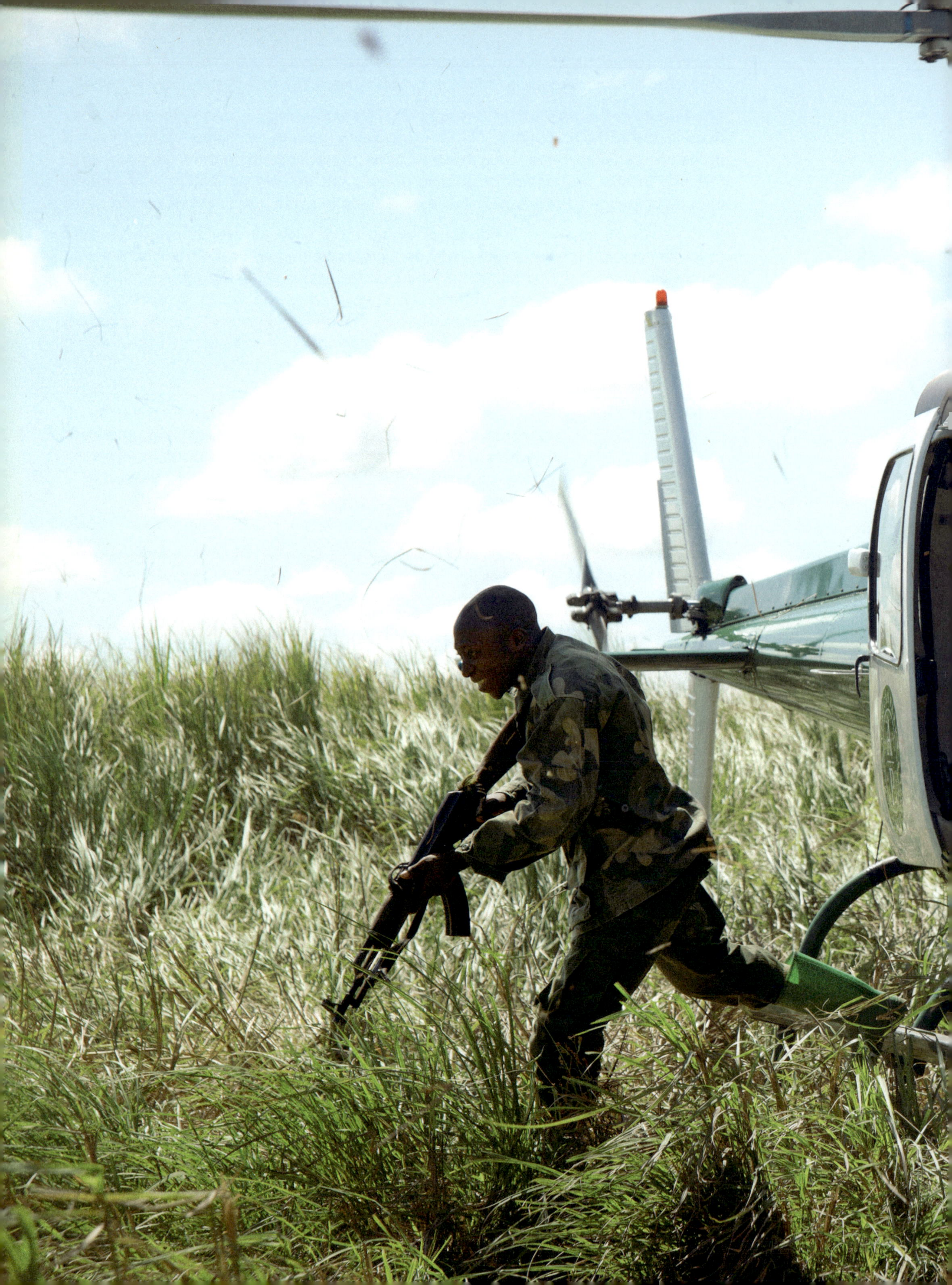

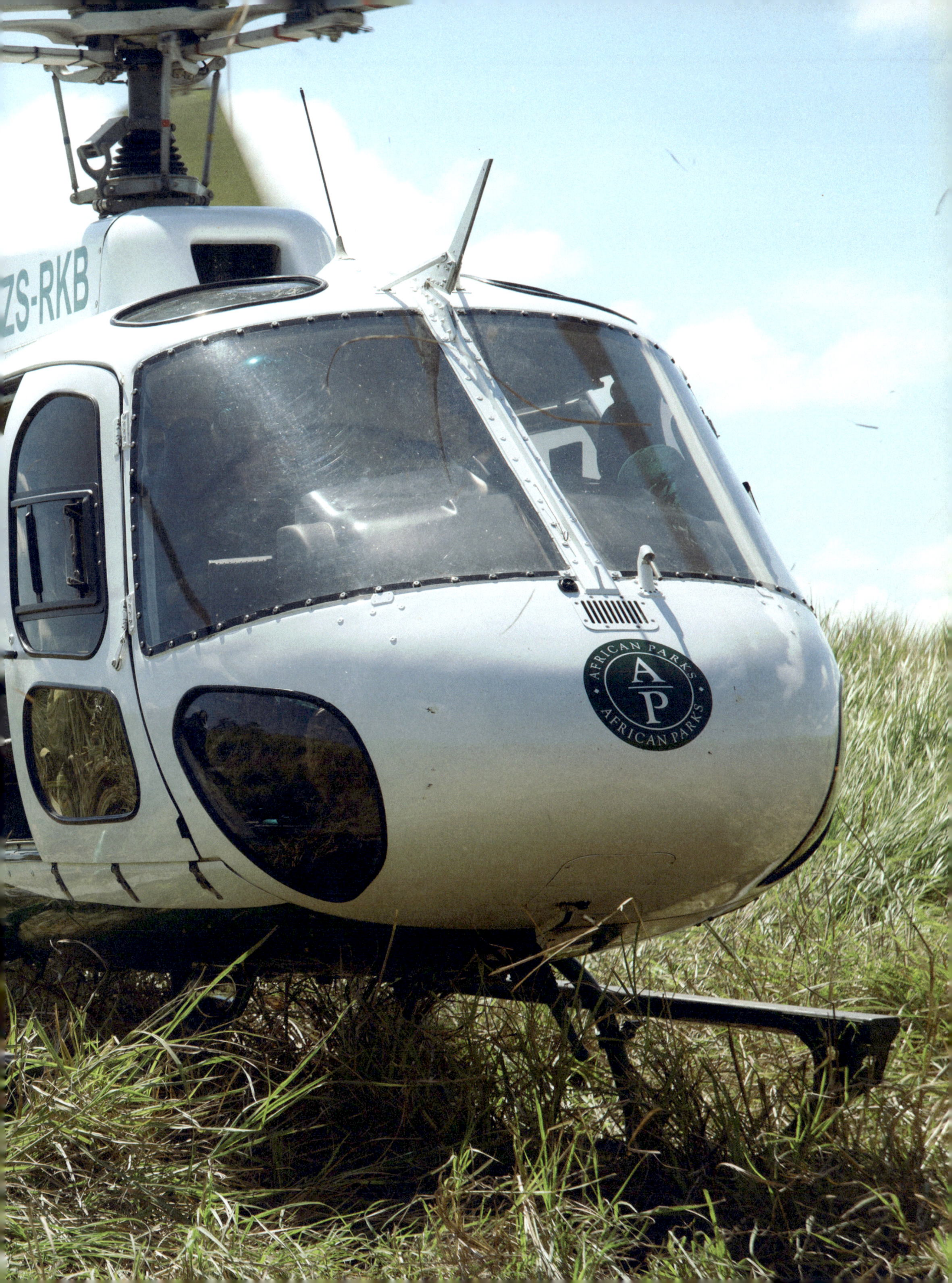

ZS-RKB
AFRICAN PARKS
AFRICAN PARKS
A
P

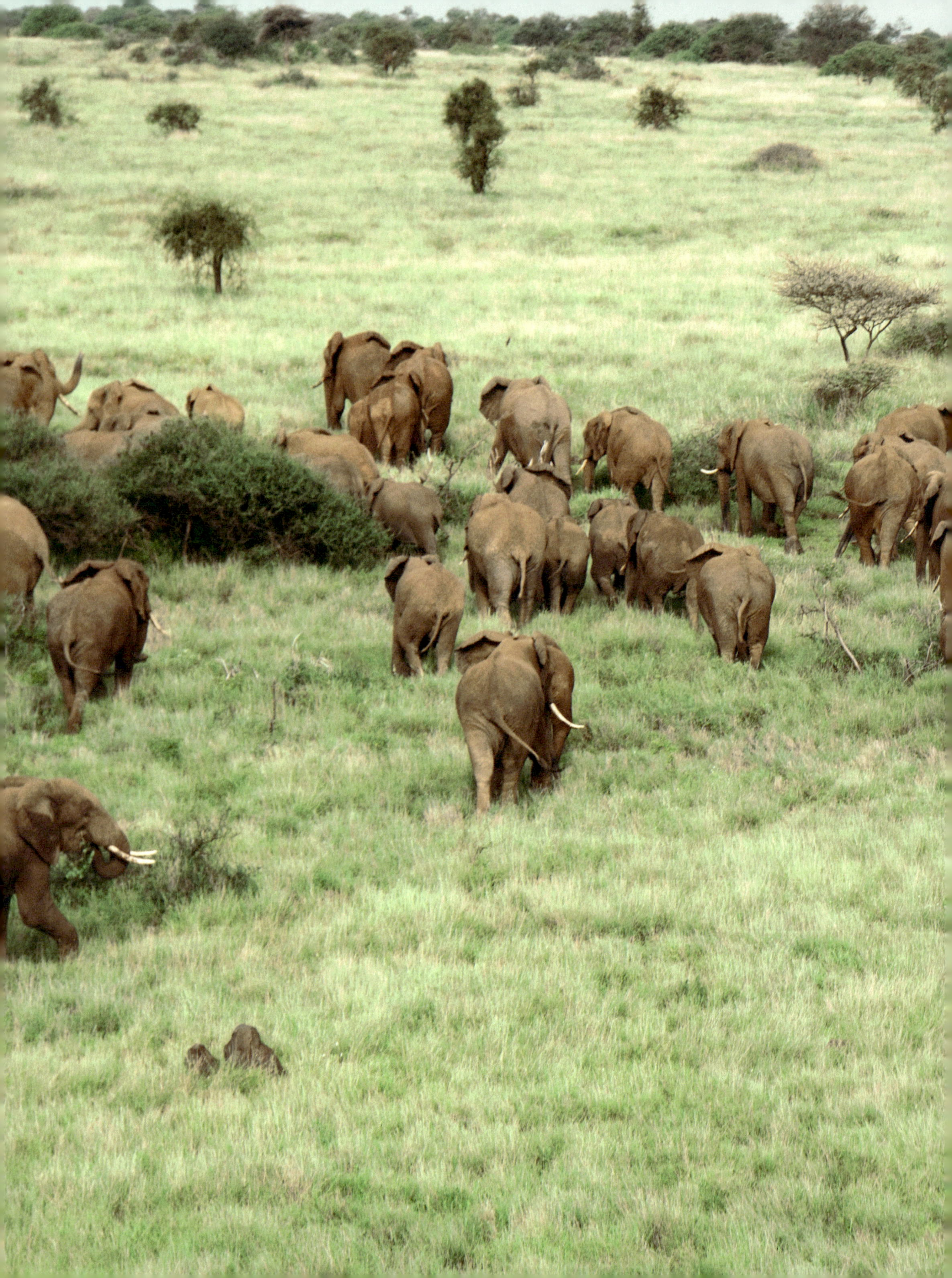

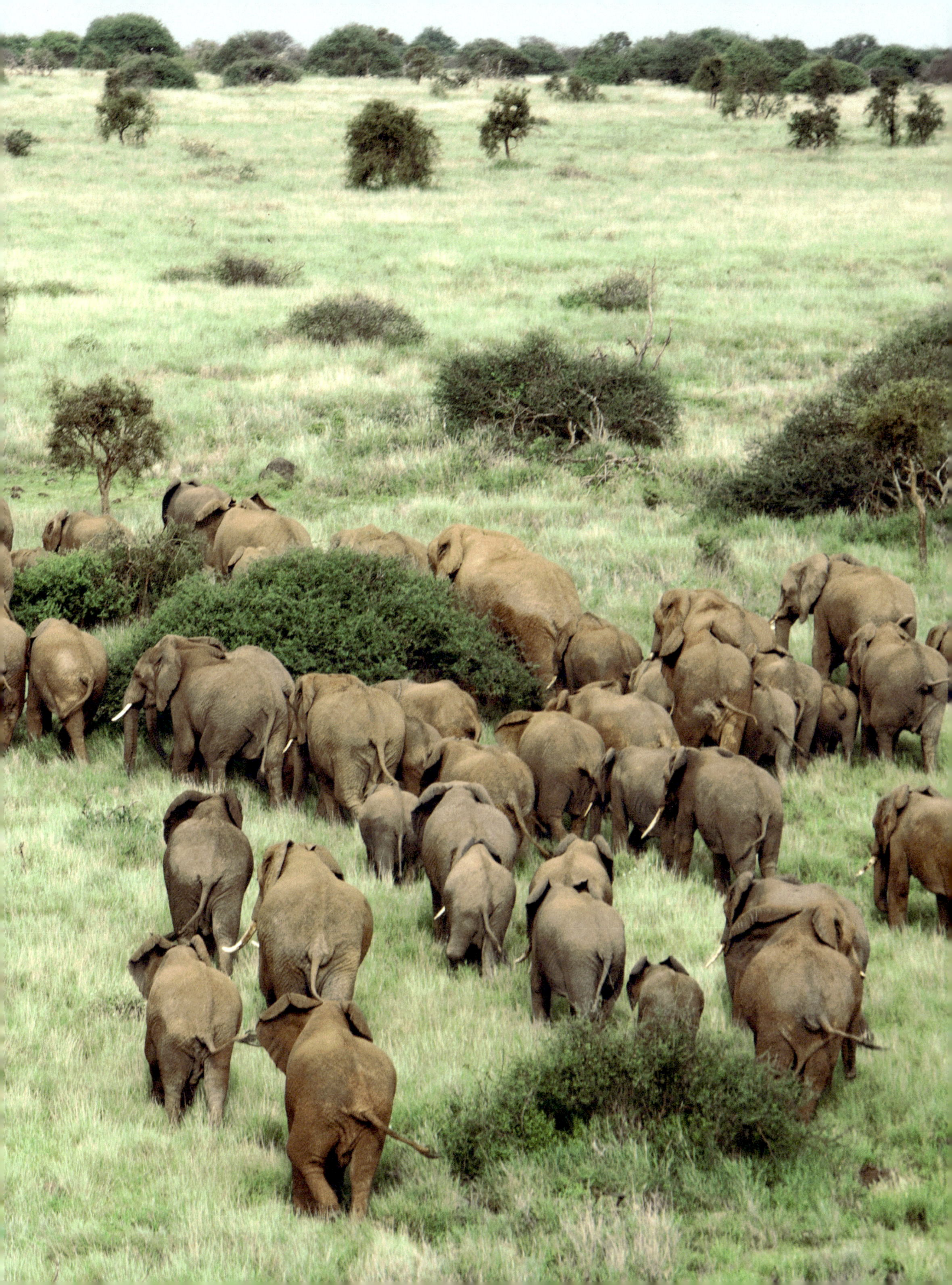

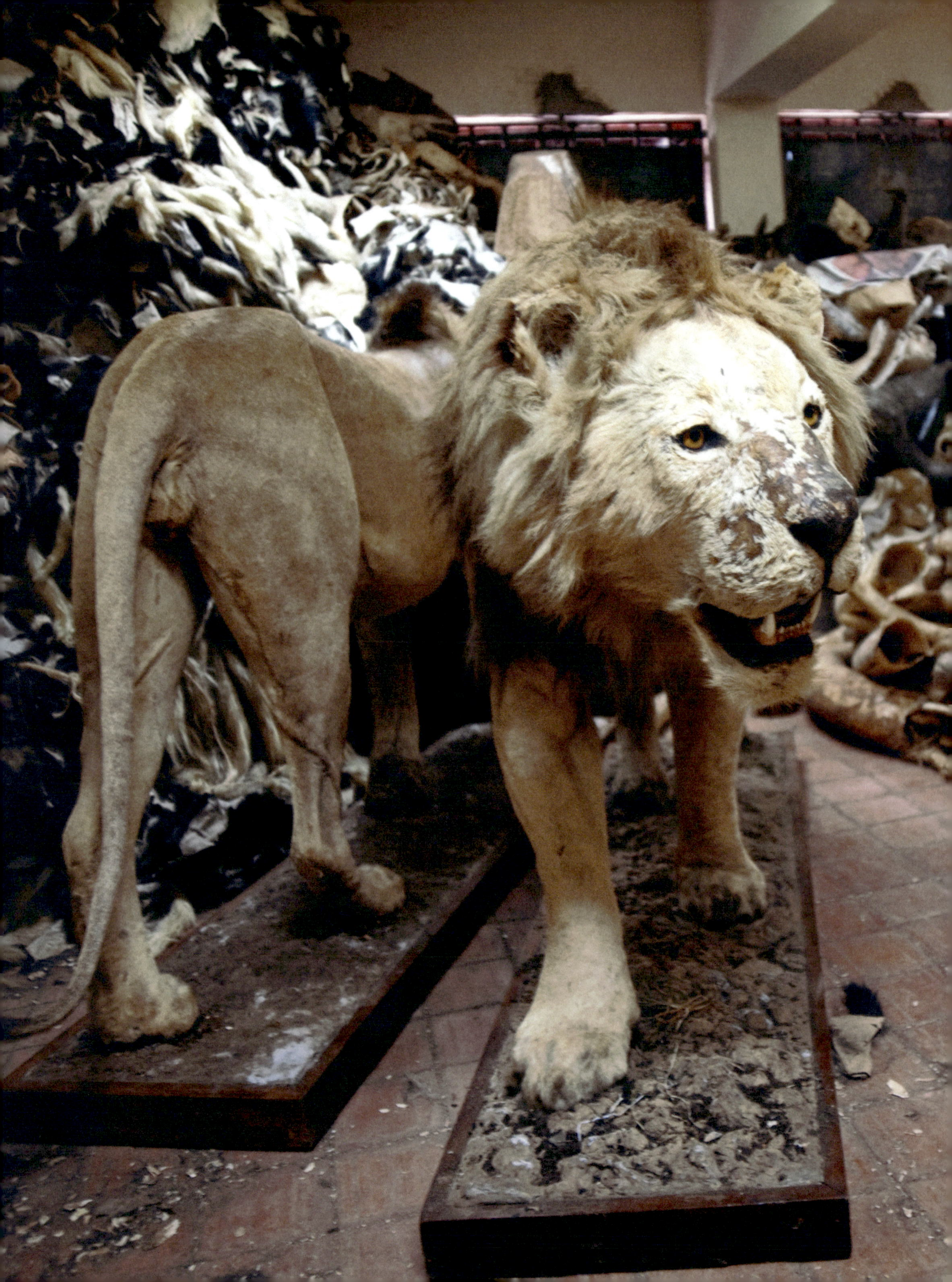

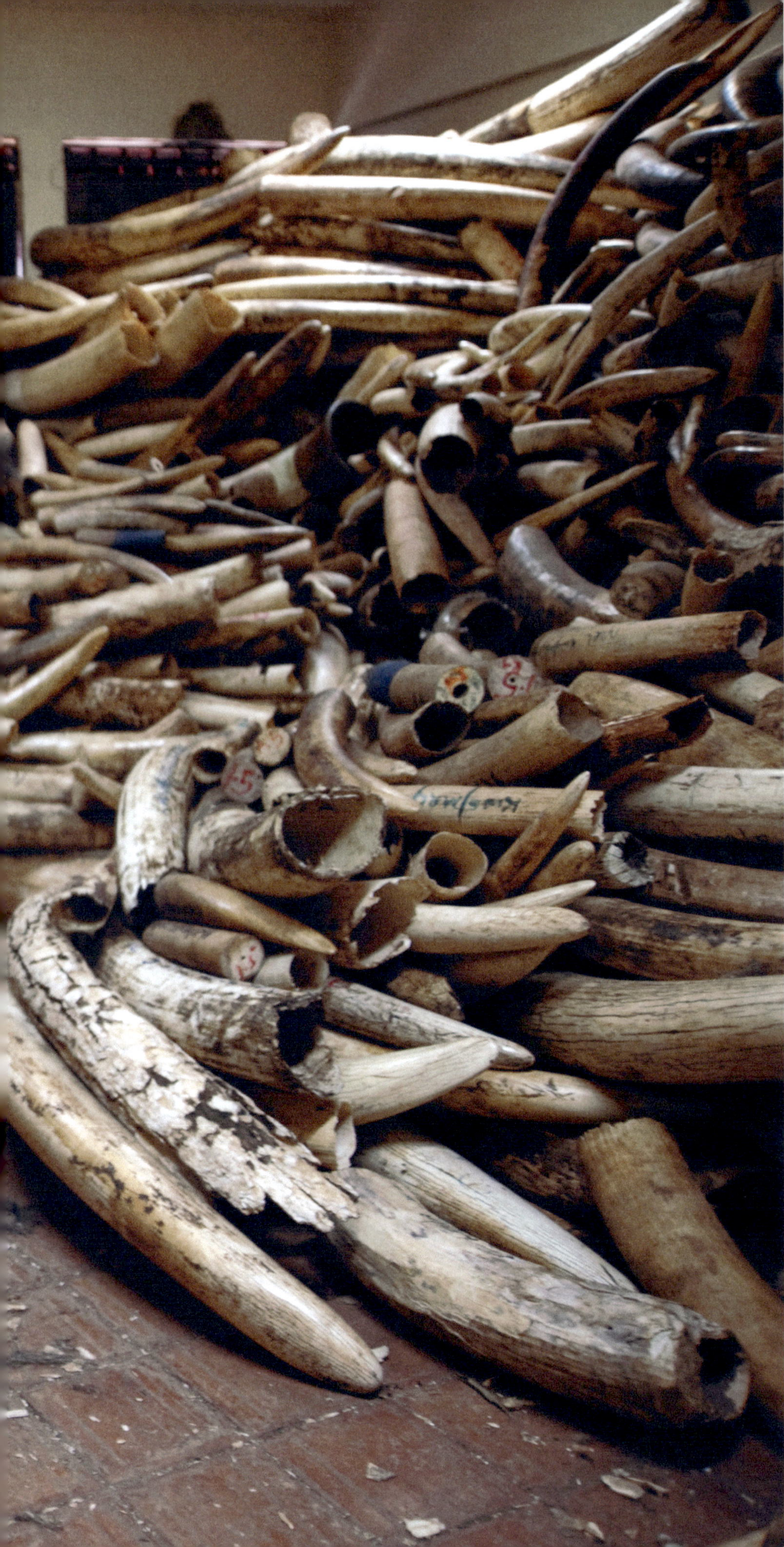

This photograph captures the trophy room at the KWS (Kenya Wildlife Service) headquarters in Nairobi, where valuable animal trophies, hides, and all illegally confiscated wildlife items, including ivory, are stored away from public view.

To burn or not to burn confiscated ivory from government stockpiles? Kenya, which introduced the world to ivory burning in 1989, still believes it's a good idea.

A debate exists among conservationists regarding how to save elephants. The Kenyan government believes that destroying ivory stocks can shame buyers whose demand for ivory carvings drives poachers to continue the killing of elephants.

PREVIOUS PAGES:
A herd of elephants in Amboseli National park. Fifty years ago, Kenya had a hundred and sixty thousand elephants. Today, there are around thirty-five thousand.

Ranger being deployed in Garamba National Park in the Democratic Republic of Congo.

Ivory stocks are increasing due to natural elephant mortality, population management practices (such as shooting problem elephants for crop raiding), and confiscations of contraband ivory. Factors related to management and security, including corruption and the high cost of protection, support the destruction of ivory. This destruction aims to prevent ivory from entering commercial markets and to curb expectations of future trade, both legal and illegal.

On the other hand, critics of destroying ivory stockpiles argue that doing so will reduce supply, increase prices, and strengthen incentives for poaching. They believe that keeping stockpiles for legal sale will increase supply, lower prices, decrease poaching, and allow profits to finance conservation efforts.

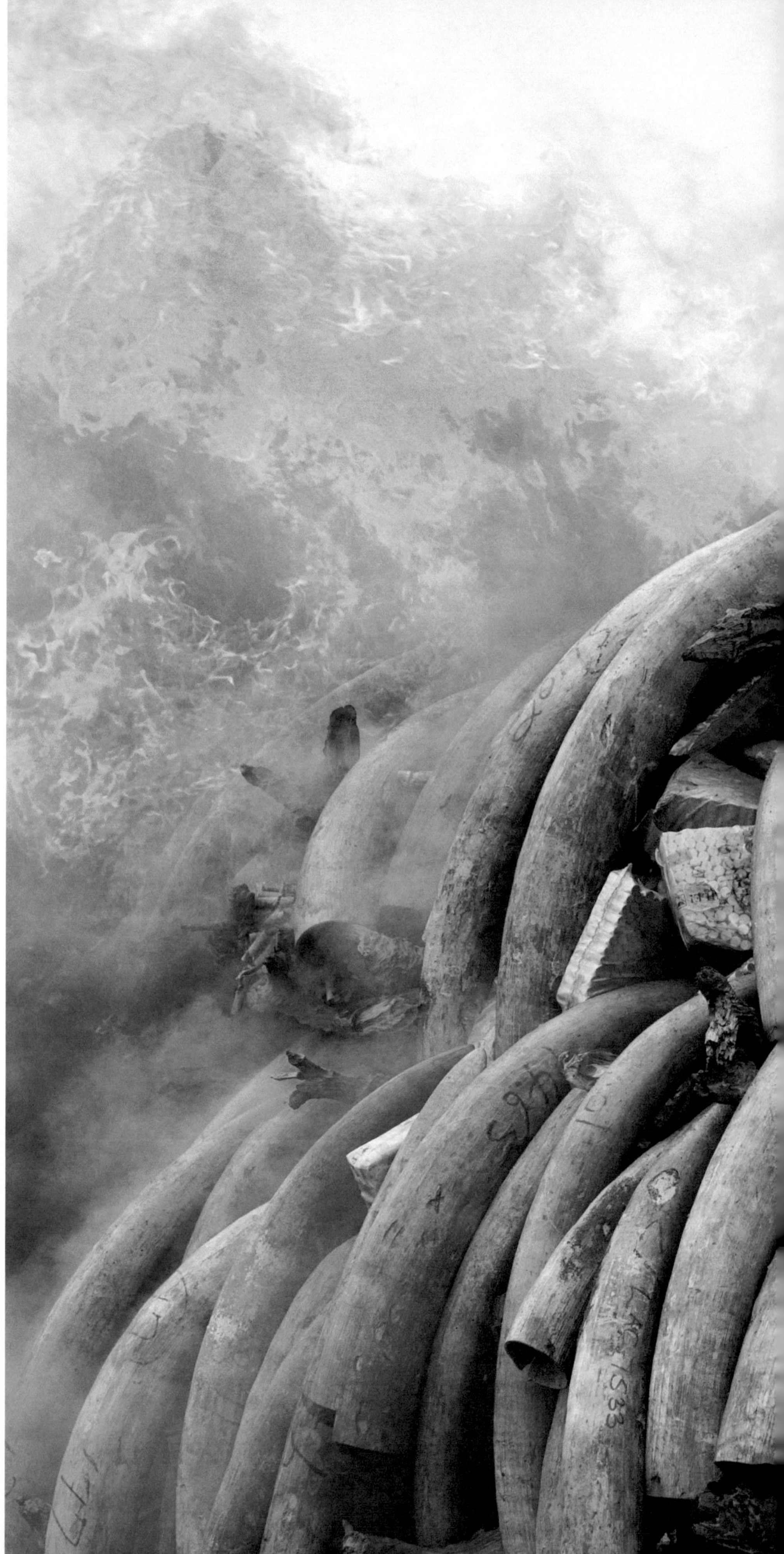

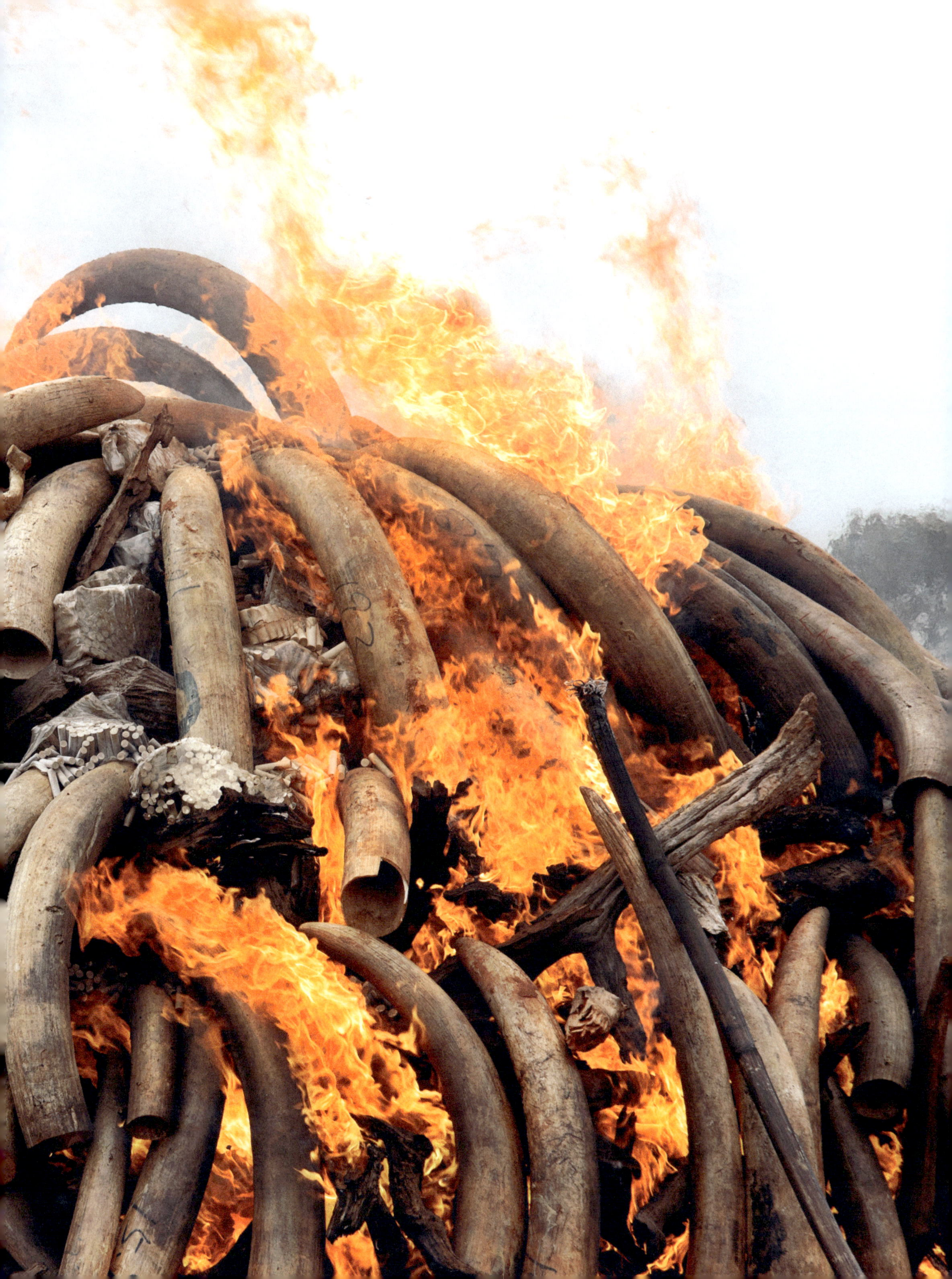

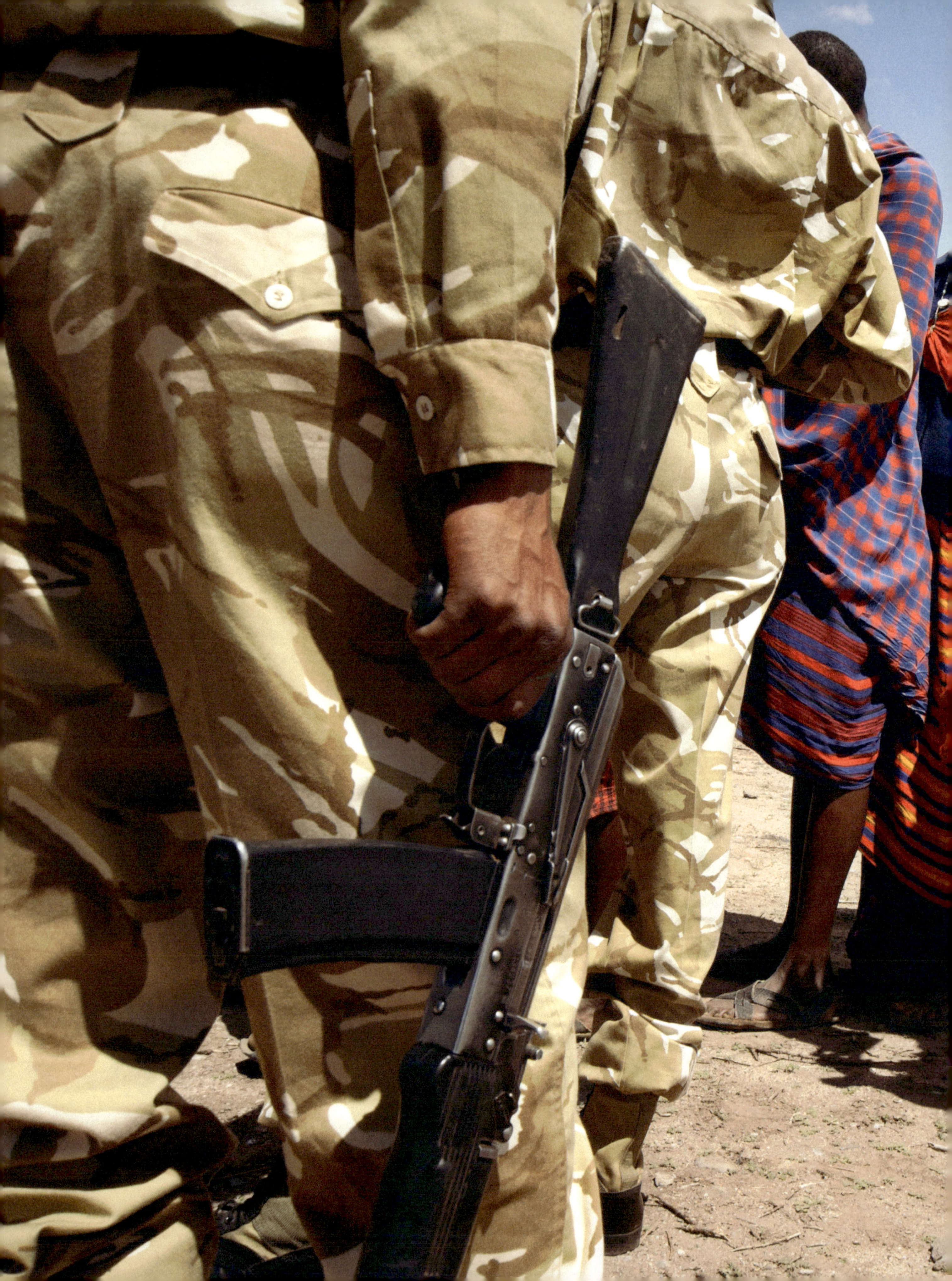

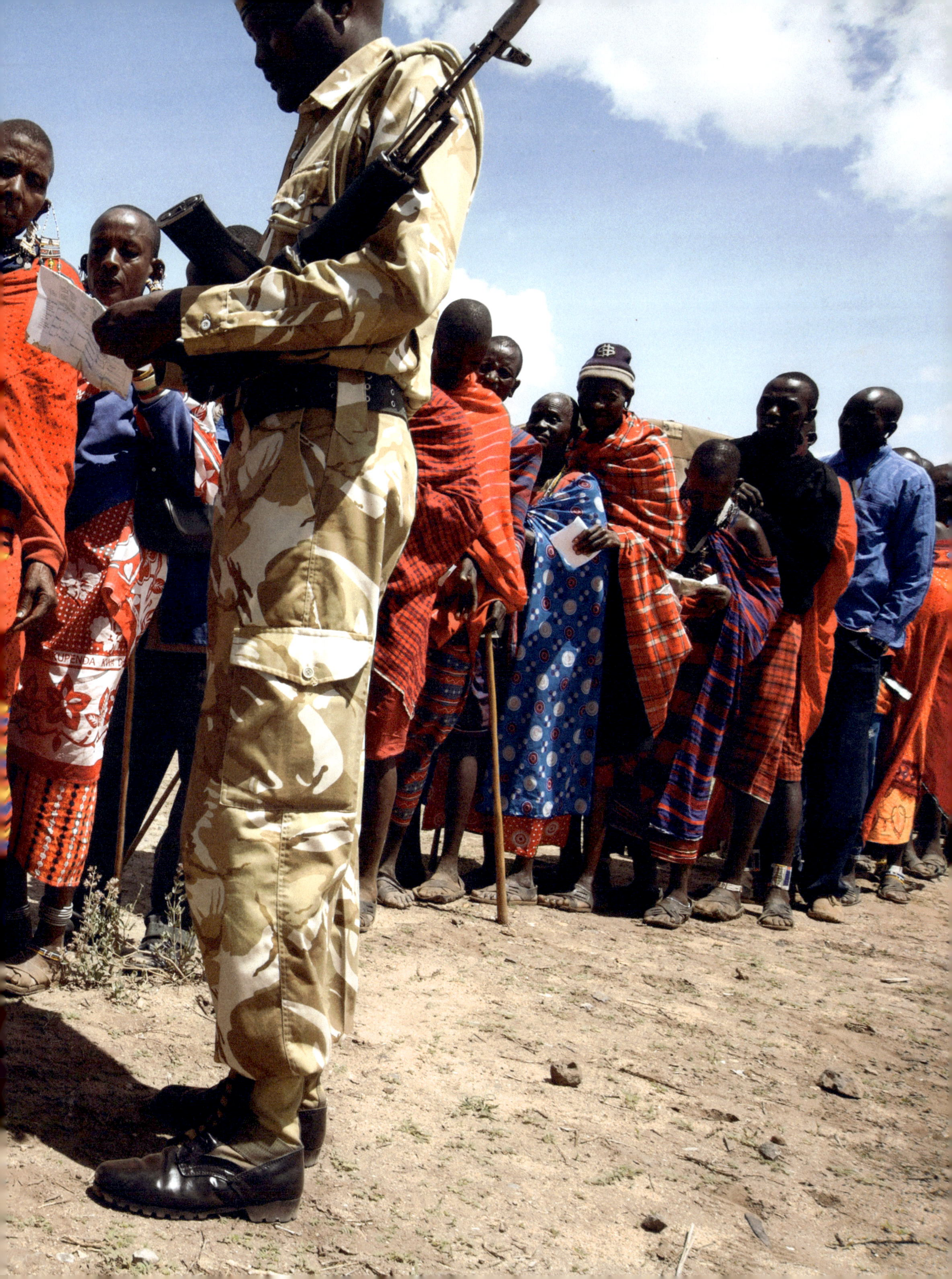

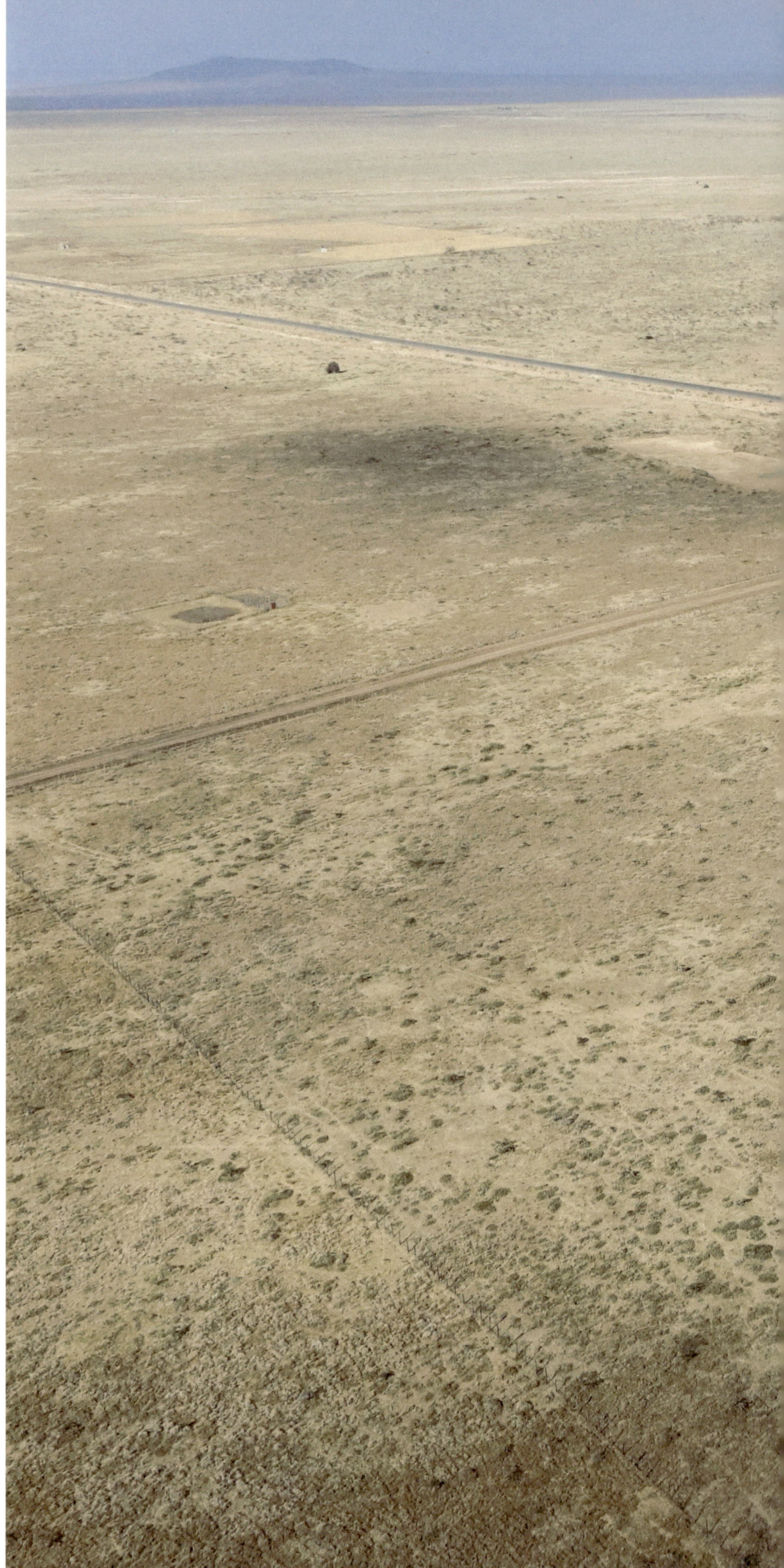

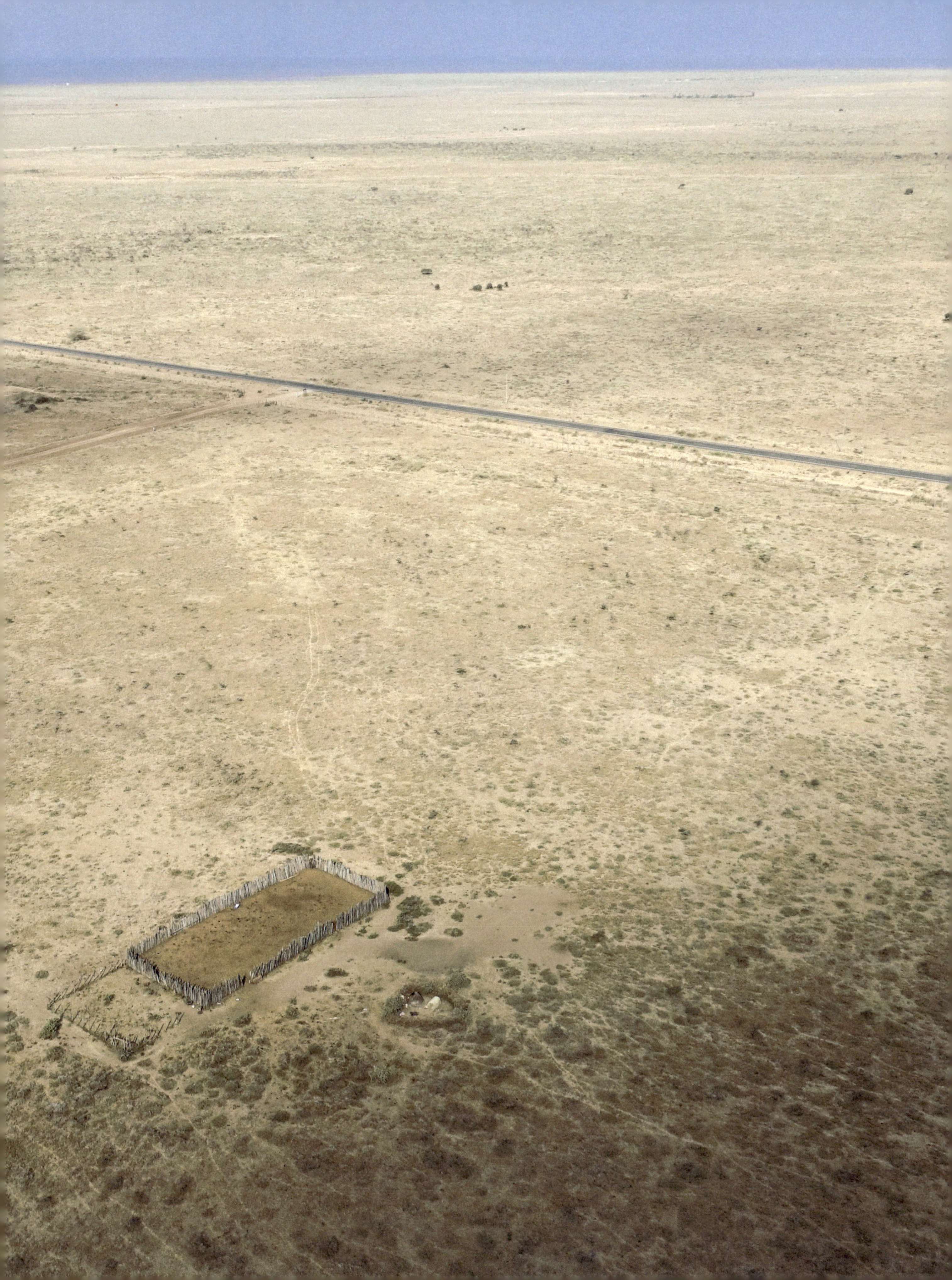

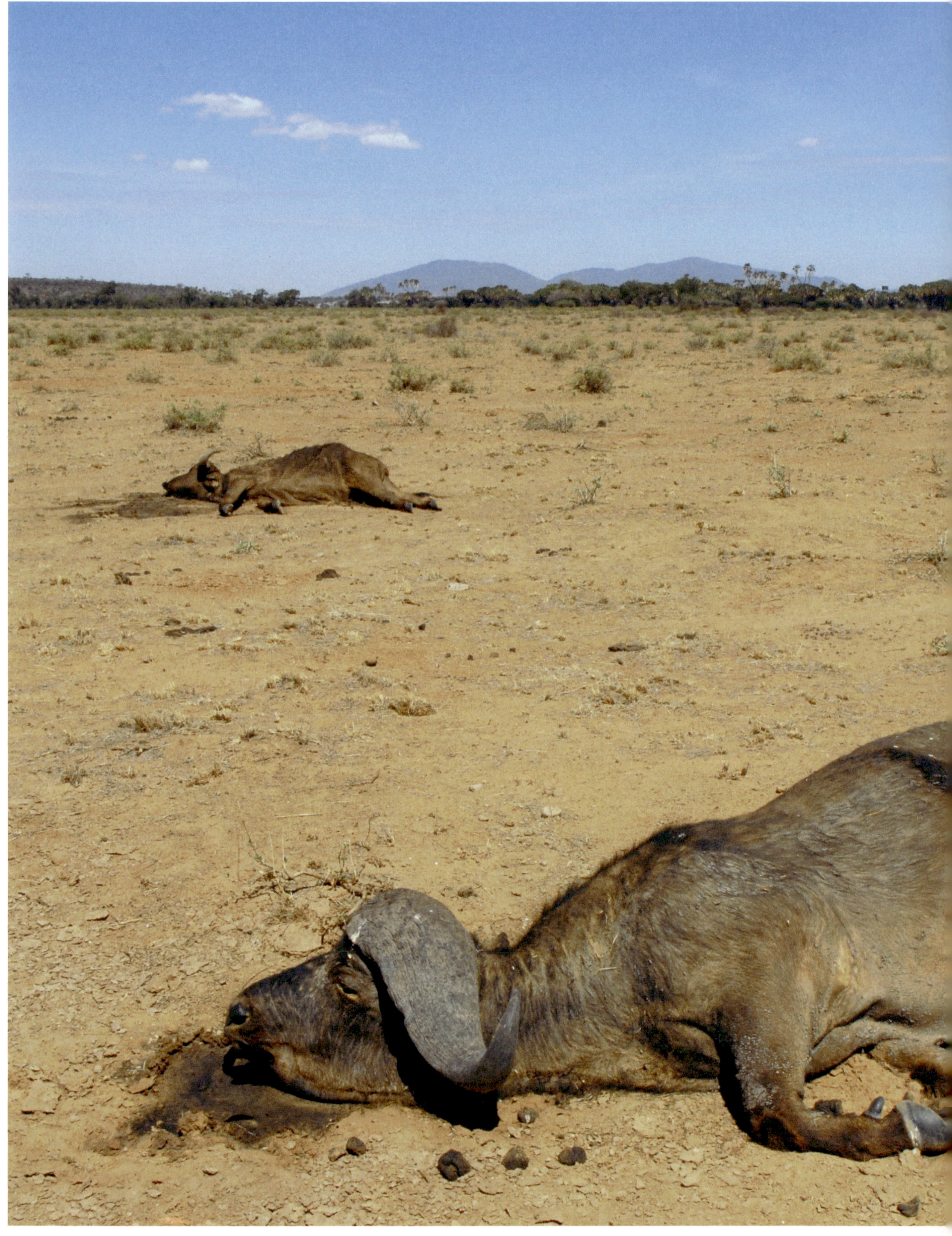

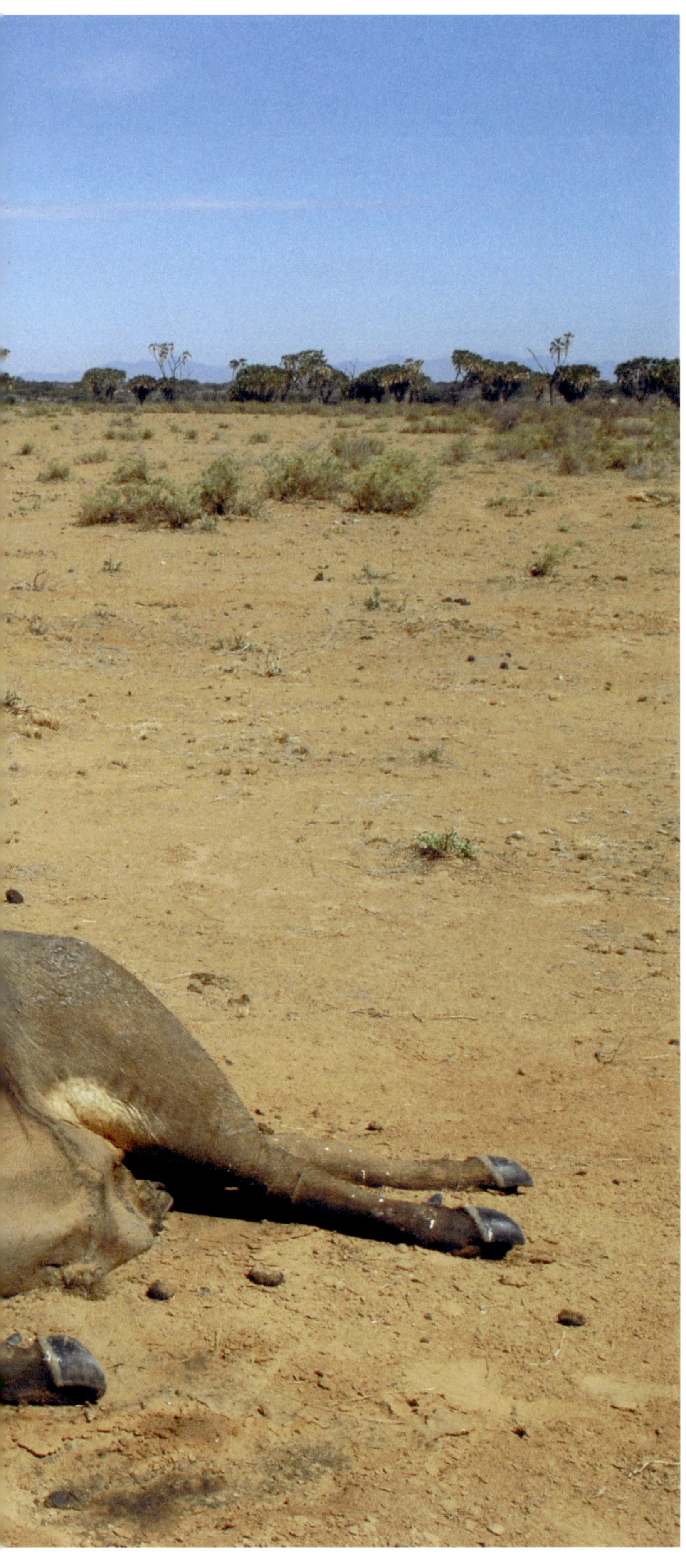

In Kenya's arid regions, droughts occur in 5 to 10-year cycles, posing a recurring challenge for nomadic pastoralists who rely on rain for their cattle. Early signs of drought appear months in advance, making proactive measures feasible to prevent cattle losses and avert famines.This is especially relevant in Kenya, where many international humanitarian agencies operate. With their resources, these agencies could act early to save lives and prevent crises.

Since the mid-'90s, I've seen an unchanging trend: emergency funding appeals often come too late. By then, severe droughts have already caused cattle and wildlife deaths, leading to famine. This delay is due to systemic weaknesses and reliance on external aid.With climate change increasing unpredictability, finding solutions is daunting. I wonder where sustainable resolutions might come from in these evolving circumstances.

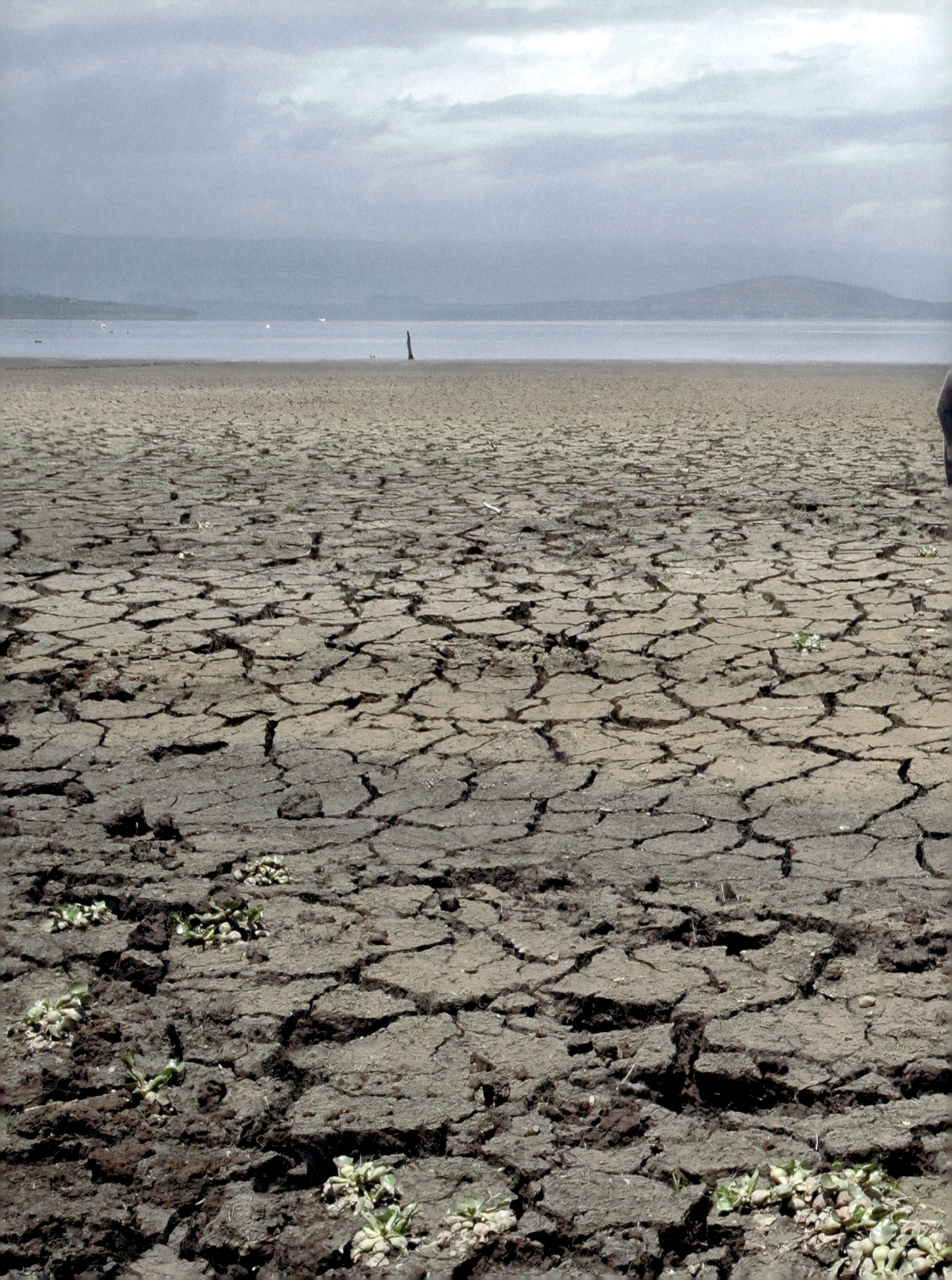

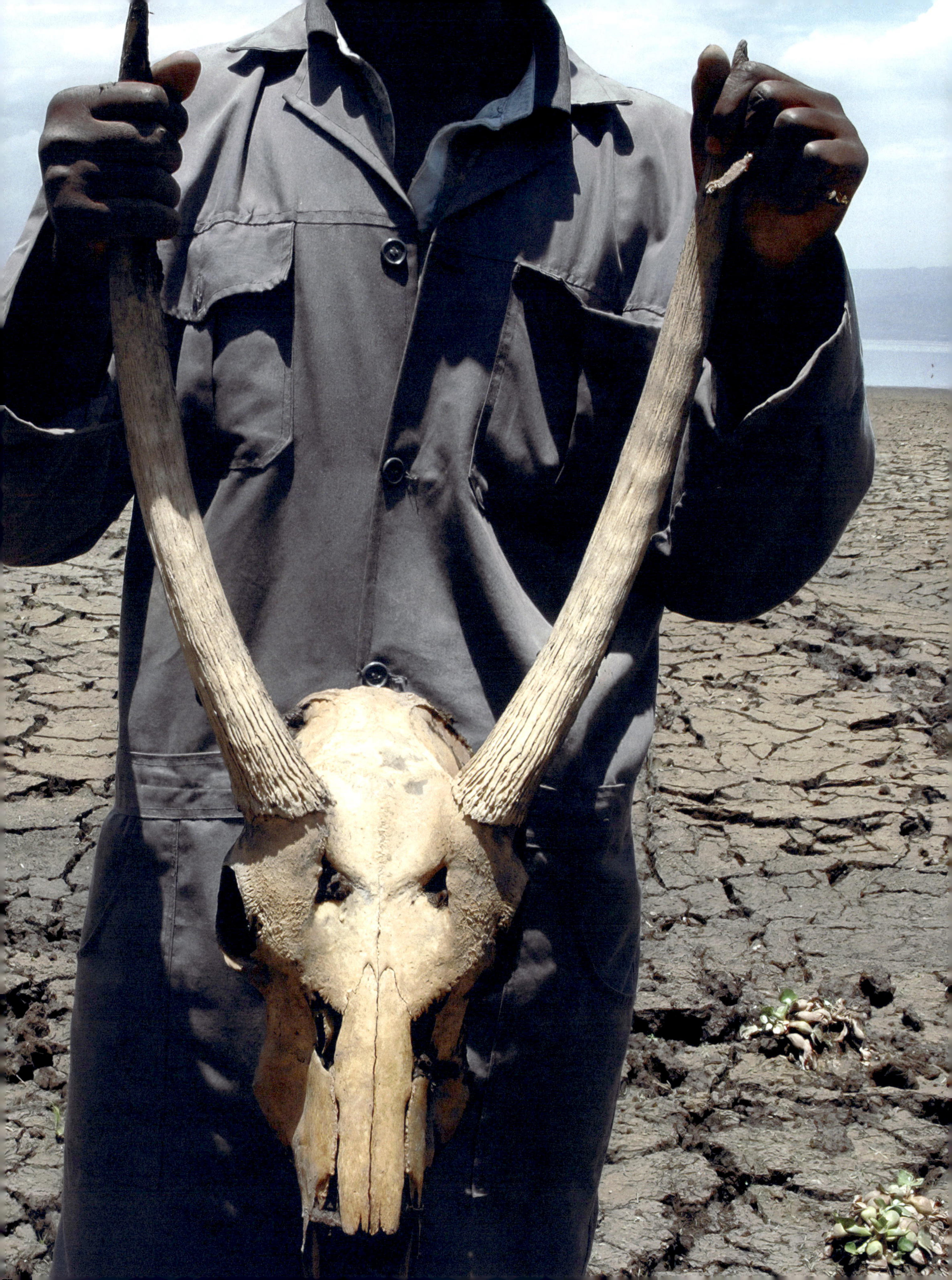

By presenting this photograph
of a crocodile hunt, taken in
Tanzania at the end of the 90s,
I am not seeking to support
the hunters' claims about the
benefits of hunting for wildlife
preservation.

However, publishing a book
about Africa that addresses
the dynamics between humans
and wildlife without discussing
hunting and its ongoing
impact on land management
would oversimplify the issue.
Hunters, often reluctant to be
photographed due to reputation
concerns, make this world
difficult to access.

After years of effort, I attended
several hunts, spending time
with them in remote areas
far from civilization. This
experience helped me understand
how hunting practices from the
colonial era profoundly altered
land management and traditional
ways of life

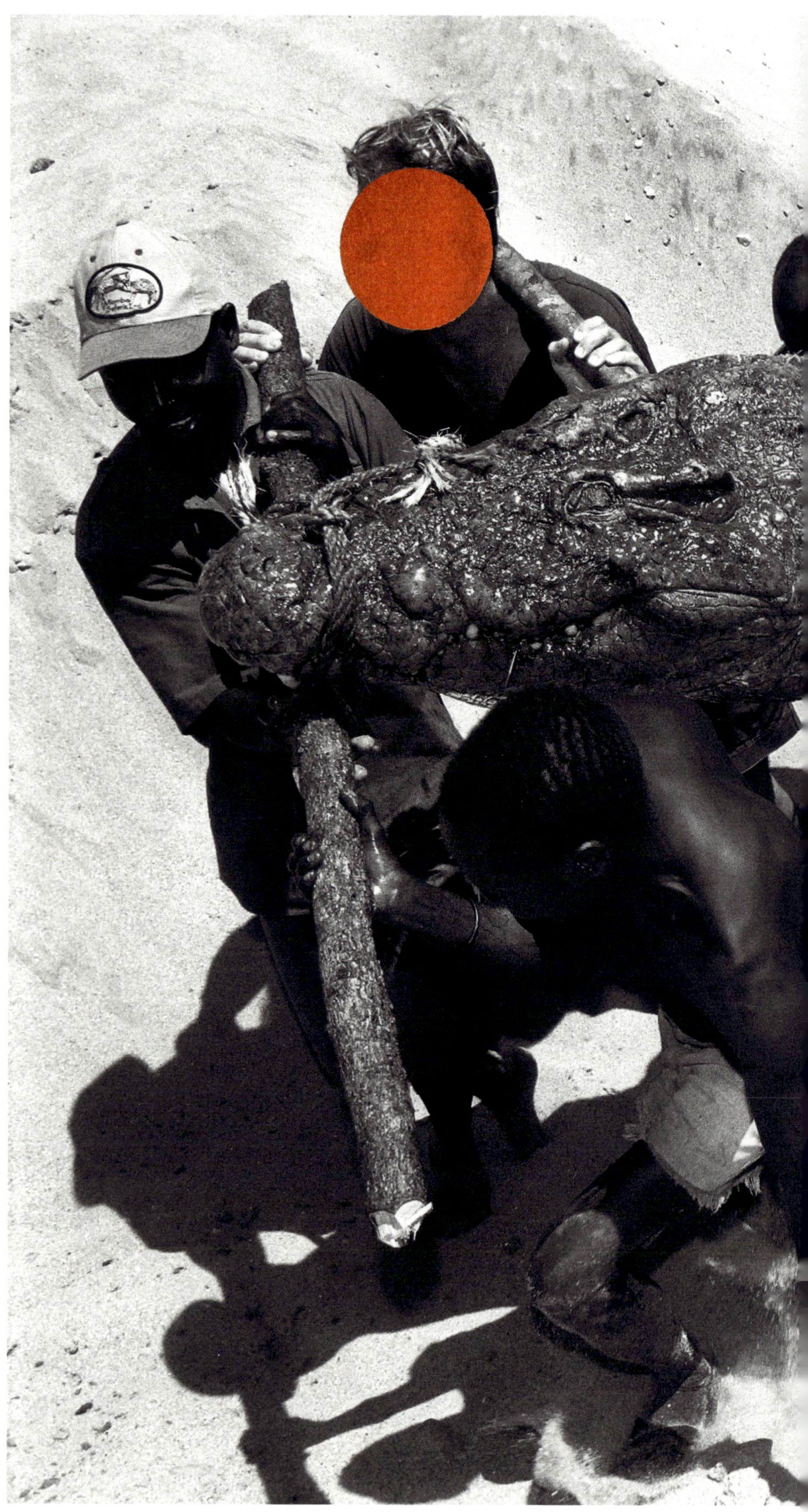

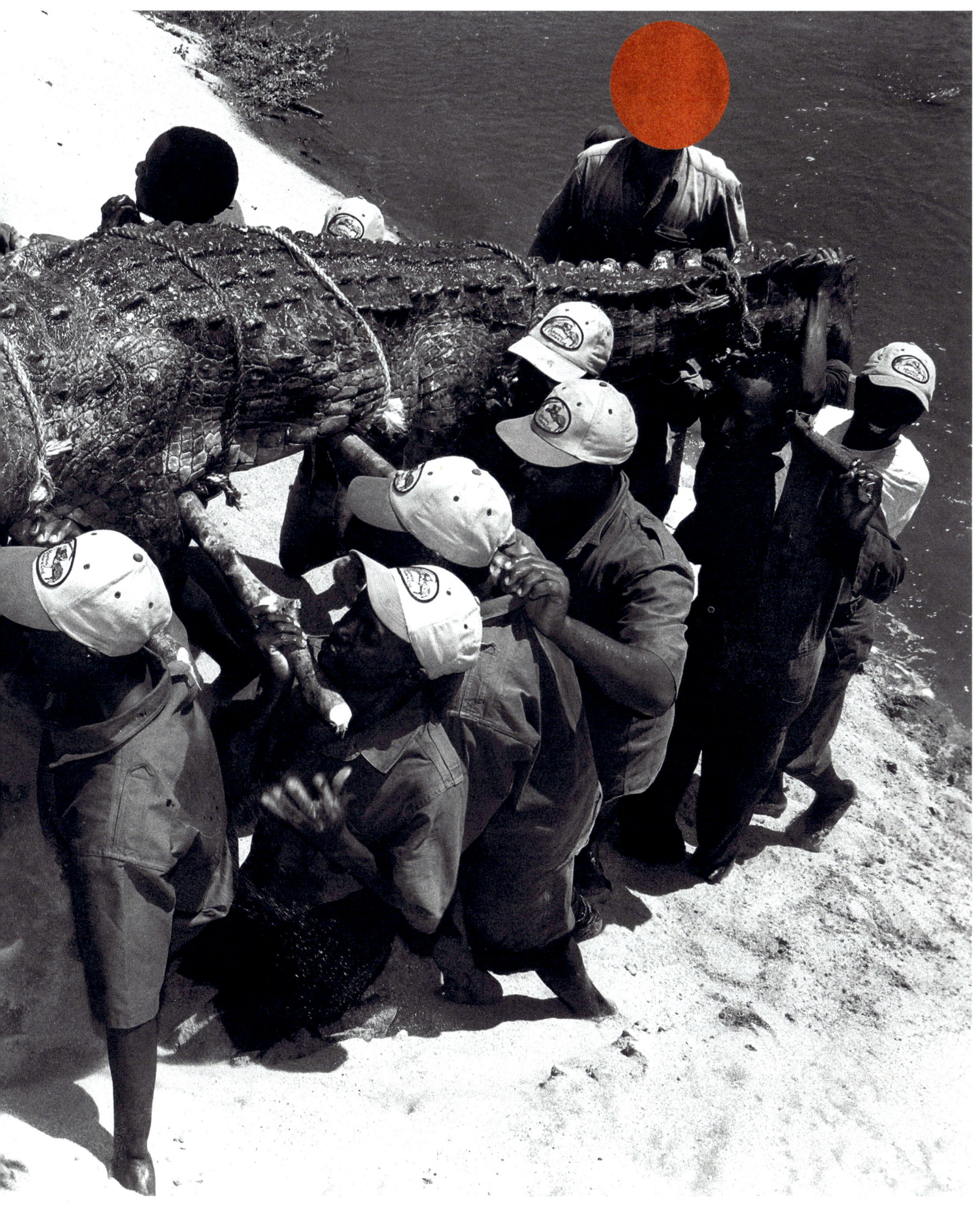

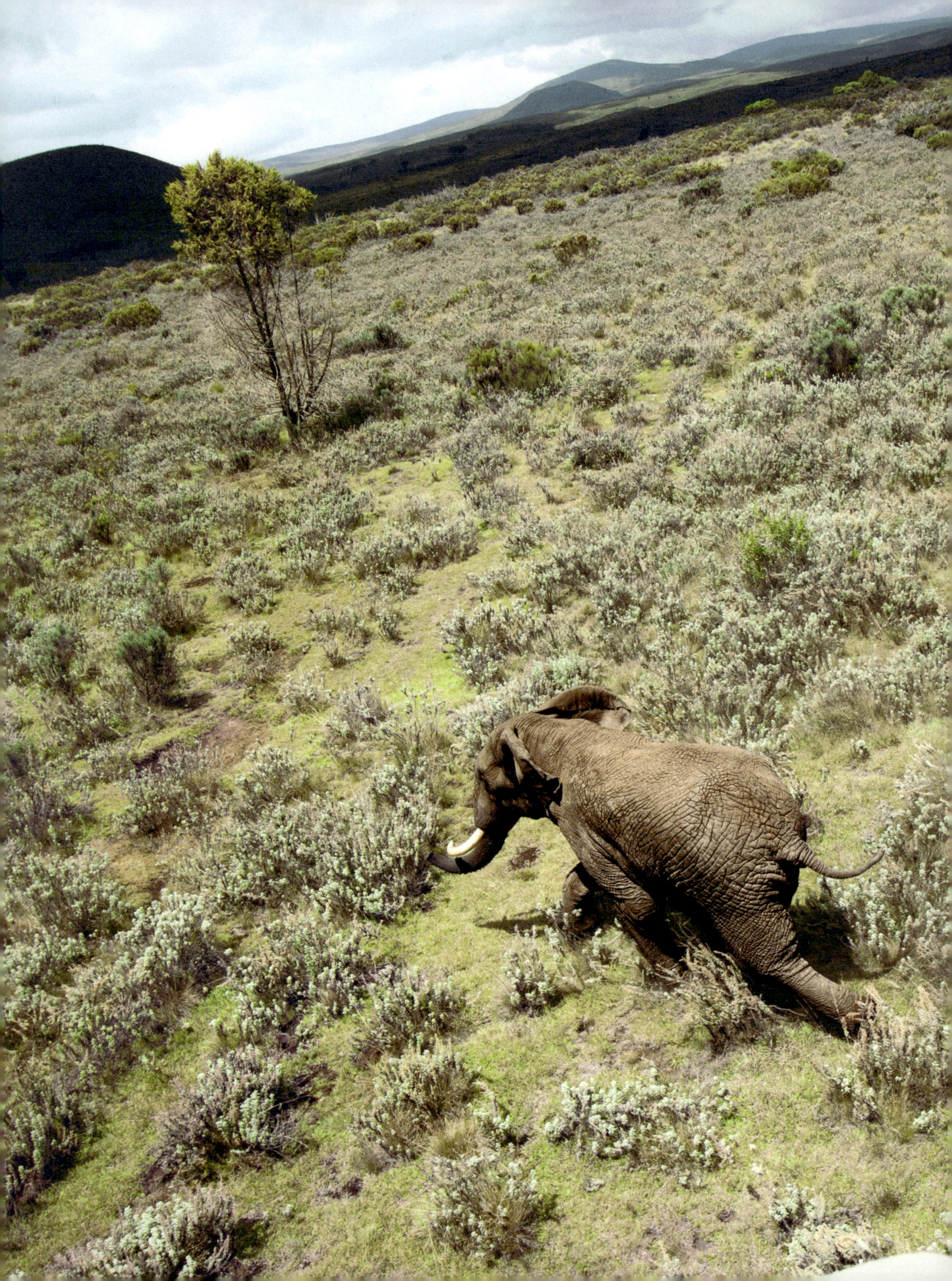

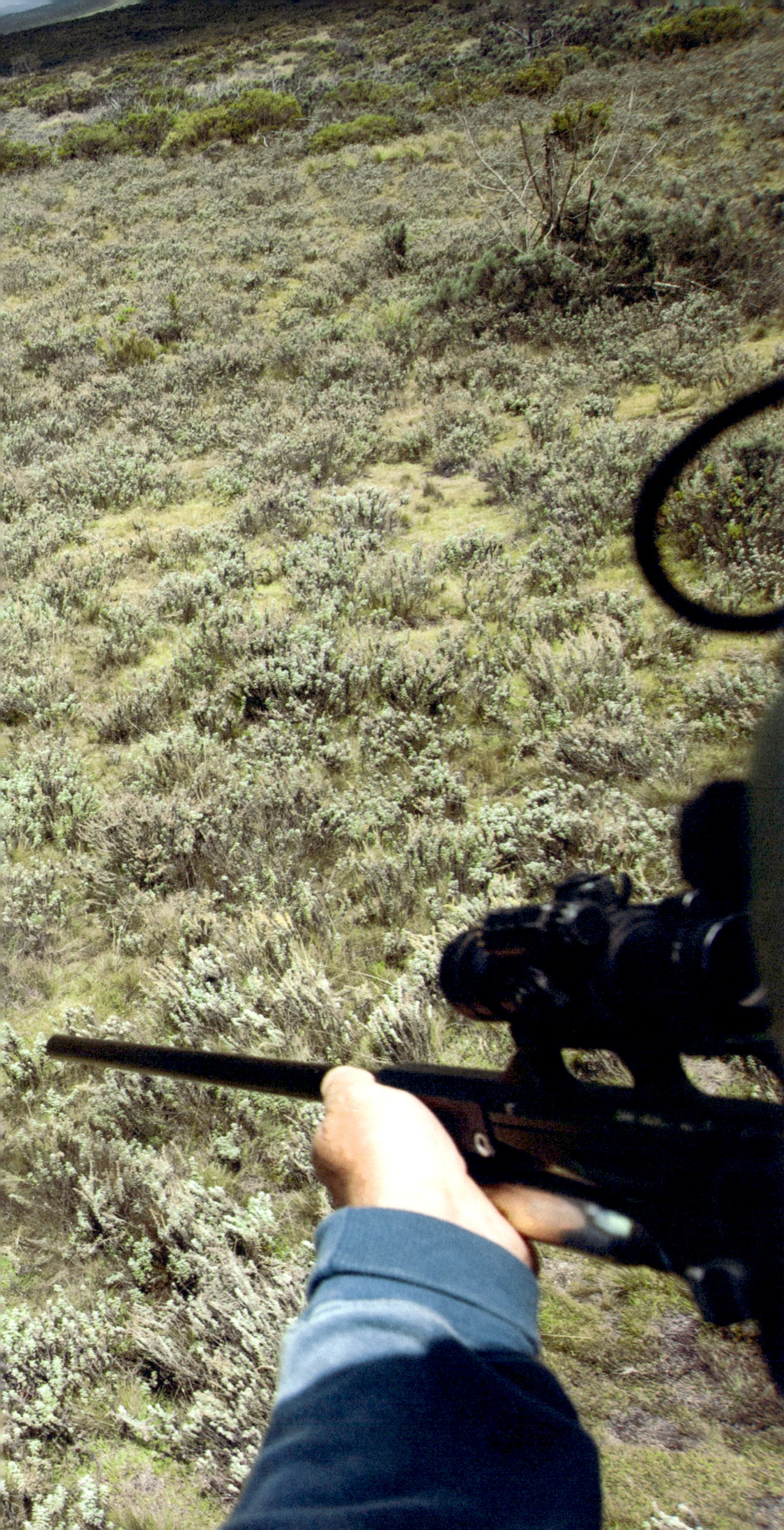

A male elephant on the eastern slopes of Mount Kenya will soon be tranquilized from a moving helicopter and fitted with a satellite-linked GPS collar. This collar will allow monitoring of its movements in an area where humans and animals are in ongoing direct conflict, aiming to reduce these conflicts.

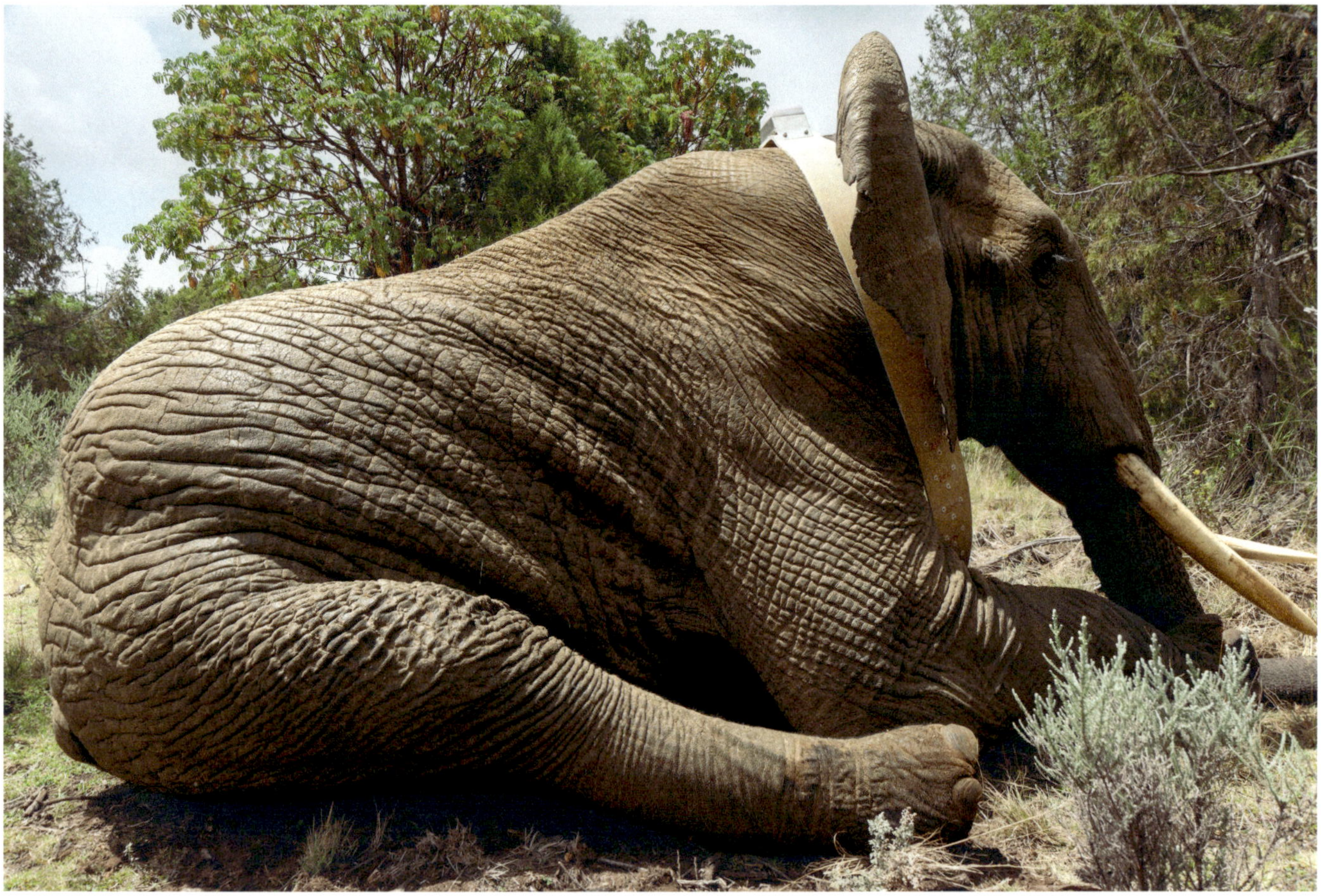

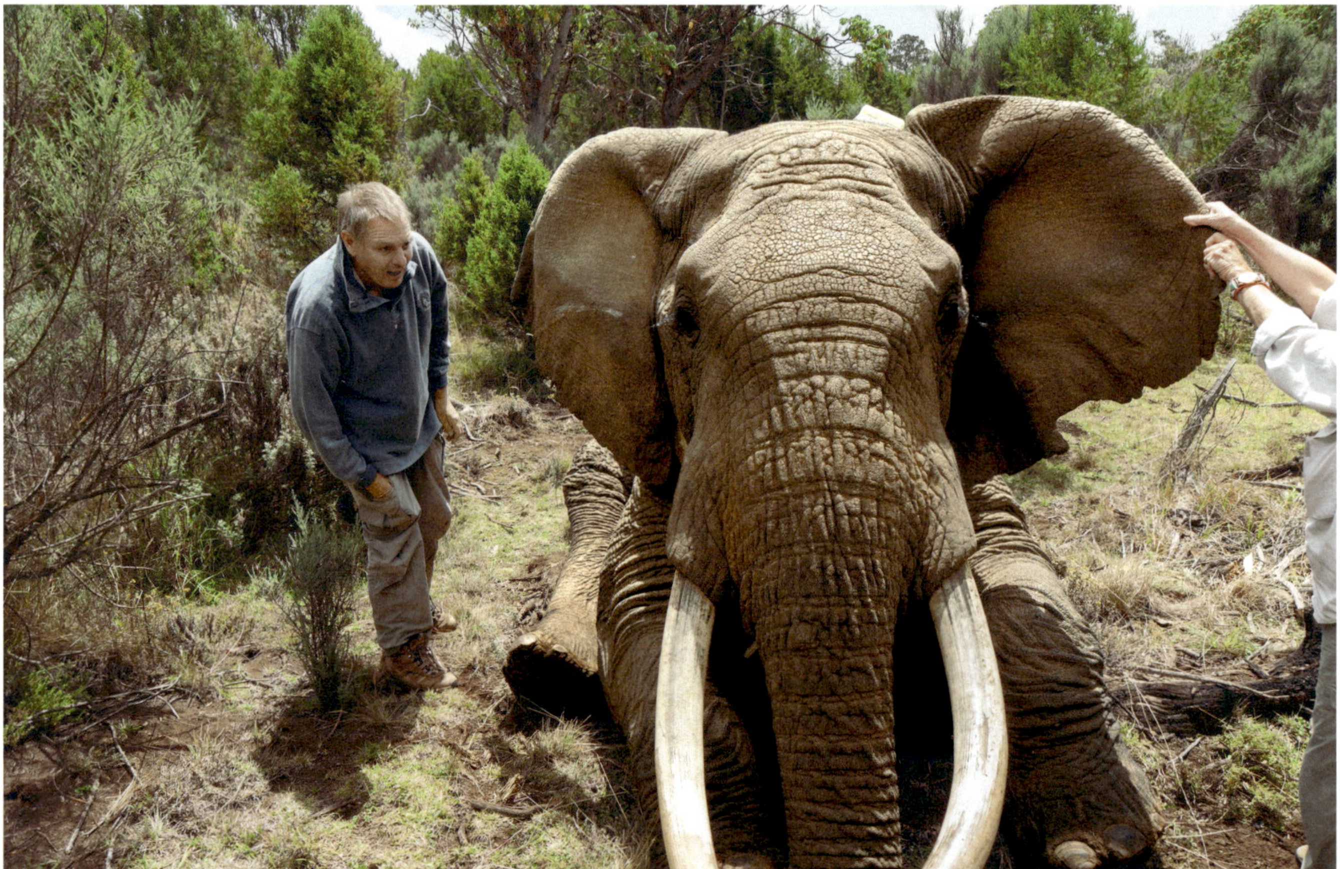

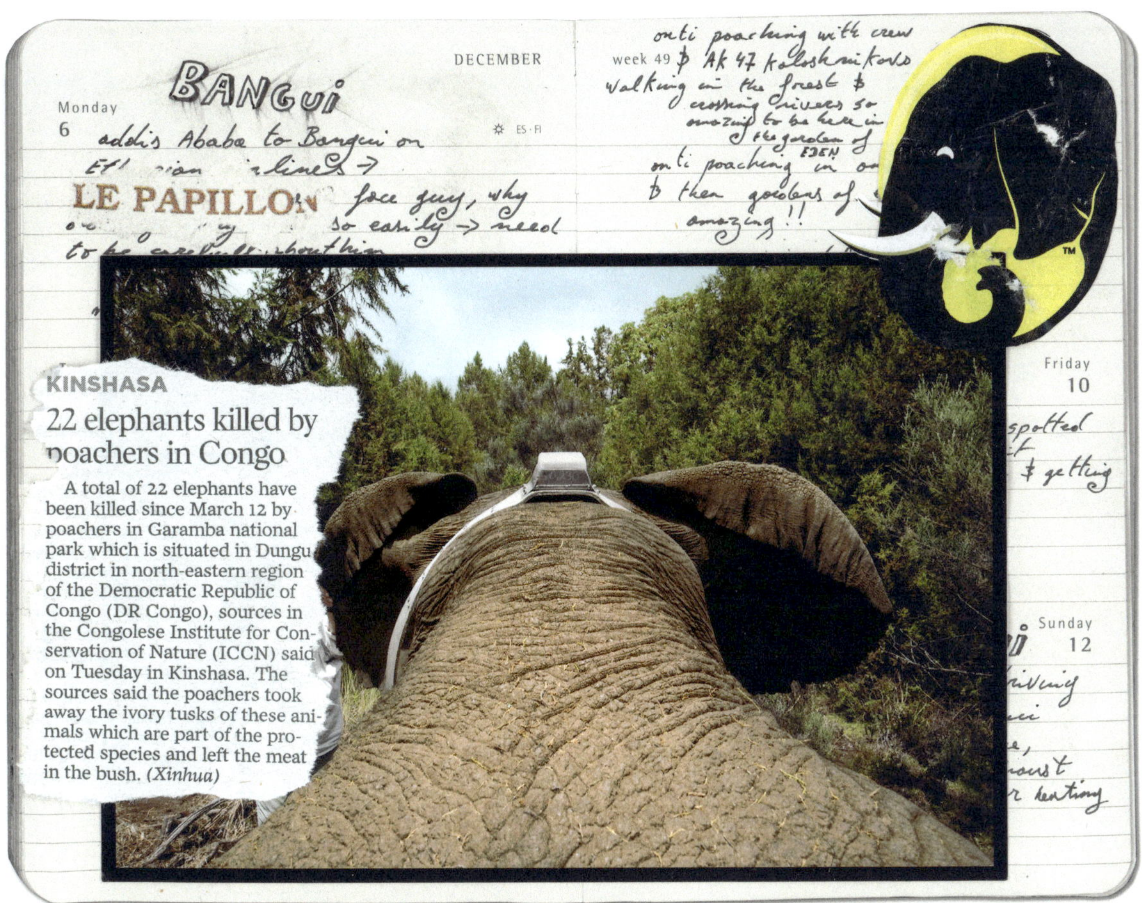

KINSHASA

22 elephants killed by poachers in Congo

A total of 22 elephants have been killed since March 12 by poachers in Garamba national park which is situated in Dungu district in north-eastern region of the Democratic Republic of Congo (DR Congo), sources in the Congolese Institute for Conservation of Nature (ICCN) said on Tuesday in Kinshasa. The sources said the poachers took away the ivory tusks of these animals which are part of the protected species and left the meat in the bush. *(Xinhua)*

In my quest to better understand how wildlife conservation could work, I needed to gain access to some of the more militaristic operations that fight poaching. These operations are financially very costly and occur either because animals need to be moved to new areas due to diminishing habitat or from areas where humans and animals are in direct conflict.

Persuading officials to let a photographer document their work is no easy task. I got in touch with Ian Craig, the founder of Lewa Conservancy, who in many ways, created a new template for conservation when he turned his family cattle ranch in the Laikipia area, into a wildlife tourism sanctuary by bringing in rhinos and other iconic species that visitors would pay to see. He invited me to join him on an expedition to locate a bull elephant with large tusks he had heard about in a very remote area and try to fit it with a GPS collar. We took off in a helicopter and finally spotted the great animal.

The pilot had to zigzag so we could find the right angle to shoot the tranquilizer dart, and then I watched as the majestic Tusker slowly dropped onto its belly and fell asleep. Jumping out of the helicopter, Craig worked fast, knowing the sedative would wear off quickly, to fit the elephant with the GPS collar that would enable him to track the bulls movements and identify the new corridors and routes he used in order to avoid the encroachments of human habitation.

GPS technology has had some success in reducing crop-raiding by alerting farmers to approaching elephants. However, these projects seem to offer only a temporary solution. Dedicated individuals like Ian Craig continue their heroic efforts, but without political will and a serious reevaluation of conservation methods and our economic and political systems, only small areas might be preserved, while the overall situation will remain unchanged.

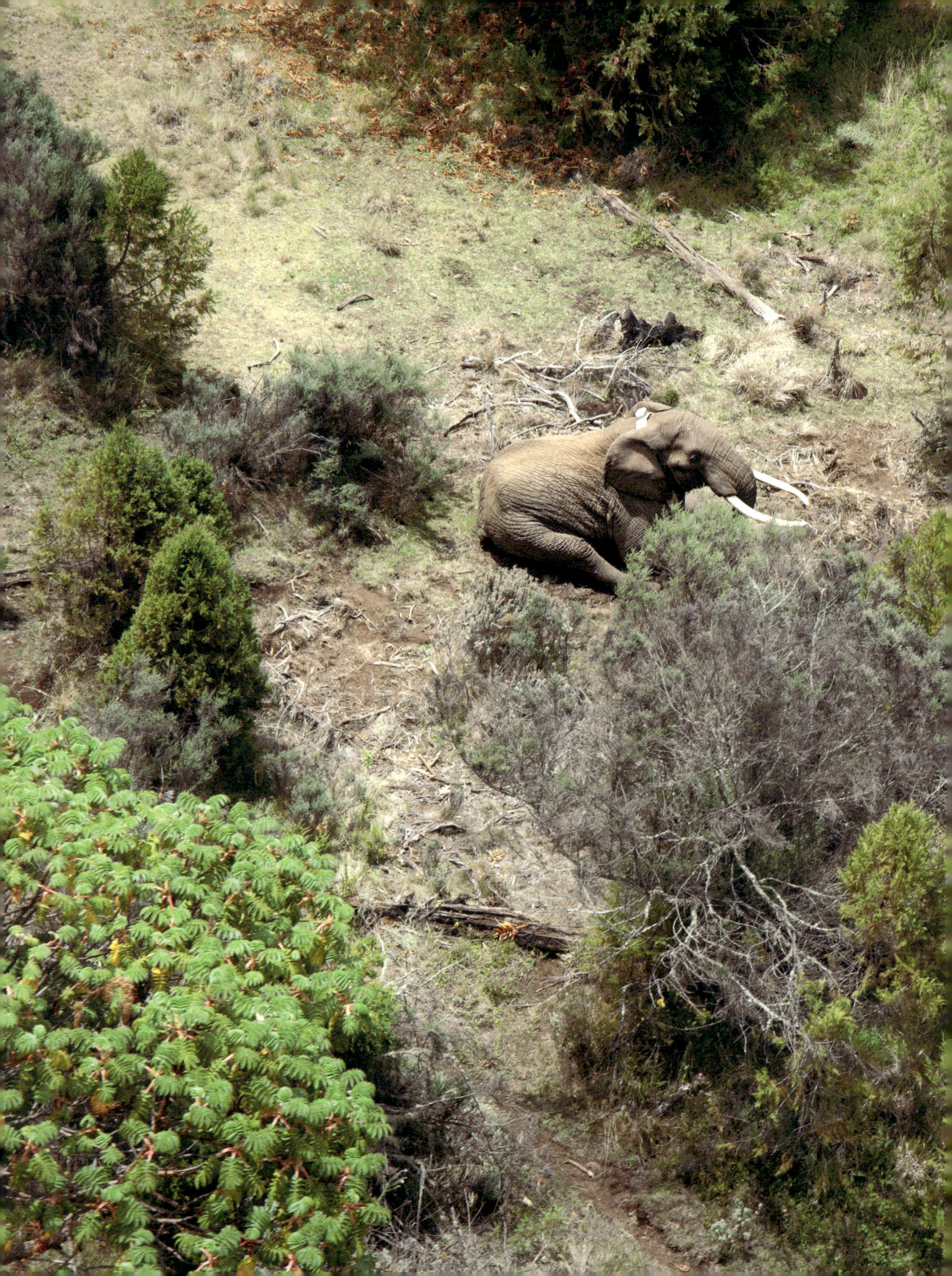

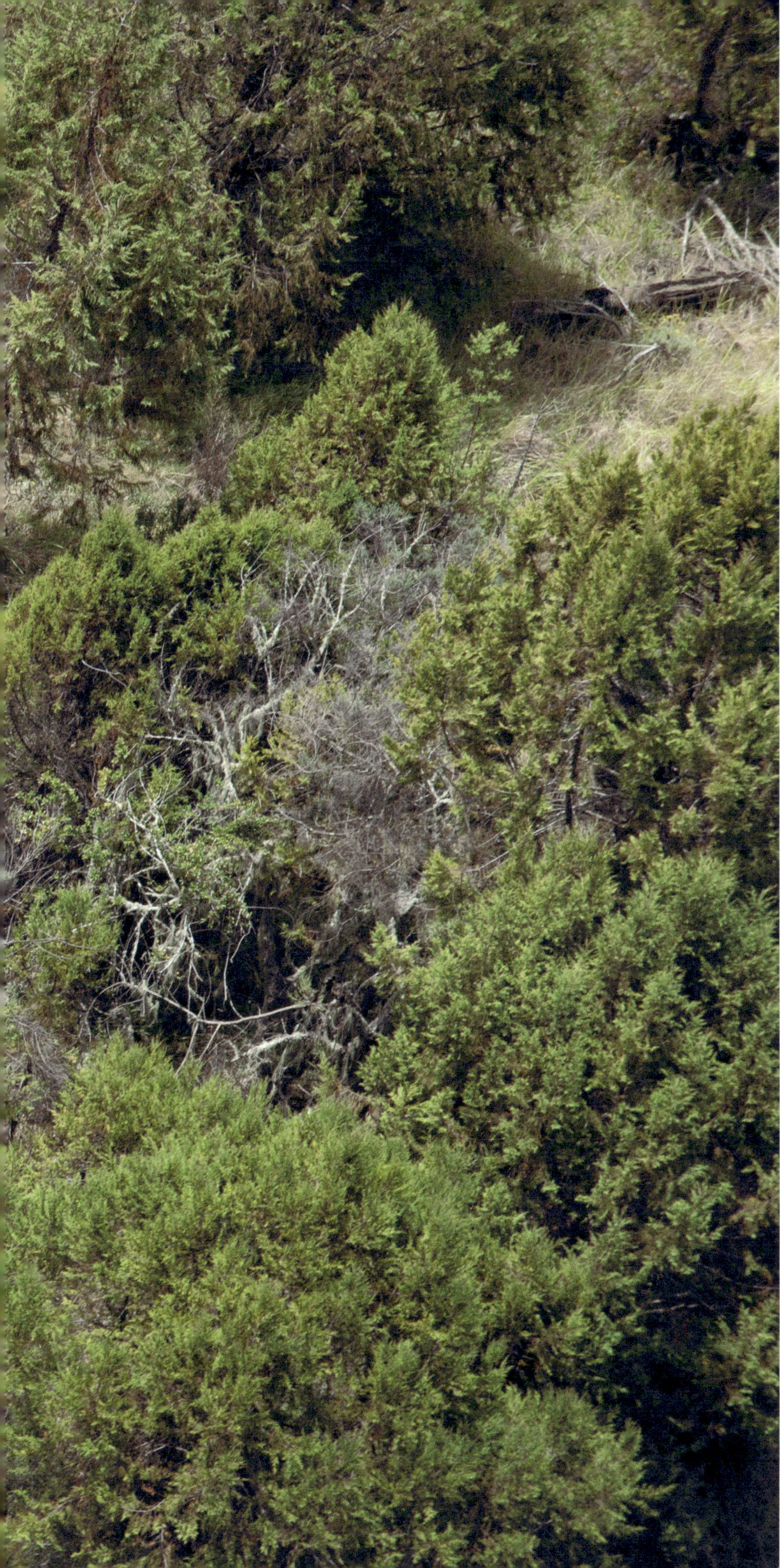

The effects of the tranquilizer eventually wear off, and the elephant gradually regains its senses, now adorned with a collar equipped with a satellite-linked GPS tracker around its neck.

Recognizing that changing human behavior is challenging, I firmly believe that the first crucial step towards saving habitats and wildlife living on it, as well as improving life on earth, effectively managing the Earth's resources, and mitigating climate change is to confront the elephant in the room—the issue of overpopulation that governments often avoid. With the current global population surpassing 8 billion, well beyond a sustainable level, it becomes imperative to address and actively manage this growth for a more sustainable future.

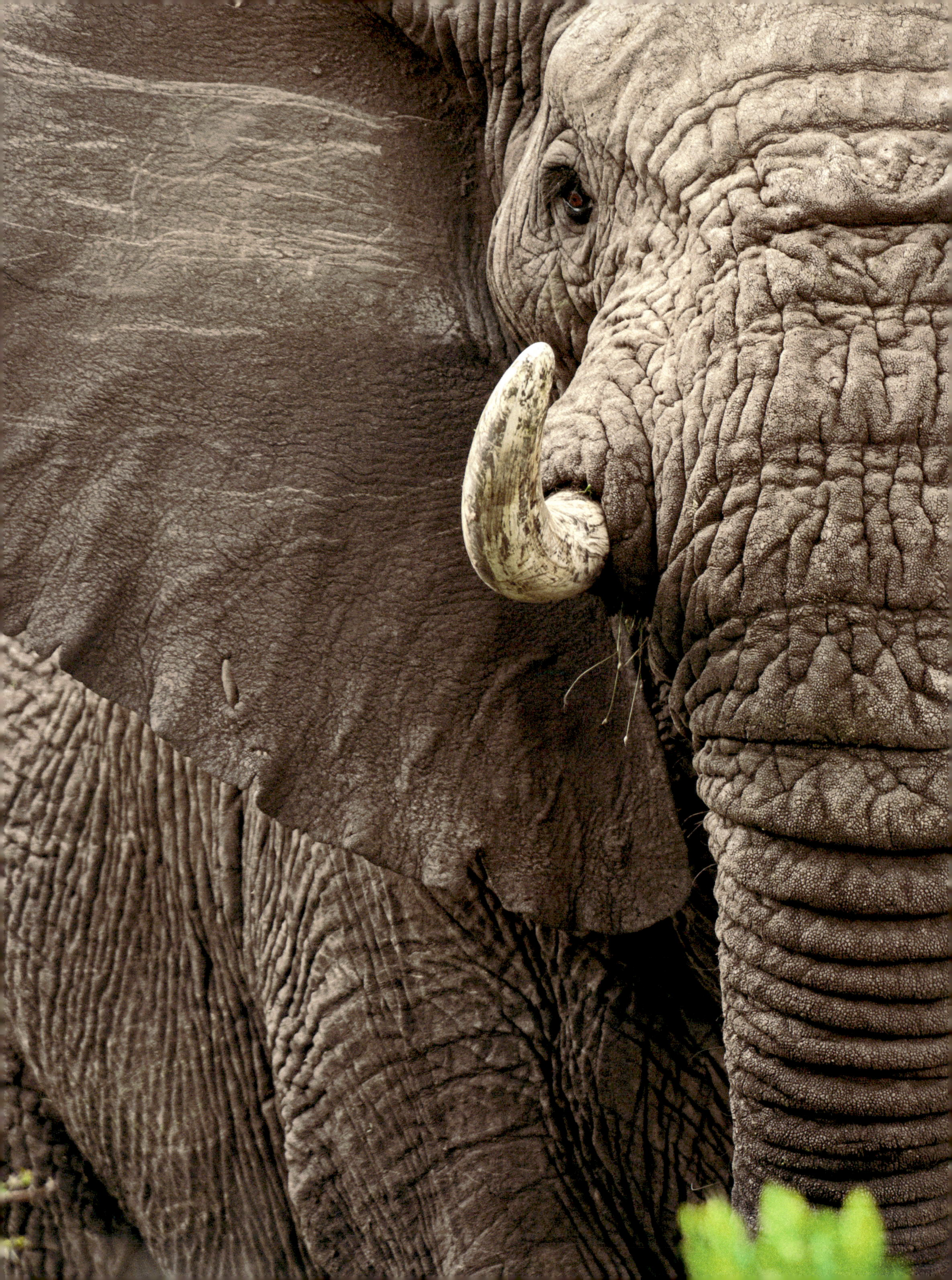

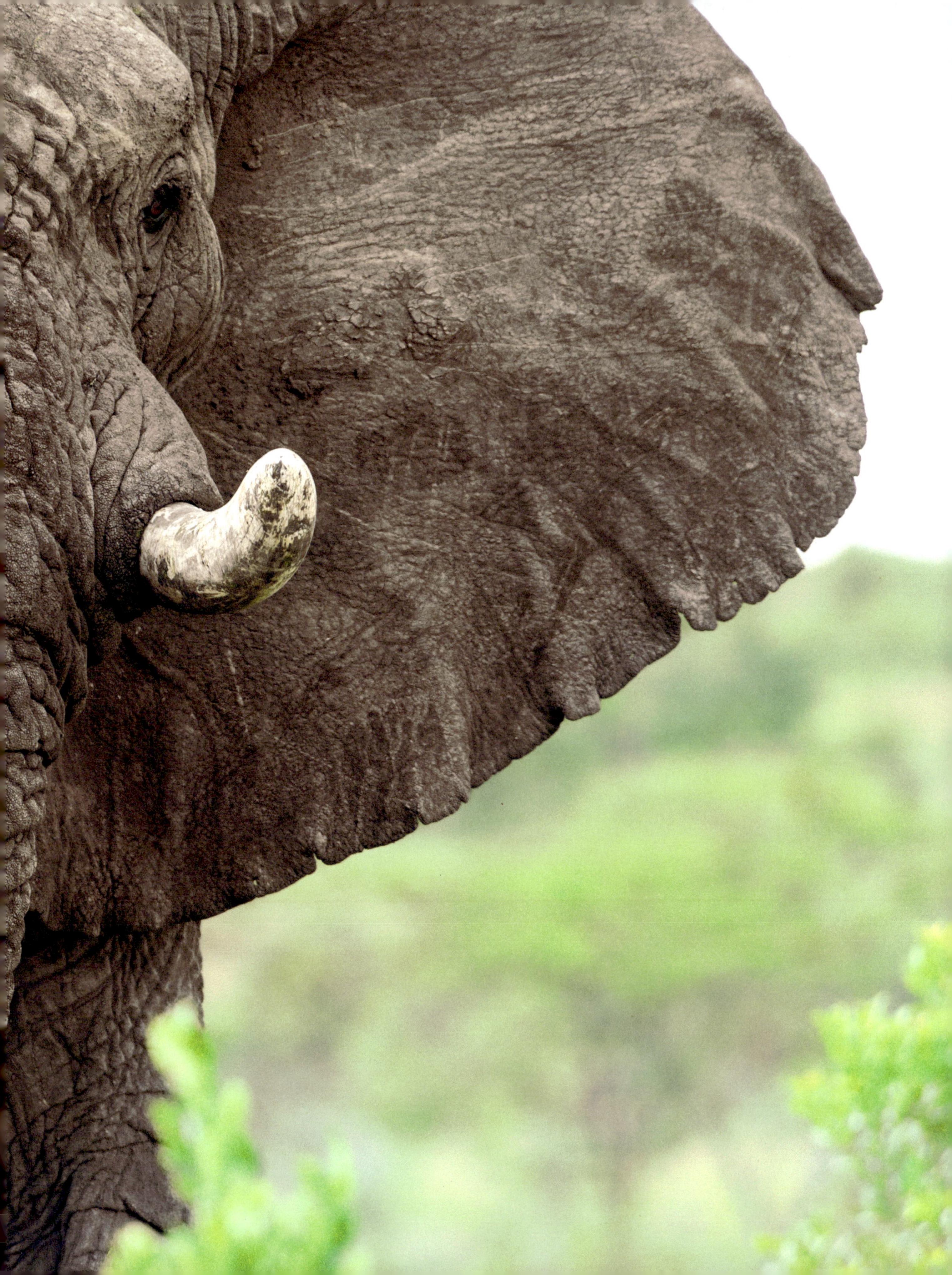

CONCLUSION

Everyone is asking the same question: What is the solution? How to stop the destruction of natural habitats and their wildlife?

There isn't an easy answer and there isn't one single answer.

In this book I am trying to show that good intentions are not good enough; that the limited and piecemeal efforts I have seen, have only a limited and piecemeal effect. So how do we find a new path forward?

One of the first things to let go of is the idea that money alone is a solution. Often donating money to what seems like a worthy cause ends up paying corrupt officials or underwriting large corporate charitable infrastructures, rather than helping people. In too many cases the people who control the funds live in London, Washington or Nairobi, removed from any of the realities on the ground.

Since 1960, when African countries began to gain independence from European empires, the continent has received billions of dollars in aid. The Zambian author Dambisa Moyo in her book 'Dead Aid' estimates that number at 1 trillion. Dr Greg Mills from South Africa thinks that in the last 30 years alone, the number is around $1.2 trillion.

It is rather disturbing to me to witness these funds being continually directed to inefficient schemes. Too often the money seems only to sustain a conservation 'industry' and perpetuate influence peddling.

The pouring of billions of dollars into the budgets of developing countries has tended to result in increasing poverty and inequality, while propping up incompetent, corrupt 'friendly' dictatorial regimes.

Richer governments have used the financial incentives of aid programs as levers of international diplomacy. African governments have become dependent on international aid packages, and in the process, have abdicated their responsibilities to foreign 'experts' and leaving it to NGOs to run projects, further disconnecting conservation from government policy and government responsibility.

There is the classic example, unfortunately often repeated, of a water well being drilled in a dry region to make clean water more accessible to local people, that ends up seeding disputes over which groups control, rights and access to the water. Another one is why does Africa need Ukrainian cereals to feed itself? Why is it not self-sufficient?

For years, international organizations have claimed to be working towards this objective.

I think we have to acknowledge that it will take years, possibly decades, to decouple the aid culture from political agendas. But more immediate remedies for conservation can and should be implemented.

First, we need the transparency and accountability brought by financial audits. Greater transparency will increase the impact money can have.

Another important change needed is to scale down the influence of academics who set too much store on data, and instead empower local people who have the knowledge and experience to be able to establish projects and deliver results. These people urgently need a seat at the table.

It is important to widen the discourse and create more awareness. To understand that the failure of creating better aid is a political failure, not an economic one and the only way to make things change, is to ask difficult questions so that governments understand they have to respond to public pressure. It is time to push back against the systems that have not served us, our environment, or our wildlife. It is no longer enough for international aid to be generous; it has to understand the root causes, it must become intelligent.

Guillaume Bonn

Trench around lake to keep hippos from straying to farms

LOISE MACHARIA/ Nyandarua is digging a 12km trench around Lake Olbolosat to keep hippos from straying into farms, attacking residents and destroying crops.

Parents are afraid to send their children to school early in the morning, lest they be attacked.

Human–hippo conflict is rampant in the northern part of the lake and the trench will help greatly to resolve the problem, Governor Francis Kimemia said.

The trench, which separates the grazing areas for hippos from pastures for domestic animals and from farmlands, will be extended to the banks of River Ewaso Nyiro.

Githunguchu, Baari and Ziwani villages will be protected by the trench.

"People living around the lake have endured huge losses as a result of hippo invasion into their farms, leaving a trail of destruction to crops, deaths and injuries to both humans and livestock," Kimemia said.

The governor said the excavation will be completed in the next month. Five kilometres have been completed.

"Due to lack of pasture, hippos go deeper into people's farms, causing interactions and injuries to humans and livestock as well as crop destruction," Nyandarua county commissioner Benson Leparmorijohe said.

BIO

Guillaume Bonn, an award-winning documentary photographer, writer, filmmaker, and picture editor, has dedicated the last three decades to capturing the complexities of conflicts, social issues, and environmental challenges across Africa. Born in Madagascar and raised in the Comoros Islands, Djibouti, and Kenya, he brings a unique perspective rooted in his French and Malagasy heritage and his diverse upbringing.

His background in Economics and International Politics, combined with his training at the International Center of Photography in New York, has equipped him with a unique perspective, offering a nuanced understanding of Africa's realities through his artistry and storytelling. Notably, for 15 years, he was a contributor to *Vanity Fair magazine* during the prestigious Graydon Carter era, widely considered the ultimate accolade for a photographer during that period—covering a broad spectrum of subjects, from captivating group portraits or royal weddings and Paris Fashion Week to addressing critical issues such as conflicts in Uganda, Somalia, and Africa's ivory trade.

Bonn's journalistic efforts extend beyond *Vanity Fair*, in groundbreaking coverage of the Darfur crisis in Sudan and exposing instances of child sexual abuse by United Nations peacekeepers in the Congo DRC, published in *The New York Times*. Renowned journalist Jon Lee Anderson of *The New Yorker Magazine* described Bonn as 'an archaeologist compelled to seek out and preserve the recent legacy of East Africa,' highlighting his dedication to documenting the changing landscapes and environments of his birth continent.

In an era saturated with unverified social media narratives, he distinguishes himself by focusing on personal projects which he describes as 'artistic with a journalistic soul'—that challenge prevailing perceptions, aiming to provoke meaningful questions and encourage deeper understanding. In addition to his contributions to print media, Bonn is the author of several books, including 'Mosquito Coast: Travels from Maputo to Mogadishu.'

For two years, he worked between Nairobi, Paris, and New York alongside American artist Peter Beard, co-directing the Canal+ produced documentary film 'Peter Beard: Scrapbooks from Africa & beyond'. The film was screened at the Sundance Film Festival and broadcast on TV channels worldwide.

He is a fellow of the Royal Geographical Society and currently is working on his next book, centered on his essay 'The Analogue Mind: The Death and Reimagining of Photography.'

SOME ARTICLES, ACADEMIC PAPERS, BOOKS USED AS RESEARCH:

Exploring Routes to Coexistence: Developing and Testing a Human–Elephant Conflict-Management Framework for African Elephant-Range Countries

Eva M. Gross / Linking Conservation and Development, 69198 Schriesheim, Germany Joana G. Pereira / cE3c-Centre for Ecology, Evolution and Environmental Changes, Faculdade de Ciências, Universidade de Lisboa, Campo Grande, 1749-016 Lisboa, Portugal; Tadeyo Shaba / Royal Place Limited, Lilongwe P.O. Box 30131, Malawi; Samuel Bilério / Wildlife Conservation Society, Niassa Special Reserve, Maputo, Mozambique; Brighton Kumchedwa / Department of National Parks and Wildlife, Lilongwe P.O. Box 30131, Malawi; Stephanie Lienenlüke / Deutsche Gesellschaft für Internationale Zusammenarbeit, Global Project Partnership against Wildlife Crime in Africa and Asia, 65760 Eschborn, Germany; Published by Diversity is a peer-reviewed, open access journal on the science of biodiversity from molecules, genes, populations, and species, to ecosystems and is published monthly online by MDPI.

Impacts of a trophy hunting ban on private land conservation in South African biodiversity hotspots

Kim Parker 1 | Alta De Vos 1 | Hayley S. Clements 2,3 | Duan Biggs 2,4,5 | Reinette Biggs 2,6
1-Department of Environmental Science, Rhodes University, Makhanda, South Africa
2-Centre for Complex Systems inTransition (CST), Stellenbosch University, Stellenbosch, South Africa
3-Department of Geosciences and Geography, University of Helsinki, FI-00014 Helsinki, Finland
4-Environmental Futures ResearchInstitute, Griffith University, Nathan,Queensland, Australia
5-Department of Conservation Ecology & Entomology, Stellenbosch University, Matieland, South Africa
6-Stockholm Resilience Centre, Stockholm University, Sweden

Are Kenyan Conservancies a Trojan Horse for Land Grabs?
"Conservancies" in Kenya are presented as an example of conservation by and for local people, but they can be a device to grab land. Unless this changes, the future for wildlife conservation looks bleak.
By Stephen Corry, published by *The Elephant.info*, April 2021.

By The Elephants, For The Elephants — How community conservancies are partnering with others to collect data from elephants to better shape conservation measures
December 2019, written and published by Northern Rangelands Trust.

Wildlife-based Tourism in Kenya: Land use conflicts and government compensation policies over protected areas
By Isaac Sindiga in *The Journal of Tourism Studies* Vol. 6, No. 2, Dec. 1995

Africa's national parks failing to conserve large mammals, study shows populations of zebra, buffalo and lion have fallen by an average of 59% since 1970, according to research. By David Adam, *The Guardian Newspaper* July 2010

Giraffe numbers in Masai Mara down 95%
Scientists blame explosion in human settlement around reserve for plummeting populations of giraffes and other animals. By Xan Rice, *The Guardian Newspaper*, April 2009

Safari: Are too many tourists killing Africa's wildlife?
After an extensive study of Africa's most famous reserves, Graham Boynton says to save its great creatures we need a conservation revolution.
The Daily Telegraph, Feb. 12, 2010

Hypocrisy and internal contradictions threatening to tear Kenya apart
By Antony Otieno Ong'ayo - 2009-07-02, Issue 440 http://pambazuka.org/en/category/features/57401 http://pambazuka.org/en/category/features/57401

Agony and Ivory
Highly emotional and completely guileless, elephants mourn their dead—and across Africa, they are grieving daily as demand from China's "suddenly wealthy" has driven the price of ivory to $700 a pound or more. With tens of thousands of elephants being slaughtered each year for their tusks, raising the specter of an "extinction vortex," Alex Shoumatoff and Guillaume Bonn's reporting and photography, *Vanity Fair Magazine*, US editions, July 2011

The Masai Mara: 'It will not be long before it's gone'
As lodges and shanty towns proliferate in Kenya's Masai Mara, drastic and urgent steps are needed to save this beautiful game reserve from becoming an environmental disaster. Jessica Hatcher and Guillaume Bonn's reporting and photography, *The Guardian Magazine*, August 2013

Short-term effects of GPS collars on the activity, behavior, and adrenal response of scimitar-horned oryx (Oryx dammah)
The National Center for Biotechnology Information (NCBI) advances science and health by providing access to biomedical and genomic information. Published online, February 2020

Hunters, Poachers and Gamekeepers: Towards a Social History of Hunting in Colonial Kenya
by E. I. Steinhart-The Journal of African History Vol. 30, No. 2 (1989), pp. 247-264 (18 pages) Published by Cambridge University Press

The Legally Permissible Traditional Customary Uses of Wildlife and Forests under Kenyan Law
by Nixon Sifuna, Open Journal of Forestry Vol. 11, No. 3, July 8, 2021

The Fate of Aboriginal Habitation of Gazetted State Forests in Present Day Kenya: A Case Study of the Agitation by the Ogiek and Sengwer Traditional Communities
By Nixon Sifuna Advances in Anthropology Vol. 11, No. 2, March 31, 2021

Assessment of Conservation Management of State Parks, Community and Private Conservancies in Kenya
Margaret Wachu Gichuhi / Institute of Energy and Environmental Technology, Jomo Kenyatta University of Agriculture and Technology (JKUAT), Nairobi, Kenya Joseph Mungai Keriko / Department of Chemistry, School of Physical Sciences, College of Pure and Applied Sciences, Jomo Kenyatta University of Agriculture and Technology (JKUAT), Nairobi, Kenya, John Bosco Njoroge Mukundi / Department of Horticulture, Faculty of Agriculture, Jomo Kenyatta University of Agriculture and Technology (JKUAT), Nairobi, Kenya

REPUBLIC OF KENYA Sessional Paper No. 01 of 2020 on Wildlife Policy
Ministry of Tourism and Wildlife, June 2020

Africa & Trophy Hunting - Current impact and future for Africa environment
Yulianita Daiva / University Prof. Dr. Moestopo (Beragama), 2015

The End of the Game : The Last Word from Paradise
A pictorial documentation of the origins, history and prospects of the big game in Africa by Peter H. Beard, published by Chronicle Books, San Francisco, 1988

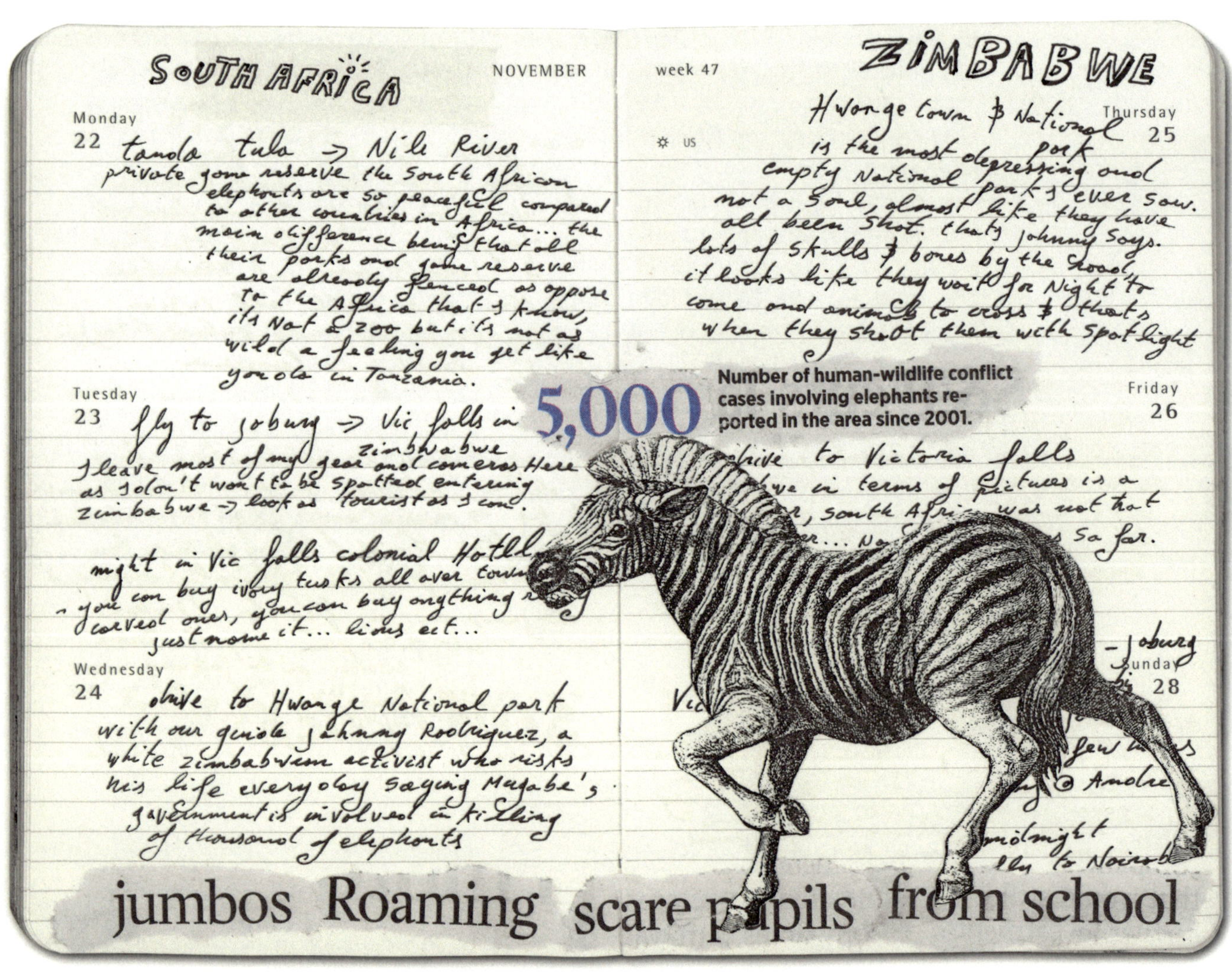

Conservation as a social contract in violent frontier: The case of Anti-poaching in Garamba National Park, eastern Dr Congo.
Kristof Titeca / Institute of Development Policy, University of Antwerp, Belgium Patrick Edmond / Independent Researcher, London United Kingdom Gauthier Marchais / Institute of Development Studies, University of Sussex, United Kingdom Esther Marijnen / Conflict Research Group, Ghent University, Belgium Political Geography Vol. 78, April 2020, 102116

(De)legitimising hunting – Discourses over the morality of hunting in Europe and eastern Africa
Anke Fischer / Social, Economic and Geographical Sciences Group, The James Hutton Institute, Aberdeen, UK - Frankfurt Zoological Society, P.O. Box 100003, Addis Ababa, Ethiopia Vesna Kereži / Biology Department, Faculty of Veterinary Medicine, University of Zagreb, Croatia. Beatriz Arroyo and Miguel Mateos-Delibes / Instituto de Investigación en Recursos Cinegéticos (IREC) (CSIC-UCLM-JCCM), Ronda de Toledo s/n, 13071 Ciudad Real, Spain Degu Tadie / Frankfurt Zoological Society, P.O. Box 100003, Addis Ababa, Ethiopia Asanterabi Lowassa / Tanzania Wildlife Research Institute, P.O. Box 661, Arusha, Tanzania Olve Krange / Norwegian Institute for Nature Research, Gaustadalléen 21, N-0349 Oslo, Norway. Ketil Skogen / Norwegian Institute for Nature Research, Gaustadalléen 21, N-0349 Oslo, Norway

The Last Place On Earth with Mike Fay's Megatransect Journals
Michael Nichols and Mike Fay. Published by *The National Geographic*, Washington, DC, 2005

It's Kenya's Farmers vs.Wildlife, and the Animals are losing
James C.McKinley Jr and Guillaume Bonn's reporting and photography in Laikipia, Kenya. Published by *The New York Times*, August 1998

Charismatic Pentecostal Churches in Kenya: Growth, Culture and Orality
International Journal of Humanities Social Sciences and Education (IJHSSE) Vol. 1, Issue 3, March 2014, PP. 27-33 www.arcjournals.org

The history of Lake Turkana fisheries and the role of TFCS and Norad
Appendix A in: Kolding, J. 1989. The Fish Resources of Lake Turkana and Their Environment - Thesis for the Cand. Scient degree in Fisheries Biology and Final Report of KEN 043 Trial Fishery 1986-1987. Dept. of Fisheries Biology, University of Bergen. 262 pp. by Jeppe Kolding

The Oil Race Is on in the Cradle of Humanity
Jessica Hatcher and Guillaume Bonn's reporting and photography in Turkana was supported by the Pulitzer Center on Crisis Reporting, and published by *Newsweek Magazine*, December 2014

Eyelids of Morning (1973) First edition
the mingled destinies of crocodiles and men : being a description of the origins, history, and prospects of Lake Rudolf, its peoples, deserts, rivers, mountains, and weather by Alistair Graham and Peter Beard, published by New York Graphic Society

The counterinsurgency/ conservation nexus: guerrilla livelihoods and the dynamics of conflict and violence in the Virunga National Park, Democratic Republic of the Congo
The Journal of Peasant Studies, DOI:10.1080/03066150.2016.1203307 by Judith Verweijen & Esther Marijnen, 2016

The 'green militarisation' of development aid: the European Commission and the Virunga National Park, Democratic Republic of the Congo

Third World Quarterly, 38:7, 1566-1582,
DOI: 10.1080/01436597.2017.1282815
By Esther Marijnen, 2017

Why we must question the militarisation of conservation

Biological Conservation Volume 232, April 2019, Pages 66-73, Rosaleen Duffya, Francis Masséa, Laure Joannya: University of Sheffield, United Kingdom Emile Smidtb: Institute of Social Studies, The Hague, Netherlands Esther Marijnenc, Bram Büscherc, Judith Verweijenc: University of Ghent, Belgium Maano Ramutsindelad: University of Cape Town, South Africa, Trishant Simlaie: University of Cambridge, United Kingdom Elizabeth Lunstrumf: York University, Canada

A Kenyan Ecologist's Crusade to Save Her Country's Wildlife

Published in January 25, 2021 in *The New Yorker Magazine* By Jon Lee Anderson

My visit with the spiritual voice of the hidden Serengeti

Published November 30, 2021 in *National Geographic Magazine* By Yvonne Adhiambo Owuor

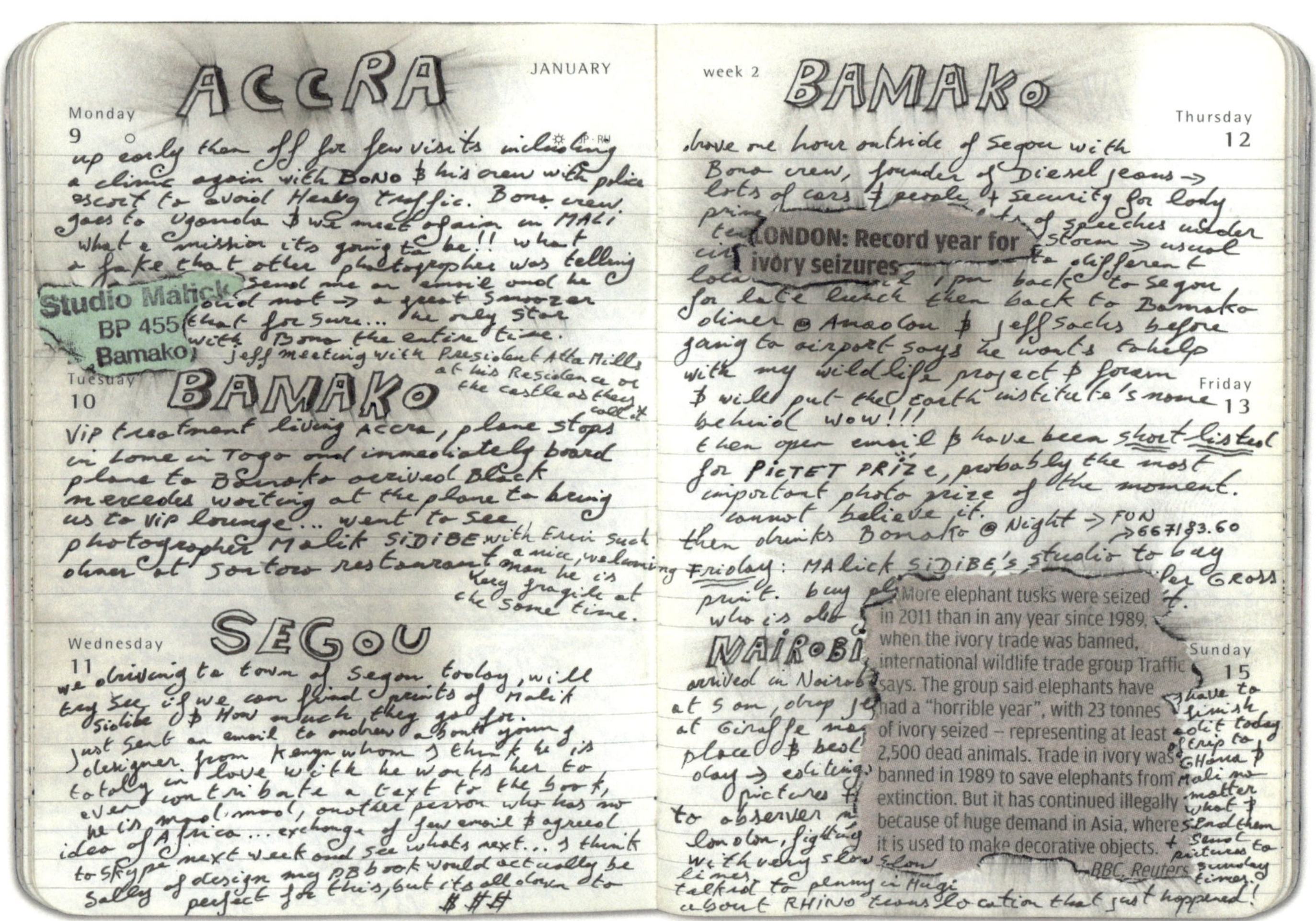

ACKNOWLEDGEMENTS

My heartfelt gratitude to the following individuals and organizations for their invaluable support and contributions:

Henry Pincus, Ezekiel Ole Katato, Richard Bonham and Tom Hill at Big Life Foundation, Michael Dyer at Borana Conservancy, Mike Watson at Lewa Wildlife Conservancy, Ian Craig, Jon-Lee Anderson, Peterson Kamwathi, Yvonne Adhiambo-Owuor, Elodie Sampere, Wendell Steavenson, RAK, Karen Howes, Mukka Fitzjohn, Isabelle Roumeguere, Anigue Malignon, James Crump, Yaron Schwartzman, Pierre Zanger, Philippe Gourdin, Gary Knight, Jean-Claude Luyat, Mary Anne Fitzgerald, Roberto D'addona, Lara Mastropasqua, Calvin Cottar, Nigel Archer, Danda Jaroljmek, Angela Fisher, Carol Beckwith, Cláudio Melo, Bruno Croizé, Rui Freire, Olivia Allard de La Villeguérin and Angela Maurice for her special support

Brigitte Trichet my publisher at Hemeria, Kathy and Amy Eldon at Creative Visions

All the Rangers in Borana, Ol-Pejeta, Lewa Conservancies & Big Life Foundation in Kenya, Garamba National Park in Congo DRC (African Parks)

Andrea Turkalo in The Central African Republic

Editors: Wendell Steavenson, Yvonne Adhiambo-Owuor and Karen Howes Book concept, content (photos / texts & design): Guillaume Bonn with contributing help in the design by Lætitia Queste and Sarah Boris

Dedicated to all the Rangers fighting to save nature and its wildlife across the African continent.

In memory of my father Yves Bonn, Tony Fitzjohn & Dan Eldon

All texts and photographs: © Guillaume Bonn, 2024 Except for texts by Jon Lee Anderson and Ezekiel Ole Katato

ISBN 978-2-490952-53-3
Image processing and printing:
Printmodel®, Paris
Printed in August 2024 in France
Legal Deposit March 2025
www.hemeria.com

A CALL TO ACTION

In Kenya and across Africa, many organizations claim to be inclusive, regenerative, and ethical in their wildlife conservation efforts, but often, this is not the case.

This book serves as the platform for the Paradise Project, an initiative born from an idealistic vision. Our mission is straightforward: to highlight those genuinely making a difference in preserving wildlife and their habitats.

Paradise Inc. also aims to show that philanthropy needs a thorough reevaluation. Using both traditional journalistic techniques and modern digital investigation methods, we are assessing the true impact of conservation organizations funded by generous donations.

Through its pages, this book seeks to shed light on new pathways, inspire fresh perspectives, and foster deeper conversations and understanding. This will pave the way for meaningful and impactful changes.

We want to engage a broad audience, especially younger generations interested in wildlife, ecology, the environment, and climate change.

The Paradise Project will start by conducting in-depth research on human-wildlife conflict to create a conservation index. This index will help environmental organizations achieve their goals.

Additionally, the Paradise Project will produce an annual list of organizations with proven positive impacts, worthy of your support. Let's align donor funds with impactful projects and together, create a paradise where every contribution counts.

Your donations to support our investigative work can be done via The Paradise Project - Creative Visions—a 501C3 nonprofit organization in the United States.

www.creativevisions.org
Tel: 310 456 1109

18820 Pacific Coast Highway Suite 201, Malibu, CA 90265
emails: gbonnphoto@gmail.com /
fiscalsponsorship@creativevisions.org

I extend my gratitude to Henry
Pincus and the Point Break
Foundation for their unwavering
belief in the transformative
potential of this book and for their
support in making it a reality.

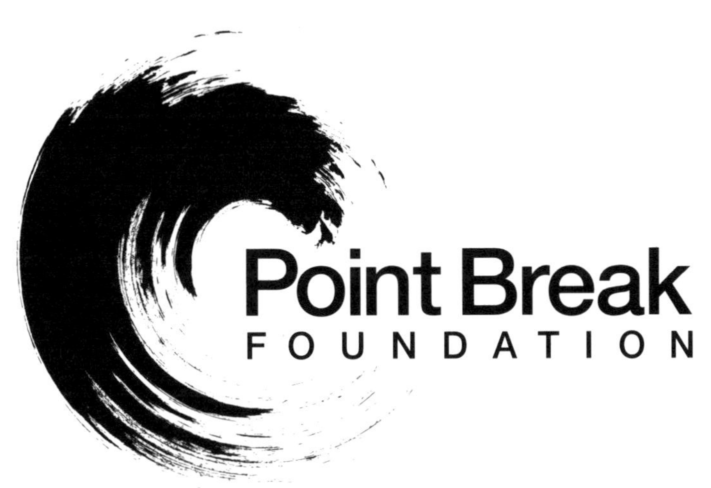

www.pointbreakfoundation.org
The Point Break foundation is a private
foundation dedicated to plastic pollution
reduction, ocean conservancy and
general environmental health.

"Never doubt that a small
group of thoughtful,
committed citizens
can change the world.
Indeed, it is the only
thing that ever has."

Margaret Mead